WANDERING HEART:
A Gay Man's Journey

Book One: The Search

JOHN LOOMIS, M.D.

iUniverse, Inc.
New York   Bloomington

Wandering Heart: A Gay Man's Journey
Book One: The Search

Copyright © 2010 JOHN LOOMIS, M.D.

iUniverse books may be ordered through booksellers or by contacting:

iUniverse
1663 Liberty Drive
Bloomington, IN 47403
www.iuniverse.com
1-800-Authors (1-800-288-4677)

ISBN: 978-1-4401-9823-6 (pbk)
ISBN: 978-1-4401-9825-0 (cloth)
ISBN: 978-1-4401-9824-3 (ebk)

Library of Congress Control Number: 2010901244

Printed in the United States of America

iUniverse rev. date: 01/28/2010

Contents

WANDERING HEART:
A Gay Man's Journey

May 30, 2018

For my friend Charles Kawiecki
with all best wishes.

John

Introduction

Every memory lives in the mind of the person who is remembering and is the royal road which connects that person with the remembered event or object, wherever in time or space it may exist. Memory is our private storehouse of psychological facts. The two ends of the memory spectrum, the internal memory (in the psyche) and the thing remembered (in the external world), are always connected, although the emphasis may shift from internal to external and back again. But the two ends of the spectrum always refer to one another.

When I started to write these memoirs, my purpose was to help others, particularly young people, recognize and deal with various difficult situations they might encounter, by describing troublesome situations in my own life and how I managed to survive them. This is not meant to be a didactic manual but is just an account of how one person managed to survive and sometimes thrive.

I have encountered many kind, intelligent, generous, and helpful people. But because I wanted to illustrate that many painful situations can be tolerated or overcome, there may be some overemphasis on problematic people and situations. It was the difficult ones who had to be carefully dealt with (or avoided). Most people don't need to learn how to survive a tea party.

When I was a child there was no one to turn to for guidance, advice, or information in many matters. Specifically, I didn't know where to turn for information or guidance about love, sex, and human relationships.

Believing from an early age that I was different from others in some shameful or dangerous way led to my belief that I was unacceptable to others, even to my mother. My father's significant hostility from my earliest age ruled out expecting any help from him.

From time to time I have been surprised, sometimes painfully so, by how similar my thinking, behaviors, and reactions are to my parents' models. There has been no attempt to emulate their behavior, but to my horror I sometimes find myself acting like a psychological clone, as if my behavior were genetically determined.

My parents cooperated to produce a physical body for me to live in, for which I am grateful. They had permanent and profound influences on my behavior, mostly good, but they were also sometimes hurtful, injurious, and crippling. Neither one was well equipped to be a parent, but both did as well as they could, even though one of them loved me and the other did not.

As I write this, they have been dead for more than forty years, and there is no one with whom to check the accuracy of my memories.

I wish I could have an hour to talk with my parents, to thank them for all the good they did for me and for the sacrifices they made for me, to forgive them for the harm they did me, and to tell them that I love them more now than when they were alive. They were my only mother and father, and until the ends of their lives I hoped for love from both of them, without expecting it.

I have had a wonderful adventure here on Earth. It seems to me that my entire life has been a pursuit, a search, for love, for someone to love. To fall in love is a precious and dangerous situation. We are fortunate if our love object, if we can find such a treasure, brings us more happiness than tragedy.

As you move through this history, please do not assume I am advocating any particular course of action or am setting myself up as a role model. Each of us must look for his own path, often in mysterious and perplexing situations.

When the gale winds of love and passion collide with the storm surge of jealousy, hope, and despair, the resulting maelstrom can whirl any of us to ruin, so don't feel too safe.

As the Buddha said, "Go and seek your own salvation with diligence."

Good luck to us all.

Note on Names and Places

All persons appearing in this narrative are/were real persons, and all the places, events, and actions were also real. None of the characters are fictitious or composite. But I have changed many of the names and some of the places so as to mask the identities of those who might not wish to be recognized.

The conversations are all reported as accurately as I can recall them. None of them have been knowingly changed, distorted, or inflated.

As William James commented, "A real difference is a difference which makes a difference."

Just as in life, there are many loose ends in this account. No tidying up has been done. Much remains unknown or mysterious.

Family

My father was descended on his paternal side from Miles Standish, one of the Mayflower pilgrims. The family was poor but respectable. His mother's family had arrived from Sweden around 1840; his grandmother, whom he particularly loved, was proud of having once baked a cake for the king of Sweden. She was also proud of the large set of milk glass which she had brought with her from the old country.

Both sides of my father's family came to Colorado by covered wagon in the mid-nineteenth century. They settled close to and in plain sight of the high snow-covered Sangre de Cristo range. His father built the family house from trees he chopped and shaped himself.

Old Loomis homestead outside Delta, Colorado, 1902

My father was born on this small farm outside Delta, Colorado, in early 1904, followed by his two sisters at short intervals. As a child and adolescent he had to do hard manual work on the farm, with its orchards, fields, horses, cattle, and chickens. One of his favorite stories was how he had to walk four miles to school, sometimes through the snow. One year the Fourth of July parade in Delta was cancelled because of a blizzard. These were what he remembered as hardships of his childhood.

He also told, with all seriousness, of occasionally hearing bells tinkling in the night, and when he looked out his window he would see the "little people" marching along, carrying lanterns, singing, and ringing their bells. He thought they were fairies or elves and knew enough not to go outside and try to approach them. He never found out who they were.

He didn't like his two younger sisters and told of how, after their grandmother died, they took her Swedish milk glass outside and broke it to bits with a hammer, saying they hated their grandmother. My father recalled that when his sisters went to college, they viewed themselves as princesses and frequently demanded new evening dresses to wear to balls. His parents were ashamed that they did not have the money to give them these luxuries. My father sometimes sent money to his parents to pay for the dresses. Not once did his sisters thank him; perhaps the parents didn't tell them the source of the money. He said his sisters were impossibly bossy and critical. I have sometimes wondered what the sisters' view of this story might have been. When I eventually met them, they were elegant and cordial. Both were talented pianists; both married and had children. Only one of them was bossy.

I don't remember his ever saying anything positive, pleasant, or cheerful about his life on the farm. He had so little to say about his parents that I don't know whether he was fond of them or otherwise.

In 1920, after finishing the tenth grade, when he was sixteen, he decided to run away from home. His uncle Pete was working in the oil fields in the Yucatan and invited my father to join him. He soon acquired the nickname *Chamaco*, meaning urchin or tough little boy. I think he liked the name; it followed him through life, and my mother and his closest friends called him by it. It was a rough and lawless time in Mexico; he told of occasionally coming across men hanging from trees in the forest.

Hanged man in the forest, Mexico, 1921

He was self-sufficient, became fluent in Spanish, learned the mechanics of the petroleum drilling process, learned to drive an automobile, and even to fly an airplane. After a series of adventures in Mexico, including being captured by a gang of bandits and being forced to drive for their chief and teach several of them to drive, he escaped.

He moved to Houston, where he opened a flying school, taught Howard Hughes and many others to fly, and met many pioneer pilots. He knew Charles Lindbergh, Amelia Earhart, Juan Trippe, who founded Pan-American Airlines, and even Orville Wright. He flew an endurance flight over Houston, attracting much attention. He was also friendly with several people who were later prominent in the petroleum industry, both in the United States and abroad.

In 1931 my mother enrolled in the flying school. My father was her teacher. They fell in love and soon married, a first marriage for both. A year

3

later she became pregnant, and he tried to persuade her to have an abortion. My mother wanted to have a child, but my father was unhappy about the prospect. I was the result of this pregnancy and was born in 1933, two years after they were married. Neither of them ever changed their minds about my birth, and he was as displeased to have me as a son as she was overjoyed to have a child. Their relationship was permanently damaged by my arrival.

1933 was an eventful year. Aside from my birth, ten thousand banks failed, wiping out my parents' finances, and prohibition was repealed: "Happy Days Are Here Again."

My father and his endurance airplane: Houston, Million-Dollar City

The same year, his uncle Donk crashed the airplane. Although Donk parachuted to safety, the flying school was finished. My father then worked as a pilot for American Airlines for two years.

My father as an American Airlines pilot, 1932

I remained an only child and don't recall ever hearing my mother say she wanted another child. My father also did not seem to want another. I occasionally asked them if they could provide me with a twin, not realizing how truly impossible my request was.

My father as pilot in front of Ford trimotor passenger and mail plane, 1931

For about the last fifteen years of his life, my father suffered from high blood pressure, was overweight, and had a severe case of gout, which caused both wrists to swell until they looked as if an egg was under the skin. This was quite painful and, combined with agitation induced by my mother's constant nagging, ruined his sleep. He was often up at 3 AM and did some of his best designing and inventing work in those early hours. Every morning he left home to go to his office by 5 AM, escaping my mother's customary daily breakfast tongue-lashings.

Later in life he invented several devices which have been successfully used in the petroleum drilling industry; he was sometimes called a mechanical genius. By 1962, at age fifty-eight, he had become affluent for the first time in his life, but two years later he was killed in an automobile accident. In spite of his lack of formal education, at the time of his death he had about twenty U.S. patents and around one hundred foreign counterparts in many parts of the world.

After his death we discovered he had been bigamous and had another wife and child in another country. Perhaps my mother had known, but when my father's assistant told me of this, I was shocked and felt personally betrayed. But I hope he had a happier life with his other family than he did with his first one. I never made any attempt to contact them after he died and have never heard from them.

Many of my father's family members kept important secrets from one another. Trust was not as important as maintaining hatred and resentment. This trait also exists in my mother's family but in a less vigorous form.

I saw my father as silent, gloomy, extremely reserved, stingy, and hardworking. I was ashamed of his gross table manners. He repeatedly dropped his utensils with a clatter onto the tabletop when he finished taking a mouthful and loudly rattling his spoon and fork against his teeth. I was also ashamed of his poor use of English, which was filled with glaring grammatical mistakes common among his peers.

He had a few fixed hatreds, aside from that for his sisters. He particularly despised Franklin Roosevelt, whom he called "limber legs," and his wife, Eleanor, whom he called "the mulatto."

I think my mother encouraged him to try to act more companionably toward me, so when I was ten years old he took me fishing, and I disliked the excursion as much as he seemed to. This was the only time he voluntarily spent any leisure time with me. It was a strained and awkward outing and was never repeated. Perhaps my mother was beginning to worry that I was overly effeminate, but being around my father did nothing to help that.

Years later, when he was forty-five, he heard the news that his father, age eighty, had committed suicide by shooting himself in the head. He was unusually quiet, and when he returned from his father's funeral, he had nothing to say.

When he died, he left behind a death letter stating that he didn't want either of his sisters to attend his funeral and he didn't want them ever to be informed of his death. My father was distant geographically and emotionally from his family. My mother also generally disliked his family. She was much closer to her own family, and I grew up in a matriarchy. The women were the rulers.

My mother was descended from English, Welsh, and Irish forebears who had been in America since the early nineteenth century. Her grandfather had died of alcoholism on skid row in Baltimore after the Civil War. Her father, my grandfather, was then an orphan and was raised by his aunt Rye (Maria), who lived in Ypsilanti, where she owned a cherry orchard. My mother was named after her (Maria Jeannette Doyle).

Great-Grandmother Robbs, Oklahoma City, 1940

Granny, second from right; her mother, far right; and five of her sisters; about 1945

My maternal grandmother was my favorite person. She was born in 1877 on a farm outside Neosho, Missouri, one of ten children, nine girls and a boy. Their mother lived to age 101. Most of the siblings had second sight: seeing dead relatives at their own funerals, seeing and talking with other deceased persons, having telepathic or clairvoyant knowledge of events happening at a distance, and sometimes having knowledge of the future. I grew up hearing about these experiences as if they were as ordinary as reading the newspaper or eating an apple, but I always knew they were special, interesting, and not threatening.

Perhaps the most colorful of Granny's siblings was her sister Kate, whose husband owned the Robinson Circus, where he was the lion tamer. One afternoon his lion killed him in front of an audience, and that was the end of the circus, which was soon sold to Ringling Brothers. When I met Kate, she was a stately matron with a twinkle in her eye.

My grandmother married at sixteen, had her first child, my aunt Nellie, at seventeen, and was a widow by eighteen. Baby Nellie was also sent to Aunt Rye in Ypsilanti to be brought up.

Aunt Nellie was beautiful, highly emotional, and musically talented, and like her father, she eventually became a severe alcoholic. My father disliked her, finding her a "troublemaker." But she lived until age eighty, with a robust constitution, detoxed for the final time the year of her death. Married three times, she had two children by her second husband. They had difficult lives:

her daughter Rosemary committed suicide a few days after the birth of Edwin, her first child, and her son Georgie was tubercular, occasionally working as a pianist. But like several family members, he had considerable musical talent and a beguiling charm of the sing-for-your-supper type—so I was told.

My grandmother soon remarried and had a second family, four more children. Her second husband, my grandfather, hard-drinking and easily angered, was a civil engineer employed by the Union Pacific Railroad. He died of a heart attack in the midst of a drunken temper tantrum. All their children were afflicted by alcoholism, which varied from mild to severe.

Maternal grandparents, New Orleans, 1931

Her third child and second son, my uncle Murray, was something of a wild man, alcoholic, and had Irish charm, energy, and fantasy. He owned a racehorse which ran at the county racetrack, as did a horse belonging to the sheriff, a drinking buddy. They had too much to drink, a heated argument ensued, and the sheriff shot Uncle Murray in the back, killing him instantly. The sheriff said Uncle Murray was threatening him, and he shot in self-defense (I suppose Murray was cleverly trying to confuse the sheriff by attacking him while walking backward).

Her next (fourth) child was my mother, who was her father's favorite. Born in 1904 in Indian Territory, which later became Oklahoma, she was a pretty and pampered little girl, who grew into a beautiful and willful woman, although she was shy, afraid of people, and insecure. She was a talented violinist and hoped for a career as a concert artist, but this was not to be. There was not enough money to pay for extensive lessons with excellent teachers.

Mother, right, and two of her brothers sitting on Old Prince, Custer City, Oklahoma, 1914

Mother, right, and a friend, Dallas, 1935

She had an unhappy marriage to my father, but they remained married until they died. This led me to view marriage, no matter how abusive and filled with hatred, as a stable and inescapable relationship, like a life sentence in a ghastly prison.

My mother (left), my father (center), and Aunt Nellie (right), White Rock Lake, Dallas, around 1932

Unfortunately, Mother became a severe alcoholic, like her sister Nellie, her father, and her grandfather, and she eventually died of the disease.

She had the most severe stutter I have ever heard, which was very frustrating for her. Oddly, it was made worse by drinking, and in later years, she often became mute when she drank. She was obviously trying to speak but couldn't get any words out.

When she was sober, immaculate clothes and grooming added to an air of quiet dignity, melancholy, and detached refinement appropriate to her view of her proper role in life.

And Granny's fifth and last child was my favorite uncle, Van. Intelligent, lively, and handsome, he sometimes came to visit us in McAllen and seemed to enjoy taking me across the border to Mexico, where we had a good dinner. He would give me my own bottle of beer. I was delighted. He was a tease and years later sometimes asked me, "How does it feel to weigh a tenth of a ton?" He often said before a festive meal, "Don't over-gorge."

Uncle Van, Dallas, 1933

I grew up a few hundred miles from any of my mother's family but saw them occasionally and thought of them as my family. I was fond of them all and looked forward to their visits once or twice a year as bright spots in a flattened and desolate childhood. When they visited us, they seemed to like me; I couldn't understand why, but it felt good.

Reviewing this group of grandparents, parents, uncles, aunts, and cousins, there are some common traits. We were mostly long-lived, independent, courageous, shy, hardworking, imaginative, musical, creative, intelligent, honest, and stubborn, and we clung tenaciously to our beliefs and fantasies, supernatural or otherwise. We were not afraid to strike out on our own, seeking greener grass or an escape from unpleasant situations. Unfortunately, we also tended to be morose, resentful, sullen, combative, irritable, reclusive, alcoholic, and tubercular. Naturally, the family was not cohesive.

From this basket of happy and unhappy traits, I can usually pick out some which have a concrete bearing on or a connection with my own current situation. These precursor traits seem to have considerable staying power. Knowing about them and having a clear view of them does not give me much ability to tame, eliminate, or control them in myself. When trying to ride a wild, runaway horse, knowledge of the horse's genealogy doesn't help much.

I believe we should learn about the psychological characteristics of our ancestors so we are not thrown into disarray when some of these traits suddenly and surprisingly manifest themselves in our own thinking and behaviors, often inappropriately. Some or all of these traits are sure to express themselves, often without any conscious planning, approval, or provocation. Are they like poisonous snakes hidden in the grass or like hidden treasures? The answer is yes. The more knowledge we have of them, the more likely we can see alternative ways for ourselves.

A few years ago I had the shocking realization that what we desire, what we want so much we will work years to obtain and make almost any sacrifice for, has no necessary connection with what is best for us, short-term or long-term. We can know what we want but not what we should have. We are lucky if what we want is not lethal to ourselves.

Unrelenting hostility from my father led me to feel my own life was evil and worthless. It didn't matter what happened to me, what I did, or what honors I acquired, as I was evil simply because I was alive. There was nothing about myself to be proud of, to protect, or to foster. I learned my lesson of self-hatred very well and very early from him. He viewed me as a piece of trash dirtying up his highway through life.

The situation with my mother was the direct opposite. She valued me and everything about me so highly and checked on me so constantly that none of my life, none of myself, seemed to belong to me—everything about me belonged to her. This led me to feel that I was only a casual tourist in my own life, that I had nothing of my own to hold on to or to take care of. In a way that I can feel but not explain, this has also produced a very fortunate lack of envy, jealousy, or competitive striving.

The formative influences of early life give us some of the tools we will carry through life, but there is also an essential "I" apart from our tools and tool kit.

Another fine legacy from my family is that I have never been bored (when left to my own devices) and have never felt loneliness in general or been bothered by being alone, although sometimes I have yearned for one particular person. Whenever I read or hear about someone being put into solitary confinement, I secretly think, "Lucky person!" The other side of the coin, an unhappy legacy, has been a persistent uneasiness in the presence of my fellow humans, an automatic shrinking away from others. Perhaps having a sibling might have ameliorated this condition; perhaps not.

Beautiful Child

With Mother, Dallas, 1933

Ebano, a small but important jungle town on the Mexican Gulf coast, lay in the center of huge oil fields. Mexico was still somewhat lawless, and the town was surrounded by a high fence and guarded by soldiers against raids by bandit gangs. Also inside the fence, but a little separated from the town, was a large expatriate camp for foreign oil workers and their families.

With Mother, Dallas, 1934

It was August of 1934. The room was dark, and Johnny, just one year old, was alone and afraid. He couldn't walk or talk yet. Voices and laughter floated down the corridor from the living room, and he could see light coming from that direction. Pulling himself upright by holding on to the bars of his crib, he was desperately afraid of dangers in the dark. Facing the sound and light, he screamed for help. No one came. He screamed and screamed, but no one came. He gave up hope someone would come to rescue him and fell into his crib, shaking and moaning.

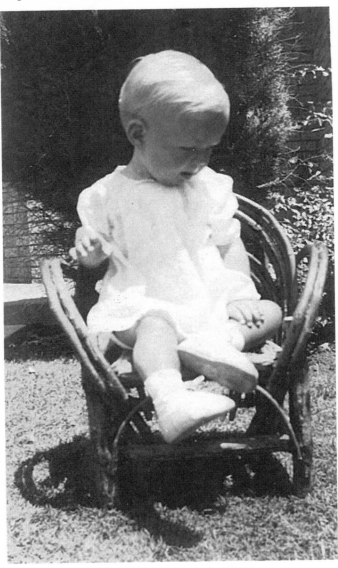

Ebano, Mexico, early 1935

Ebano was a few miles from the main railroad line and was connected to it by a spur line, which had a railroad cart big enough to carry eight people. There was a bench down the middle of the cart, a canopy against the rain and sun, and a man on each end to operate the up-and-down pumping handles. The man-powered cart could scoot along the rails at a good speed between the town and the railroad junction.

Age two, Ebano, 1935

Two years passed, and it was now August of 1936. Little Johnny, an only child, enjoyed riding the cart to the railroad junction on the occasional trips to Tampico with his parents. There the local ladies sometimes picked him up and kissed him, saying, *"Que chulo! Que chulo!"* (How beautiful!) The highlight of the trip was a visit to the big Tampico market where chocolate rabbits were for sale. Johnny always got one.

Age three, walking with his mother, Tampico street scene

He was a beautiful child, with platinum hair, blue eyes, a bright smile, and an air of quiet reserve. He had turned three earlier that August and had enjoyed a birthday party attended by his friends Mikey and Sharon Douglas and

Johnny with his friends Mikey and Sharon

Emma-Lou Ruby. Sharon was not really a contemporary, as she was already four. Mikey was almost three, and Johnny and Emma-Lou were the same age; their birthdays were only a week apart. Johnny was still having some difficulty learning to walk, especially going down stairs, but Emma-Lou was more proficient. Although she was a very sweet, pretty little girl who often gave Johnny a hug, he was jealous of her stair-descending ability.

Johnny had two other good friends, also three years old, who lived at his house. Tubby was a male Norwegian elkhound, genial, with liquid brown eyes and long brown fur, who was protective of Johnny, carefully inspecting people who got close.

Johnny with his best friend, Tubby, Ebano, 1936

Poochey was a Dalmatian, not too smart, with soft black eyes. He made up in character and disposition what he lacked in intelligence. Though a male, he took a maternal attitude toward Johnny, often giving him big wet kisses on his eyes. Tubby and Poochey were best friends, and they could run up and down the hill beside Johnny's house a hundred times better than Emma-Lou.

Author at his home in Ebano, 1936

Johnny's mother, Jean, was a shy, perfectly groomed, sensitive, overly intense woman. She was beautiful and looked younger than her thirty-two years. She was careful to see that Johnny got good care but was too busy going to parties with the other expatriate wives, playing cards, and smoking and drinking heavily to spend much time with him. She hadn't bothered to learn Spanish—there was no need.

Glenn, Johnny's father, a handsome, brilliant, adventurous man, was the same age as his wife. He had run away from home at sixteen and had gone to the Yucatan to work in the oil fields with his uncle Pete. Living in Mexico for several years, he became fluent in the language. With his dark eyes, black hair, swarthy skin, and perfect Spanish, he could pass for a Mexican. Glenn was friendly to all except Johnny, whom he didn't like. When Jean had told him she was pregnant, he ordered her to have an abortion. She refused, and their relationship had never fully recovered. He was jealous of Jean's attention to Johnny and saw him as a rival. Jean enjoyed Glenn's jealousy of Johnny.

Glenn was a hard worker, spending much time out of the house, perhaps on purpose, as Jean was already becoming a serious scold, especially when she was drinking.

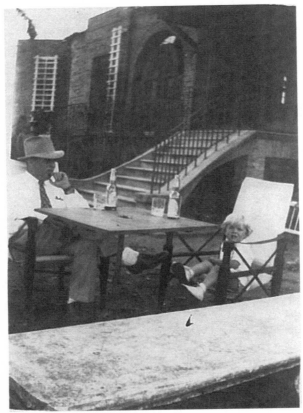

Author and his father drinking beer, Tampico Country Club, 1936

Both parents had grown up in the United States, neither one in a supportive family, and neither one knew much about being a parent.

Johnny's nurse, Chencha, was a middle-aged Mexican woman from the village. She was like a real mother to Johnny, which he needed. She gave him his breakfast, bathed him, helped him get dressed, went for walks with him, and watched him play with his friends. After making his lunch, she sat with him during his afternoon nap, then gave him his dinner and put him to bed. She hugged him and held him on her lap, and Johnny loved her smell of woodsmoke, onions, and perfume. He loved touching her face and hugging her, which he was not allowed to do with his mother or father. She offered Johnny the only human warmth he knew in the ice house of his early childhood. On Sundays, when she usually spent the day in the village with her family, Johnny missed her and was sad.

Chencha spent a lot of time talking to Johnny. She only spoke Spanish, so Johnny learned to speak Spanish, not English; there was no need. Jean and Glenn thought it amusing that their little boy could speak Spanish but couldn't speak with them in their native language. Johnny didn't care. They had nothing to say to Johnny, and he had nothing to say to them.

So, Johnny's world was tranquil and secure, and he liked being with his customary bunch: Mikey and Sharon, Emma-Lou, Tubby, Poochey, and especially Chencha. His parents were of very little interest to him. They were like furniture to him.

At ten o'clock one Sunday morning, Jean was still in bed nursing a bad case of the "flu," as she called her hangovers. Glenn sat in the living room cleaning his fingernails with a kitchen knife. Johnny played with his blocks on the floor. Jean called out in a hoarse, commanding voice from the bedroom, "Glenn, take Johnny for a walk." Glenn frowned, looking angry, but after a few seconds he smiled slightly and said, "Oh, yes."

Going for a walk with his father, Dallas, 1936

So Johnny and Glenn set out. It must have been a charming sight—the little platinum-haired boy with his handsome, dark-haired father, walking hand in hand.

They climbed to the top of a small hill, where there was an abandoned, dilapidated bandstand, with concrete pillars and a domed roof. It had a good view over the camp, the village, and the countryside, as far as the house of the doctor who kept cages of rattlesnakes to use in his experiments.

Johnny didn't like that house. His father sometimes took him there to see the snakes and held him up close to the cages. The snakes stared at Johnny. They coiled and rattled and made Johnny scream with fear as Glenn laughed.

After surveying the scenery from the bandstand, Glenn picked his son up and held him close; Johnny was surprised, but he liked being held. Sometimes he hoped that his father loved him. Glenn smiled at him with his mouth and his teeth, but his eyes were like the snakes' eyes in the cages, hard and cold.

Speaking in Spanish, he said, "You're not our child. We don't like you at all. We hate you. We're going to take you back where we found you and leave you there."

Johnny's world collapsed. The light got very bright, and sounds seemed to die away. Johnny couldn't get enough air. He didn't know what he had done to cause this.

He began to cry, to scream in abject sorrow and terror, and he waved his arms helplessly. What had he done? He didn't know how to atone. What would he do? Where would he live? Who would take care of him? The top of his head seemed to be melting away. He felt an excruciating, searing, crushing pain in the back of his head, as if his head were being shot to pieces.

Glenn smiled. "Quit crying, you brat," he said. "If you *ever* tell anyone what I said, I'll cut off both your hands."

Johnny abruptly quit crying and was immediately paralyzed with horror and despair. His spirit fled, and his body became like a mute, stiff wooden doll.

Glenn began to laugh softly. He enjoyed the effective and successful psychic rape and amputation he had just accomplished.

Johnny Crying, Father Smiling. Torture Bandstand, Ebano, 1936

They walked slowly back down the hill and went home. Johnny tried to look his usual self. Jean didn't notice anything wrong. Even if he had dared to tell his mother, he couldn't, because he had never learned her language.

Jean smiled at him. "Did you have fun on your walk?" Johnny didn't understand her. Glenn smiled smugly at them both.

Johnny hugged his father's leg, already learning the importance of saving the face of his tormentors, of colluding with them to conceal their crimes, even if he were the victim. He was afraid his father might cut his mother's hands off too.

Tubby and Poochey knew something bad had happened, and they stayed close to Johnny the rest of the day.

When Chencha arrived the next morning, she too knew something was very wrong. She tried to comfort him, but Johnny feared that Chencha would be in danger and might have her hands cut off if he confided in her. And he didn't tell Mikey or Sharon or Emma-Lou what had happened either. He didn't tell anyone. From then on, life seemed dangerous and frightening.

Once or twice a month, Glenn would take Johnny for a walk up the hill to the bandstand and would repeat the torture. He always enjoyed these occasions, and the more Johnny screamed, the better Glenn liked it. Johnny knew that no degree of submission or obedience could save him from the monster's hatred—there was no escape.

The usual details of life went on: Mikey and Sharon and Emma-Lou came to play, Tubby and Poochey were sweeter than ever, and Chencha was more loving than ever. But Johnny was being destroyed.

Early in December 1937, the Mexican government decided to expel all foreign oil field workers and their families and to expropriate all foreign oil properties. Christmas Day was chosen for this to be executed. President Roosevelt intervened with President Cardenas of Mexico, and a one-day postponement of the expulsion was granted.

On Christmas Day, Johnny received a wonderful present: a little barn with a wooden fence and wooden farm animals. He loved the little animals and hoped they would be his friends. There had been much packing, and Johnny's parents were nearly ready to leave Ebano.

The next morning, December 26, Chencha was crying, but she gave Johnny his breakfast and his bath and helped him get dressed. He started to pick up his Christmas present, the wonderful farm set, to take with him, but his mother said, "No. Leave that here." He began to cry in disappointment. He saw his father smile.

He hadn't said goodbye to his friends and was not allowed to say goodbye to Tubby and Poochey, who were sitting on the steps outside the front door. Chencha, tears in her eyes, gave him a last hug, he got into the little Oldsmobile car with his parents, and they started the drive north to the Texas border.

He had lost everything: his farm set, his friends, Tubby and Poochey, his home, and worst of all, he had lost Chencha. And now he was at the mercy of his demonic father. Johnny knew better than to cry again.

After they reached their new home, the small Texas border town of McAllen, they moved into a small apartment building which did not permit pets. Glenn continued his tortures for another eighteen months, always in private, always in secret, with threats of mutilation if Johnny tried to reach out to anyone for help.

Jean saw him cringe and look frightened whenever Glenn came close to him. She knew there was something sinister going on between her husband and son, but she was not inclined to help. Johnny clung to her as his only protection from his father. As long as he stayed totally under her control, never showing any signs of independence, she was content with the situation. Glenn was as thorough as he knew how to be in his destruction of Johnny's soul, but eventually he became bored with his sadistic game.

Some years later, Johnny worked at his father's machine shop in the summers. He had powerful impulses to stick both his hands into the milling machine, which would have mangled and amputated them. These impulses have never entirely left him; his father's psychic wounds and mutilations have never completely healed.

Glenn would be proud and pleased at the permanent damage he had done but disappointed that he had not succeeded in eliminating Johnny entirely.

Johnny survived because he never confronted either of his parents. He tried not to think about what they did or said and tried to act as if all were well and as if he loved them. Every morning he hoped he could hide from his parents for another day. He tried to believe in the love that sometimes came his way from his grandmother, teachers, or from his aunts and uncles.

Emma-Lou and her parents moved to Egypt; Johnny never saw her again. Mikey and Sharon moved with their parents to the same south Texas town where Johnny and his parents moved. They came over to play with Johnny occasionally but eventually moved away, and they forgot the friendship. Tubby and Poochey were also shipped to Texas, to a family with a big house and yard. Johnny occasionally saw them and never stopped loving them, but they gradually forgot who he was and were no longer friendly, sometimes even growling at him if he wanted to hug them. He never saw or heard from Chencha again. Sometimes he could recall her smell, and tears would come. Years later he learned she had died in Ebano.

Johnny began to learn English and was able to talk with his mother. Eventually he learned to play the piano.

Now, seventy years later, Johnny can still look back and see his friends in Ebano, and he still yearns for those far away beings shining with innocence and love.

Johnny and his dear Chencha, Ebano, 1936

The Search Begins

My mother was a serious and dedicated violinist from early teen years. As a distraction from her intense preoccupation, two of her friends suggested that they all might enjoy taking flying lessons, and so they enrolled at the Houston airport flying school. My mother and her teacher, who owned the flying school, fell in love and soon were married.

Three years later, I was born. My mother continued her violin study, which included several hours of practice each day. When I turned one, my mother suddenly stopped practicing, put her violin away, and did not play again for many years.

Three factors caused her to stop playing: the physical difficulty of practicing, her realization that a concert career was becoming more unlikely, and most importantly, I cried when she played.

Years later she told me which compositions she most loved to play—pieces by Fritz Kreisler: *Schon Rosmarin, Caprice Viennoise, the Old Refrain*; the Bruch G minor Concerto, pieces by Sarasate: *Zigeunerweisen, Spanish Dances,* and others. I had heard all these pieces repeatedly before I was born. I may have been crying when I heard these pieces at age one from joy, not from misery, at again hearing music I had heard in the womb. Unfortunately, my mother had no way of knowing this, and she had already died before I came to understand the true situation. I have no conscious recollection of having heard my mother play them, but even today, when I hear these pieces, my eyes fill with tears and I feel a piercing emotion: part joy, part loneliness, part sadness for something once loved and now lost forever. Like love, the feeling is unbelievably painful and immensely precious and desirable. The grieving never finishes, even if what was lost is forgotten.

XXXXXXXXXXXXXXXXXXXXXXXXXXXXXXXXXXXXXXXXX

We each have a yearning, a drive, a desire, a movement toward ecstasy. Many supposed experts are eager to tell us in what direction and where our ecstasy lies and how we may reach or regain our goal. Some of these guides may be correct but only by coincidence. If their facades were transparent, we could see the guides themselves are lost and wandering in a desert of misery and pain.

It is almost impossible to say where our ecstasy lies, as many miseries successfully disguise themselves as ecstasies. It is even more difficult to outline a path to the goal. Perhaps there is no path, no way to reach the goal. By accident, or by random imagination, we may brush up against our ecstasy, but this is rare and completely unpredictable: it may occur in any circumstance and at any age.

Sometimes it is like a glimpse of the lost beloved from the window of a speeding train. In a shimmering moment, our beloved is lost again. When great ecstasy comes to us, its twin—great, piercing, unbearable pain—always accompanies it. Eve's apple is sweet and full of poison.

XXXXXXXXXXXXXXXXXXXXXXXXXXXXXXXXXXXXXXXX

In 1937, when I was four years old, for the first time I had the good fortune to stumble by accident onto the road to ecstasy. One day, when left alone by my mother in the bathtub, with the water running, I explored the sensation of the water as it gushed against various parts of my body. To my bewildered delight I found that the water running against my peepee produced a very intense pleasure. I was disappointed that I could not find any other part of my body which gave me pleasure anywhere close to the peepee pleasure.

In my household there was very little discussion of bodily parts or functions. The word *peepee* served as a noun and a verb. A peepee peepeeed peepee. *Weewee*, likewise, served as a noun and a verb. A peepee weeweeed weewee.

Fortunately for me, my mother was not interested in my peepee function, but she was definitely interested in my bowel function and insisted on examining my bowel movements until I was fourteen years old.

She insisted on administering enemas to me two or three times a month until then. At that time I rebelled, we had a big quarrel, and she gave up. However, frequent dosing with laxatives continued until I was seventeen. Until the time she died nineteen years later, she inquired from time to time as to the condition of my bowel movements and sometimes suggested she should inspect them. "No, everything's okay," I replied, and she grudgingly pulled in her horns and acted offended for a while.

I have never seen any research showing at what age mothers usually stop wanting to inspect the BMs of their sons and/or daughters. Perhaps fathers are generally not so interested.

At any rate, I understood in a dim way that running the bathtub faucet onto my peepee was not acceptable. A couple of times my mother caught me doing this and scolded me and said I must never do it again. "Why?" I asked. "Just because. *Don't do it again*," she yelled at me. She made her point, which was that I should be careful to hide any peepee play from her and from my father, who was becoming her puppet. This was the first installment of my childhood sex education.

Within two years I had grown so tall that I could no longer maneuver myself under the bathtub faucet, and so I said a hesitant farewell to my faucet-lover. My first small bites of Eve's apple were tainted and sorrowful.

XXXXXXXXXXXXXXXXXXXXXXXXXXXXXXXXXXXXXXXXXXXX

The apartment where we lived was in a building with three other apartments. The walls were so thin my mother said, "You can hear the neighbors eating toast in the morning. What a hellhole." My mother usually referred to McAllen as "this hellhole."

The landlords, the Nelsons, lived across the street in an old two-story house with a big porch. Mrs. Nelson would sometimes invite me inside her big house to sit down and have a little chat. She would give me a piece of candy, which I did not tell my mother about, as she did not approve of candy.

My mother seemed particularly annoyed when we went out, perhaps when we were getting in the car to drive to the grocery store or do some other errand, that the slats of the venetian blinds in each apartment could be seen to separate enough for the people inside to peek out to see who was doing what. The same thing happened when we came home. My mother disliked being watched, or as she put it, "spied on." She and I did the same spying when we were inside and heard a noise outside. We thought of this as perfectly harmless curiosity but of course not as peeking or spying.

Mrs. Nelson always looked sad; I expect she was lonely. Her daughter, Nanette, and husband, Jack, lived in the complex, in a garage apartment right next to our apartment. It seemed to me that living in a garage apartment was very glamorous. They went flying on the weekends in their own airplane. We could sometimes hear them quarreling and screaming at one another. My parents agreed that they drank too much and that was the cause of their arguments.

After a while, Jack crashed the airplane when he was drunk, and he and Nanette were both seriously injured. After they recovered, they were divorced. Apparently glamour and domestic happiness did not go together. I wondered why some people seemed happy and others didn't.

Nanette always smiled at me and usually had something cheerful and kindly to say. The result was that I fell in love with her. I told my parents and some other neighbors about it but never had the nerve to tell Nanette herself. Perhaps she knew intuitively; perhaps someone told her how I felt about her. Nanette continued living alone in the garage apartment until she was found dead one morning. Nobody explained to me what had happened; perhaps the cause of her death was unknown. *Maybe a broken heart*, I wondered.

XXXXXXXXXXXXXXXXXXXXXXXXXXXXXXXXXXXXXXXXXX

There were only a few apartment buildings in McAllen. Most people lived in houses, or in trailer-houses in the trailer courts. Other children teased me about living in an apartment and said only bums and white trash lived like that. I believed what they said and was suitably embarrassed and ashamed. But it didn't matter, as nobody liked me anyway.

Author and his father, McAllen, Texas, 1939

In spite of what the other children said, there were some advantages to living in the apartment complex. There were various trees growing in the yard—grapefruit, orange, mesquite—and shrubs, too: hibiscus and oleander. Sammy and Johnnie, two neighborhood boys my age, and I often played together. We liked to climb in the trees, eat the fruit when it was ripe enough, and look in the windows of the apartments, spying on the neighbors.

Once we saw Matilda, one of the housewives of the neighborhood, emerge from her bathroom with nothing on. We could see *everything* as she stood in front of the window slowly drying herself before she sat down at her dressing table to comb her hair and play with her breasts. We almost fell out of the tree from embarrassment and of course did not tell anyone what we had seen.

The neighborhood dog, Cookie, a friendly and enterprising dachshund, lived in another garage apartment with her owners, Dolly and Roger. Each evening about 7 o'clock, Cookie would come to the back door of our apartment and bark to be let in. My mother would let Cookie in, and we would all talk to her. I could pet her and play with her for a while, and she would give me some kisses, which I loved. We would usually save her a small piece of meat left over from dinner, or a little milk, sometimes even a little ice cream.

After about ten minutes, Cookie would scratch at the back door, and we would let her out. She would go immediately to the next apartment and repeat her visit and snack consumption. Of the thirteen apartments in the complex, including her own, three had occupants who did not like Cookie, but nine apartments welcomed her most every evening.

Cookie was fat. Like most dachshunds, she could sit up and beg persuasively for an extended period. In spite of her obesity, she was agile and active. She could make a running start and run right up the slanting trunk of the biggest mesquite tree in the yard. She liked to go dangerously far up in the tree. Barking with pride, she seemed to say, "Look at me!! Look at me!! What a special dog I am!! Oh yes." We were all proud of Cookie's unusual tree-climbing ability and bragged to our friends about her. If they were skeptical, we would invite them over to see Cookie climb up into the tree. She was always happy to show off, and our friends were always suitably impressed.

Then sadness came to the neighborhood. Dolly, Cookie's owner, was pregnant and gave birth to a daughter. Everyone went to see the new baby. She was very ugly and screamed from time to time. The grown-ups said, "Oh, she's so beautiful, so cute, so darling," and touched her hands and feet. We children knew they were lying, but grown-ups often did unexplainable things.

After three months, Cookie suddenly disappeared. We were told that she had been jealous of the screaming little newcomer and had growled at her. Dolly and Roger felt they had to exile Cookie, so she was sent to live with a family a mile away. A week later, she ran away and came back to her old neighborhood. We all hoped she could stay at home, but she was sent into exile again. We were all sad to lose Cookie, who, like most dogs, was a bundle of love. We children hated the ugly newcomer. We didn't like Dolly and Roger anymore and wouldn't speak to them. They were obviously stupid, mean, and crazy. We all agreed that they should have kept Cookie and sent the ugly little screamer away to live somewhere else, perhaps to an orphanage.

A few months after Cookie was sent away, another family in the apartments got a new puppy named "Puppy." He was a friendly little being and soon developed his own route around the neighborhood to visit the various apartments. He liked to jump and play with me, and I soon began to love Puppy. I looked forward to his visits and sometimes went to his house and knocked on the door, asking to play with him. I would be let in, and sometimes his parents gave me a cookie.

One Saturday morning, I looked down from our second-floor window and saw Puppy lying by the side of the road. I told my mother about this, and she looked out the window. "Uh-oh," she said. "I hope he hasn't been run over by a car." I yelled and ran down the stairs and across the street. Puppy was lying very still.

As I got closer, I could see something which looked like a heavy red glass around his mouth. I called to him, but he didn't move. When I got even closer, I could see that it was shiny red blood wrapped around his mouth. He didn't move. I touched him, and he still didn't move. I lifted one of his little legs, which was totally limp and fell back to the ground with a tiny thump when I let it go. I knew he was dead.

He had been hit by a car, which had not stopped. Perhaps the driver didn't know that an accident had happened—Puppy was only a little dog and would not have made much of a bump as the car ran over him. I ran home crying and told my mother. She asked me to go to his house and tell his owners. I did this, and they rushed out to go to him. When they saw him, they too began to cry.

I had seen my little turtle dead, also some cockroaches, and once I saw a dead bird, but I had never before seen a dead animal, especially not one that I loved. It was terrible. It left a hole in the middle of my chest. A permanent scar formed inside. Seventy years later, I can still see little Puppy with the blood red cuff wrapped around his mouth and can remember how it felt to cry for him.

XXXXXXXXXXXXXXXXXXXXXXXXXXXXXXXXXXXXXXXXXXX

Across the street from our apartment house was the Lincoln Elementary School, where I was enrolled in the first grade in September of 1939. In the schoolyard there were teeter-totters, slides, jungle gyms, and swings. The six swings hung in a row from iron pipes welded into a triangular shape, with a horizontal connecting pipe. All the boys liked to slowly shinny up the pipes, and I found out why. Wrapping my legs around the pipe and then squeezing and pushing produced an even better sensation than the bathtub faucet.

Small boys in various sizes hung from the pipes in paralyzed ecstasy until the sensation began to diminish. Then we gave another push or two further up the pole and the ecstatic feeling returned. The boys hanging on the poles resembled bats or coconuts—minimal activity from these lumps of flesh. The real activity was not pole-climbing; it was ecstasy-making. For many of us, it was our introduction to sex; we were having sex with a metal pole and already feeling guilty about it too.

A few tomboys would also shinny vigorously up the poles, much faster than the boys, but they didn't seem to have the same paralysis problems that the boys were enjoying. Occasionally, the teachers would urge us to go on to the top, or else to climb down, and we would. The teachers, all female, perhaps did not realize exactly what was going on, but they knew it was something *wrong* and *bad*.

So, I soon realized with a pre-verbal understanding that both peepee play and ecstasy would lead to being scolded and shamed and threatened by adult bullies, like parents and teachers. This was my second lesson in sex.

XXXXXXXXXXXXXXXXXXXXXXXXXXXXXXXXXXXXXXXXXXXX

Most summer afternoons, my mother took me for an hour or two to the big public swimming pool, the Cascade, about two miles out of town on the road to the Mexican border, which was five miles farther along the road. In the summer, the Cascade was open daily, except when there was a polio epidemic. At those times, all pools would be closed, along with many public gathering places, such as movies, auditoriums, bars, dance halls, and such.

People were terrified of catching polio. No one knew what caused it or how it was transmitted, although it was suspected that crowds, or water, or flies, or lower-class people might have something to do with the transmission. There was no protection or immunization or effective treatment. The illness could be of any degree of severity, from barely noticeable, to a permanent mild or severe paralysis, to living the rest of life in an iron lung, or to dying, which was not uncommon.

When a polio vaccine was eventually announced, bells rang across the country, and an announcement was made in the Supreme Court, interrupting a trial.

In that era, in the late 1930s, segregation was still widely practiced. In those days "Whites Only" was the policy in many places, at least in the Southern United States. Not only were blacks not permitted in the pool (there were no blacks living in the little south Texas border town of McAllen, Texas, anyway), but no Hispanics were permitted either (they might be spreading disease), with one exception: the son of the local internist, a Hispanic man highly respected in the community.

Since there were no blacks living in McAllen, or Negroes, as was the term in those days, Mexicans were substituted as objects of bigotry and discrimination. McAllen was divided equally between the "Anglos," or "Americans," or "whites" and the "Mexicans," which included residents of Mexico, illegal entrants (wetbacks) now called "undocumented aliens," and also Mexican-Americans.

The town had four movie theaters, none of which would admit blacks, if any had shown up to buy a ticket. There were two theaters in the Anglo section of town. The better one, the Palace, which played first-run movies with stars like Bette Davis, Joan Crawford, and Betty Grable, would not admit Mexicans. The second-rate theater, the Queen, played B movies, cowboy films, serials, and such and was the Saturday afternoon hangout for many of the white kids.

The Queen would admit a small number of Mexicans, who had to sit in the rear section of the balcony. The two theaters in "Mexiquita," as the Mexican section of town west of Fourteenth Street was called, would of course admit Mexicans, and also Anglos, although Anglos did not attend the Mexican theaters unless they were perhaps interested in something other than seeing the movie. Mexicans were also unwelcome in the better clothing stores, restaurants, drugstores, and pharmacies, and they generally cooperated by keeping timidly to their places. This kind of segregation seemed okay to us unthinking kids—it was just the way things were.

However, there was one exception to this general bigotry and discrimination. The Garza family owned a tract of several thousand acres northwest of McAllen, in Starr County. They had received their property in a land grant from the king of Spain some centuries earlier and therefore antedated any of the other locals, Anglos or Hispanics. Their property had numerous productive oil and gas wells. The Garzas were wealthy, socially exclusive, and reclusive. They did not mingle with any of the locals, their friends being in Monterrey, Mexico City, and Madrid.

I knew their daughter, Jesusita ("little girl Jesus," not an unusual name), who took singing lessons from my piano teacher, Esther Lee Blakemore. Jesusita had a clear lyric soprano voice and made rapid progress in her singing. She had fair skin, large brown eyes, light brown hair, and wonderful posture.

She had exquisite manners and seemed very kind and intelligent but often looked melancholy. In other words, she was a paragon. She was tutored privately at home, traveled by chauffeured limousine, always had a stern and capable chaperone in attendance, and of course did not date any of the local boys.

In a dim way, I realized that here was a person quite outside the usual social norm who was having an exceptionally good life. This gave me a little hope about my own situation as an outsider. Eventually I lost track of Jesusita, but I hope she made a happy marriage and has had the radiant life she seemed destined for.

But back to the swimming pool: I greatly enjoyed swimming. It was a noncompetitive sport, the only kind of athletic activity I liked. I would change into my bathing suit in the men's locker room or would wear my bathing suit from home. I hated to put my feet in the smelly chlorine water, which was mandatory going into and coming out of the pool.

There were drawings on the locker room walls. I knew these were peepee drawings, showing something like a cannon with wheels underneath. I knew the pictures showed something dirty, that nice people were not interested in such things. Even worse, I understood that this had something to do not only with dirty people themselves, but it also had something to do with girls and something nasty they did with boys or men.

In some way I could not clearly visualize, I thought that weewee and bowel movements were somehow involved in this whatever-it-was. I wanted no part of this but had the good sense not to mention these drawings to my mother. She might have forbidden further visits to the pool, which would have taken away one of the few pleasures I had as a child.

Sometimes on weekends my father would also go to the pool, and we would change in the locker room. When I thought he wasn't looking at me, I would take a quick and furtive glance at his peepee, but I didn't recognize what I saw. There appeared to be some lumpy arrangement of flesh with a lot of hair around it. I thought it looked disgusting, but I was curious anyway. I hated the thought that something like that might eventually grow on me. I didn't want to believe it.

The swimming pool visits concluded the third installment of my childhood sex education. Pure poison, no pleasure at all. Eve's apple was not offered at the swimming pool, at least not to me.

XXXXXXXXXXXXXXXXXXXXXXXXXXXXXXXXXXXXXXXXXXXXX

My next steps along the road to the land of ecstasy occurred at school, with my classmates in the first grade. I liked a few of the little girls in my class and even occasionally proposed marriage. My proposal was usually accepted, and my new wife, who would call herself "Mrs. Loomis," and I would hold hands and hug and kiss on the cheeks for the next few weeks. This never felt quite right, and it was boring anyway, so presently there would be a divorce by mutual agreement, and I would choose a new wife from among my classmates.

Some of the little girls wanted to do their own choosing, and so they attempted to choose a husband. This behavior was too aggressive to be acceptable to the teachers and was discouraged. Only the ugliest little girls proposed marriage to me (like Willie-Maude, with her dirty hands, bad smell, freckles, and buck teeth), and I didn't want to marry them, so nothing came of their gender-reversing behavior.

A number of my other first-grade classmates were getting married and divorced on a regular schedule, and I suppose that for some of them these casual uploads and downloads continued for the rest of their lives. The teachers found this behavior amusing or charming, and it was never discouraged.

My parents were told that I was mentally retarded, that I could not learn as well as the other students. They were shocked and unbelieving and consulted local physicians about this problem. It was discovered that I was extremely nearsighted. I could not see the blackboard and therefore could not learn from it.

I remember the first day with my new glasses. I was astounded and overjoyed that I could see the leaves on the trees and birds flying in the air. I knew that trees had leaves and that birds flew in the air, but I had not been able to see them before if they were more than two or three feet from me. And for the first time, I could see the writing on the blackboard. I turned from the worst student into the best, and my classmates disliked me more than ever.

They called me "four-eyes," "loony," "fangs" (I had very crooked teeth), and other names which hurt my feelings. I was the worst athlete in the school, a fact which stimulated my classmates' contempt even more.

Perhaps unknown to the teachers, there was a kind of secret talk among the children: "Can I park my car in your garage?" and similar questions, followed by much giggling. We didn't know what we were saying but understood that it was something grown-up, dirty, and not to be repeated to the teachers or parents. By the time I reached the second grade, I realized that the marriages, despite the teachers' amused approval, and secret talk were only leading me into blind alleys, like infantile marriages of convenience, and no real love was involved.

Eve's apple was not at the end of any of these alleys, or perhaps an easily detected fake apple was being offered.

On the other hand, my interest in little boys was much more urgent. From the standpoint of an adult, all little boys may seem rather similar, but from my viewpoint as a child, there was as much variation in my little friends as there now appears to me to exist among adults. I preferred boys who had clear skin, blond or brown hair, and blue eyes, who were strong and had well-developed muscles. It helped if they were intelligent and friendly, but the physical attributes were more important.

In my first-grade class there were three outstanding objects of desire. This desire didn't have any definite form or sexual content, but I wanted to touch or hug my desire objects.

The first was Homer, who was an infant Hercules, eventually becoming an amateur boxing champion. He was of Hispanic background, from a large Catholic family. They lived in a small house in Mexiquita. Even in the second grade Homer was very busy with his exercise and boxing practice. He didn't seem particularly intelligent, which made no difference to me.

Sometimes I felt desperate to hug him. My attempts to "wrestle" with Homer were met with bored passivity. Homer knew I liked him and was remotely friendly in return, but we had so little in common that it never occurred to either of us to pursue the friendship.

The second object of my hug obsession was Harold, a tall brown-haired boy who worked at the grocery store on afternoons and weekends. He was the youngest of three brothers. All were handsome, good athletes, popular, friendly, and had even, cheerful dispositions. Harold was intelligent, although he took some pains to hide the fact so as not to alienate his classmates.

I often tried to wrestle with Harold, but he wasn't very interested, as he was much stronger than I, and this mismatch didn't challenge him enough. The wrestling matches consisted of my (unsuccessful) attempts to hug Harold, and his (successful) attempts to hold me off.

Two years later, I found a book on hypnosis in the public library and imagined that if I could hypnotize Harold, I could then hug him as much as I wanted. I invited him over to my house one evening when my parents had gone out and made an attempt to hypnotize him. He was willing to try this, but the only result was that his eyes got tired from looking upward, which was part of my routine. My lack of success was disappointing to me and probably also to Harold.

Word of this experiment somehow circled back to my mother, who scolded me severely and said I must never do such a thing again. I didn't tell Harold or anyone else that the real point was to hug him. I realized that my desire to happily hug Harold was hopeless, an early bitter disappointment.

The third object of my adoration was Charles. He had a crew cut, which was unusual in those days. Probably his mother cut his hair, as the family was poor. He also had a dark suntan and dark hair and eyes, was quiet and shy, and kept mostly to himself. Charles lived with his family on a farm and had to do hard manual work to help out. This resulted in his becoming very strong, and he was a mass of rocky-hard muscle. I liked to feel his fuzzy crew cut, and he seemed pleased to have me run my hands over his head from time to time.

When I tried to wrestle with him, he would just stand still and let me try to twist his arms, trip him, put my arms around him and throw him to the ground, or whatever other maneuver I might dream up. He did not budge. It was like trying to throw a tree to the ground. His arms were so strong they could not be twisted. He just smiled at me and invited me to keep trying. I had the chance to repeatedly feel most of Charles, which I enjoyed greatly, especially squeezing his shoulders and biceps. He knew I liked him and was pleased by my admiring attention. I invited him over to my house a number of times, but he always had to go home right after school to help with the farm chores. What happiness might have happened if he had come over?

Sometimes I would stare at the Tarbutton boys, three handsome, athletic brothers who generally kept to themselves and had a reputation for being tough and mean. Sometimes I caught the middle brother, my favorite, staring back at me. This gave me a thrill; the meaning was unknown to me. We eventually became friendly.

There was no conscious sexual/genital component to my desires. I wanted genuine, friendly close physical contact. I am glad that I did not understand more, confused and yearning though I was.

About this time, my mother, whom I usually addressed as "Honey" and "Sweetie," had a somber talk with me in which she told me that these names were not good and I must not use them anymore. From then on, I was to address her as "Mother," which I did. Perhaps she was aware of some overly close element in our relationship; perhaps my father didn't like my calling her by names of endearment. When I addressed my father, I called him "Daddy," which he did not like, but perhaps he could not think of any other form of address he would dislike less. I was told to speak to him as little as possible in public. I guessed that he was embarrassed by being associated with me.

XXXXXXXXXXXXXXXXXXXXXXXXXXXXXXXXXXXXXXXXXXX

My sociable and friendly wrestling daydreams were interrupted by ugly reality in the second grade, which I started in September 1940 at age seven. One of my classmates, Bobby, was a tough little boy from the wrong side of the tracks. He was a fighter and a bully. He started on me by demanding that I give him my eraser and said he was going to beat me up if I didn't give it to him. After two days of threats, I finally surrendered and gave him the eraser.

He said if I told anybody about this, he was going to beat me up, and he gave me a hard punch in the stomach as a token of his intentions.

The next week he wanted my fountain pen, and I again slowly gave in to him. Then he wanted my notebook, and then my Crayolas. Then he began taking my schoolbooks away from me. The last indignity was his demand that I give him my lunch money, so I had no money left to buy anything in the school cafeteria. I had to go hungry for the rest of the school day. The no lunch situation went on for about two weeks.

I had never had a fight, didn't know how to fight, was afraid of Bobby, and didn't think there was anywhere I could turn for help. I was a defeated seven-year-old sissy, and the situation became intolerable. Perhaps my father had been right when he wanted to abort my birth.

One morning after breakfast, instead of getting ready for school, I told my mother that I wasn't going to school anymore. Because I was a good student and had always liked school, she knew that something was seriously amiss. At first I wouldn't tell her what was wrong, but after about two hours, I broke down crying and explained that somebody had taken all my school supplies, that I had nothing to work with anymore, that I would no longer be permitted to have any pencils, pens, paper, Crayolas, books, or any other school supplies, that I wasn't going to be permitted to have lunch anymore, and that I was afraid of being beaten by Bobby. Obviously, I couldn't go to school ever again.

My mother looked at me thoughtfully, then combed her hair and put on her street clothes. She told me to wait at home, and that she was going to see Victor Fields, the school principal. She came back in about an hour and told me that she had explained to Mr. Fields that I was too intimidated and terrified by one of my fellow students to be able to come to school anymore. At first Mr. Fields found the story hard to believe. He couldn't imagine how one of the best students in the school could be in such a predicament without any of the teachers knowing that anything was wrong. Even then I was expert at hiding and dissembling my feelings.

He called the second-grade teacher, Miss Beasley, along with Bobby, to his office, and after a few minutes Bobby confessed to his misdeeds. He had taken some of my things to his home; others he still had secreted in his desk. Mr. Fields told Bobby to go home and bring back my things. He asked my mother to go home and to bring me back to his office after lunch.

The scene in his office, attended by my mother, Mr. Fields, and Miss Beasley, was very distressing to me, as I was afraid to tell my story. Then Bobby was summoned to come to the office and to bring all my things with him.

I was terrified, and the three adults could see the extent of the fear that Bobby had put into me. When Bobby appeared, I expected him to start beating me in front of the others, but to my surprise, he looked sheepish and kept his eyes down. I had assumed the grown-ups would take his side against me.

He was told to apologize to me and to give my things back. He complied without meeting my eyes. He was told that his parents would be notified of what he had done and that he was to leave me strictly alone. He was never to try to take anything from me again, or else he would be expelled from school. I believe that the teachers recognized a budding criminal in Bobby. I was told that if Bobby bothered me again, I should immediately go to my teacher or to Mr. Fields's office.

I viewed myself as thoroughly disliked and unlikeable, and therefore I was very surprised that my story had been believed and that the adults had been willing to protect me or to support me or to correct the wrong done to me. I was surprised that they cared whether Bobby beat me to a pulp or whether I ever returned to school again.

Unfortunately, the lesson I learned was not that I would be protected and might have some of my rights preserved. The lesson I learned was to be afraid, to be wary, to guard my possessions, and not to trust my fellow students. I actually had not expected any of them, or any other adults either, to act toward me with goodwill. I thought I could not rely on such an unlikely event in the future, and this outlook has not changed much even now. I remained terrified of Bobby, who glared at me and occasionally punched me when nobody was watching. However, he did not try to practice extortion on me again.

Looking on the positive side, perhaps the early experience of being a victim of extortion stood me in good stead later on, so I was not more trusting and vulnerable to being tricked. I am not a trusting person even today, years later. Sometimes I think with surprise and gratitude of the kindness of my mother, Mr. Fields, and Miss Beasley in helping me with the Bobby situation, which was completely beyond my capacity to manage by myself.

XXXXXXXXXXXXXXXXXXXXXXXXXXXXXXXXXXXXXXXXXXX

In December 1940, when I was seven years old, the school put on a Christmas pageant. I was chosen to play one of the numerous angels. My mother made me an angel costume out of an old sheet. It was like a floor-length dress, fairly wide, with long, very floppy sleeves and small droopy blue wings attached in the back. I loved it. My part in the pageant called for me to stand still most of the time, but now and then I could swish and twirl around the stage, along with the other angels, flapping and fluttering my sleeves.

Imagining myself to really be an angel, I was in another and better world for a while. When the pageant was finished, all the children took their costumes home. My outfit hung in the clothes closet, and I often looked at it. Occasionally I would try on my mother's high-heeled shoes, but this was only mild fun, not serious like becoming an angel.

A couple of weeks later, I put the angel costume on and then went outside into the yard and pretended to be a flying, twirling, leaping, fluttering angel, far surpassing my stage performance. It was heaven. My mother said nothing when I came back into the house. Over the next month, I spent more and more time dressed to show the real me—a twirly angel. My parents showed no reaction. The neighbors smiled and asked me if I liked being an angel.

One day after school, when I hurried home to get dressed for my angelic outing, I could not find my outfit. I looked everywhere. I asked my mother where it was, and she said she didn't know. That evening, I even asked my father, and he also didn't know. I searched through all the closets every day for a week, but no costume was discovered. Over the next year, I looked about once a month but didn't find it. Eventually I knew that even if it should reappear, I had grown too large to wear it, but I still wanted it. Years later I asked my mother if she might have hidden the costume away from me, but she denied any knowledge of the matter.

After thinking the matter over for about sixty years, I have concluded that my parents were embarrassed by their sissy child and by the backyard spectacle I had been putting on. It was beyond their tolerance to have me prancing around the yard in what looked to most eyes like an evening dress. They decided to eliminate the angel outfit but somehow didn't have the nerve to tell me, realizing how attached I was to it. Perhaps since there was a hint of homosexuality and/or cross-dressing, they were unable to deal with the matter and so just eliminated it. I would be happy to get my purloined costume back even today, but I know that will never happen.

Because I was a poor athlete, when teams were chosen to play some sport such as baseball or football, I was always the last one chosen by the team leaders. Whichever team I landed on gave a collective groan. Although I did my best, I just wasn't good at sports. I was afraid of the other students too, both of their scorn and of being physically hurt by them.

I was always apprehensive about being killed, thinking that some of my apparently friendly classmates might suddenly and without provocation turn murderous. Of course, this represented, in my mind, an extension of my father's attitude toward me.

The coach, who was in charge of the athletic program for the elementary and high schools, was somehow able to show some warmth and caring for me. I felt that he understood my fear and despair and was on my side, at least to the extent of thinking I should be allowed to remain alive, which was a great comfort to me. He was more important to me than I realized at the time, and I wish there was some way, even at this remote time, that I could thank him for his kindness.

And so my education and search for love was off to a shaky start.

Summer of 1941

These were the final years of the Great Depression. There was very little surplus money anywhere, and only a few families were financially safe, even on a modest scale. My father's new little machine shop in McAllen made just enough to pay the rent and buy food. We were poor, often on an overextended credit from the grocery store, with no money for anything extra. Most people were in the same situation.

In September of 1939 I started the first grade at the Lincoln Elementary School in McAllen, having learned enough English to get by. There was a question of whether I could have shoes to go to school or perhaps should go barefoot like the other poor children.

XXXXXXXXXXXXXXXXXXXXXXXXXXXXXXXXXXXXXXXXXXXXXX

Shortly before Christmas in 1939, my mother suffered a ruptured tubal pregnancy, a very serious, potentially fatal, event. She had an emergency operation at the McAllen hospital, lost a lot of blood, and for four weeks drifted between life and death. After a month in the hospital, she came home, very weak and fragile.

Within a few days, the surgical incision became infected and opened up, another serious and sometimes fatal complication. There were no antibiotics at that time, and the sulfa drugs were not yet in use, so the danger from an infection was very serious. My mother returned to the hospital, this time to stay for four months. During this time she slowly recovered from the surgery and the infection with its complications, but she became a morphine addict while in the hospital, a problem which was to plague her intermittently until the end of her life.

Our Mexican servant, Belin, who did the house cleaning and looked after me, stayed on for two years after my mother came home from the hospital. I liked her and could speak with her in Spanish, my native language. She took me for a walk every afternoon to a secluded section of the school yard, where we shared a cigarette, which I took to be a sign of her love for me.

45

This abruptly ended when Belin was found to have advanced tuberculosis and was sent away to a sanitarium to die. This was probably when I myself became infected with tuberculosis, which was discovered by a routine skin test. Luckily I have never had any symptoms, signs, or physical manifestations of the disease.

My father, who had always preferred that I should not exist, was too concerned with my mother to inflict his usual torments on me, so at least her illness relieved me of most of his baleful attentions.

In March of 1940 my grandmother came down from Houston and stayed with us in our one-bedroom apartment, cooking and taking care of my father and me. I was very happy to see her arrive, as she was affectionate and had a loving heart, and to me this was like putting water on a parched plant.

She was fifty-three years old, about five feet seven inches tall, slight, with piercing, kindly blue eyes behind rimless glasses, mostly gray hair in a simple bob, a few wrinkles, and hands roughened by years of work. She always wore her plain gold wedding ring and another ring with a small diamond held in an upright prong setting, along with a silver watch set with tiny diamonds and a loose band that was more like a bracelet. Years later I still treasure her watch and her two little rings.

When my grandmother arrived, she brought me a gift in her suitcase, which she always referred to as her "grip." The present was a small ceramic horse with a hussar rider, about two inches tall, the horse painted white and the rider painted with a blue and red costume, black boots, a gold turban, and one dark blue eye. I had never seen anything so beautiful and couldn't believe my good fortune.

Granny often gave me a hug and a kiss and would sometimes pat me on the head. These were gestures of affection which I had not known since I was torn away from Chencha two years before. Of all the people in the world, my grandmother was the one I loved the most, and she knew it. It seemed to me that I was her favorite too.

When my mother eventually came home from the hospital for good, in the early summer of 1940, I was very sorry to see my granny return to Houston.

By the spring of 1941, my mother had partly recovered and was in fair condition, although she tired very easily and needed a three-hour nap every afternoon. By this time, she had developed severe bronchiectasis and lung cavities, which sapped her strength. From time to time she coughed up blood clots, which frightened us all.

I had finished the second grade in June, 1941, and it was summer vacation time. My parents decided we would drive in our 1936 Oldsmobile up to Houston to visit my grandmother. So in late July we drove the 360 miles to

Houston, a trip that took about fourteen hours, on good paved two-lane roads all the way—deluxe modern travel. We started at 4 AM, with a large block of dry ice in the car to help us keep cool.

There were only a few cafes along the way, and we stopped for lunch at the best one, known for having edible food that wouldn't make you sick. About a hundred miles south of Houston, the south Texas scrub vegetation gave way to oak trees; some even had hanging moss, so I knew we were getting close.

Houston was a huge city, with over 200,000 people, a few fifteen-story skyscrapers, streetcars, and even some four-lane streets. My grandmother lived in a two-story house in the Southampton section of town, on Castle Court Boulevard, Number 1555. The street was so wide it even had an esplanade, which I had never seen or heard of before, with crepe myrtles and other flowers growing right in the middle of the street.

My grandmother and I were overjoyed to see one another again. I was relieved to see my mother looking happy, smiling, talking and laughing with her mother. I was puzzled to see my father also smiling, talking, and acting polite but appreciated the change from his usual sullen silence.

A week later, my eighth birthday arrived, and my grandmother made an angel food birthday cake, with white icing and eight candles. We had a fine birthday party, with ice cream too. What a treat!! The next day my parents drove back to McAllen, planning to leave me with my grandmother until school started early in September.

Days of Heaven

I did not know why they decided to go home and leave me behind—perhaps to have some private time with each other (not very likely), or so that my mother could get more rest (perhaps), or to let me practice being away from home (maybe), but whatever the reason, both my grandmother and I were delighted, and we soon settled into a routine that was bliss for me.

Every morning we got up around 6:30. My grandmother would wear her "wrapper" over her nightgown, and I would be in my pajamas. She would cook breakfast—usually one egg apiece, with toast and jelly, sometimes bacon too, and pancakes on Sundays, or sometimes she would get out the waffle iron, which I really liked. Afterward we would wash and dry the dishes.

Then it would be time to wash the clothes. There was no washing machine; we washed the clothes in a big galvanized tin tub, using a washing board, with bluing in the water to make the fabrics whiter. I enjoyed using the washboard and was diligent in scrubbing the clothes up and down on the board, splashing, making a lot of noise, and generally having a good time.

We would rinse the clothes and then wring them out by hand, being extra careful with the delicate items. For these, my grandmother would take over. We put all the laundry into two big wicker baskets and put on our clothes-hanging aprons, regular aprons with a big pocket on each side to hold the clothespins. My apron hung almost to the ground.

In the backyard, behind the fig tree, were four droopy clotheslines hooked to a support on each end. We were very careful about hanging the clothes neatly, similar items together. I could only reach the lower central sections of the clotheslines, and my grandmother used the higher end sections. When we were done, we went inside, took our baths for the day, and put on our daytime clothes, but usually no shoes or socks.

Houston is a rainy place, and if rain started, we would run out, unpin the clothes, and carry them back inside. Later we would take them outside again. This in and out with the clothes-drying process would sometimes go on most of the day. If it was too rainy, we would have to hang the clothes around the house on coat hangers and on the furniture.

My grandmother would boil starch in a pan on the stove and would dip the collars and cuffs, the napkins and the doilies and whatever else needed starch, into the mixture once or twice or even three times, depending on the degree of stiffness we wanted. I only watched, as this step was too precise for me to join in. The ironing was usually done the next day, as part of a separate social ritual.

After the clothes had been taken care of, we would sit on the front veranda in a large hanging swing. We would swing and talk for a couple of hours, a time I treasured. My grandmother always dignified my comments by listening with serious attention, and I did the same for her. We were both sincere in our interest.

Occasionally, her face would suddenly turn red, her eyes would bulge out, her mouth would open wide, and a roar would emerge: "Git! Git!!!!! GIT!!!" She would rise menacingly from the swing (or from her chair if we were inside) and step down into the yard. She had seen her enemy, one of the neighborhood dogs, standing or squatting there. She was of the rock-solid opinion that these malicious dogs deliberately came to her yard to do their duty rather than dirty up their own yards.

One look at the menacing apparition coming toward him was enough to cause the dog to stop whatever he was doing, even if in the middle of his delivery, and leave the premises as fast as he could run, glancing back over his shoulder to check on the monster's progress.

Granny appeared to truly despise dogs. They always returned, no later than the next day; perhaps they were playing a mischievous game with her. These were the only times I ever saw my grandmother angry. On resuming her seat, she would roll her eyes, sigh, flutter her hands, smooth her dress, and would soon resume her usual sweet and tranquil mood. The storm was over.

One of the highlights of the day took place around 11 AM. We could see the mailman coming down the street with his big leather bag slung over his shoulder, stopping at each house to leave off the mail. As he came closer, we got more curious what he might have for us. About half the time there was no mail for us, and we would sigh with disappointment, but the other days he gave us a big smile and handed the mail to my grandmother, usually a handwritten letter or a postcard. After a little polite banter, he would go on with his route, and then we could look at the mail—a true matter of interest. Sometimes there was a penny postcard from my mother for me.

Most of the time the mail was for my grandmother, and she would read the letter aloud, usually from one of her five grown children, sometimes from one of her eight sisters or her brother. The letters all had three-cent stamps, and I wanted to save the stamps for my collection. Granny obliged, carefully removing the stamp, trying not to destroy the envelope. We would talk about the letter and gossip about the sender. What happiness!

XXXXXXXXXXXXXXXXXXXXXXXXXXXXXXXXXXXXXXXXXXXX

Her eldest sister, Ethel, lived in Oklahoma City, but sometimes visited Houston, and I always looked forward to her visits. She was the most psychic of the sisters, frequently seeing deceased spirits or other beings from the next world. She would stop in the middle of a conversation and say, "Oh, here's Aunt Annie. She's looking quite well. She says to tell you watch your step going downstairs. Is there anything you want me to tell Annie?" (Annie was her old aunt who had died twenty years before.)

These episodes always made me envious, as no matter how hard I looked, I could never see Annie or any of the other departed souls who made their appearance in Granny's living room. If Ethel suggested something in the form of a warning, such as "Check your spare tire before you drive down to the border," you could be pretty sure there would be a flat tire before reaching home. She would send advice like this in her letters too. Ethel was a grave and timid soul, but her psychic pronouncements were often amazing.

Another sister, Kate, had married a man who owned the Robinson Circus, well-known in its day. She toured with her husband and the circus, selling tickets and watching the money. Her husband was the lion tamer, but one afternoon in the middle of a performance, his bad lion killed him. Soon the circus was sold to Ringling Brothers and lost its separate identity. I used to say his bad lion ate him but I just made that up. It wasn't true. The truth was that his bad lion killed him, but didn't really eat him up.

Robinson Circus, circa 1920, Great Aunt Kate at far left

Their sister Nina had been the girlfriend of one of the big-time prohibition-era gangsters. My recollection is that the man was known as Pretty Boy Floyd, but perhaps it was Machine Gun Kelly or Bugsy Siegel. The mists of time are obscuring my memory of these events. The family legend was that it was quite a fiery romance. He was shot to death in a police encounter, and his widow, Aunt Nina, was perhaps somewhat consoled by his legacy: six substantial pieces of Los Angeles, Hollywood, and Beverly Hills real estate. He left her in excellent financial condition. She was pretty, vivacious, charming, and had a jolly gleam in her eyes.

When I went to visit her years later in Beverly Hills, she asked what I would like to see. The botanical garden was my choice. So she took me to Forest Lawn Cemetery, a large place where many celebrities were interred. There was also an auditorium which displayed a colorful glass-bead curtain showing the crucifixion of Jesus. When that curtain was pulled open, it revealed an even larger (largest in the world, they said) glass curtain of the Resurrection. After gazing at this for a while and hearing hymns played on the organ, the audience exited through an exhibition of replicas of the crown jewels of England. It was an interesting afternoon.

Two of Granny's older sisters died in somewhat unusual circumstances. Both had been happily married for many years and were in their late eighties when they died. They lived only a few miles apart in southern California; one lived in Santa Monica, the other in Long Beach. Gertrude, the oldest of the sisters, suddenly and unexpectedly died one morning. Her husband suddenly and unexpectedly died the same afternoon. A month later, Madeline, two years younger than Gertrude, suddenly and unexpectedly died one afternoon. Her husband had suddenly and unexpectedly died two hours earlier. These spouses were so intertwined psychically that one could not survive without the other.

Granny's oldest sibling, her brother Ed, opted for a calmer life, and had remained a bachelor, tending his moderate and modestly profitable chicken farm outside Neosho, Missouri. He lived to a very old age.

My early life was full of strange and improbable coincidences, apparitions, incursions from the next world, and other entertaining surreal events.

XXXXXXXXXXXXXXXXXXXXXXXXXXXXXXXXXXXXXXXXXXXXX

After we had finished with the mail, we had lunch at the kitchen table, usually a butter sandwich or a bowl of soup, with milk for us both. Then we both had a nap from about 12:30 to 1:30. I napped on a sofa in the dining room, and Granny napped in her little room off the kitchen. I loved her little room, which was just long enough for her bed (with porcelain potty underneath), with its small bookcase and dresser with her button box on top, which she would give to me to look through on rainy days. The room smelled of her Cashmere Bouquet talcum powder. I would sprinkle some on myself too from time to time.

XXXXXXXXXXXXXXXXXXXXXXXXXXXXXXXXXXXXXXXXXXXXX

In the afternoon, I would join two other neighborhood boys, Maurice and Herman, and two girls, Ruthie-Ann and Maudine, all about my age, and we would knock on the back door of one of the five houses in the same row as my grandmother's. The lady of the house would be ready to start the ironing and would invite us all in to keep her company while she did this chore, which took two or three hours.

We would sit on the floor in a semicircle around the ironing board and try to be quiet and polite. If we got too noisy and didn't pay attention to the warnings to hush, we would be invited to go outside. This was a big disappointment, and we tried not to be expelled from the party.

We listened to the radio all afternoon: *One Man's Family, Ma Perkins, Stella Dallas, Portia Faces Life,* and *As the World Turns.* The six of us were enthralled by the ongoing eventful lives of all our friends in the soap operas. If one of us missed an installment, the others would fill in the missing story next time with exaggerated voices and gestures, sometimes not comprehending the more grown-up nuances of the love stuff. Sometimes there was not enough ironing to last for the whole afternoon, so the process might get much slower, or perhaps we would all be treated to some lemonade or glasses of ice water while we finished listening.

The next afternoon we would knock at another door, and so all five weekday afternoons were passed in this fascinating way. The ladies all seemed to enjoy these matinees, although my grandmother probably pretended to be more interested than she really was. I was dimly aware we were spending afternoons in paradise!!

After the radio shows were finished and the ironing done, I would go home. Usually the morning's wash was dry by then. Granny and I would put on our aprons again and bring the clothes inside and fold them up in a damp towel until it was time to iron them. Then we would sit in the kitchen for a while.

I remember the old-fashioned gas stove, enameled white and black, standing on four high legs, with a raised oven on one side. The burners all had round black iron covers which had to be removed with a tong device before lighting the gas with a match. She had bought a refrigerator two years before, getting rid of her faithful icebox, which had needed a new piece of ice delivered by the iceman every morning. He unloaded the block of ice from a flatbed wooden trailer drawn by his patient old horse. Rest in peace, all.

Dinner would be on the table by 6 PM. I am sorry to report that my grandmother's cooking was not up to her other high standards. Yellow, flabby-skin fried chicken, hard as a rock inside, cold turnip greens and leftover grits fried in the chicken grease, buttermilk, and half a cookie, or sometimes banana pudding with vanilla wafers, made a frequent menu. Other times, perhaps fried eggs with toast, or sliced tomatoes sprinkled with sugar, or highly overcooked green beans, or horrible slimy boiled okra would make their appearance on the table. I think my grandmother had lost interest in cooking (if she ever had any) during the many years she had to cook three meals a day for six or seven people.

XXXXXXXXXXXXXXXXXXXXXXXXXXXXXXXXXXXXXXXXXX

Granny had married Alfonse Dagernet, a good-looking half French, half Wea Indian man, in 1894, when she was sixteen. By age seventeen, she had had her first child, Nellie-Mae. By the time she was eighteen, Alfonse had died of tuberculosis, and she was a widow.

In 1896, Granny married her second husband, Edmund Henry Doyle, a civil engineer for the Southern Pacific Railroad. She had four more children,

Edmund, Maria Jeannette (my mother), Murray, and Van. The family moved frequently because of E. H.'s work building railroads and lived in various locations in Texas, Oklahoma, Kansas, Arkansas, and Louisiana. All the children were born in different locations, my mother in 1904 in Custer City, Indian Territory (later called Oklahoma after it was admitted to the Union in 1907).

As E.H. rose in the Southern Pacific hierarchy, he was given the use of a private railroad car to take the family on vacations. I have a number of photographs of the family inside of and in front of the private railroad cars. The adults are smiling and holding rifles, as if they were on a hunting excursion, and are wearing sort of rough-rider outfits, as if waiting for Theodore Roosevelt to appear.

Nellie-Mae was sent away to be raised by E. H.'s aunt Rye (Maria, pronounced "Mariyah," after whom my mother was named). When Aunt Rye died years later, she left her cherry orchard and house in Ypsilanti, Michigan, to my grandfather, E.H., whom she had raised.

He died suddenly in 1936, when he flew into a drunken rage at work and had a fatal heart attack. My grandmother was again a widow but had inherited the Ypsilanti house and the cherry orchard. Most years Granny would spend some time there. Despite greatly liking the cherry orchard, she eventually had to sell it, along with the house. Afterward, my grandmother was pleased when two great trunks full of Aunt Rye's linens and household items arrived in Houston. Aunt Rye was exceedingly stern-looking in her photos. I was convinced the poor lady was a witch and refused to go near the trunks or to touch anything that was inside, fearing that she herself might be inside, in a ghostly and menacing form.

I never learned why Nellie was sent away to live with Aunt Rye. Perhaps E.H. didn't want another man's child, perhaps because she was part Wea Indian. She was for the most part educated in convent schools and was the only Catholic in the family. Nellie frequently visited her mother for short periods and was friendly with her four half siblings, who all regarded her as their older sister. She and my mother were especially close, later having a common bond of depression and alcoholism.

At the time I am remembering here, Nellie was about forty-four and had been widowed once and divorced once. She was a beautiful woman, emotionally labile, laughing and then crying, charming, generous, and fond of me. She could sing very well and was a talented pianist too. By this time she had become a severe alcoholic, which was to damage the rest of her life.

Nellie's two children by her first marriage, Georgie and Rosemary, were about ten and twelve years older than I and were closer to my mother and her generation than to mine.

Rosemary, who had been very close to my mother, committed suicide in a post-partum depression a few days after giving birth to her first child, Edwin. His father, Ned Armstrong, later wrote a book, *Man and Boy*, describing his experiences as a single father bringing up his son. Years later I met Edwin in New York.

Nellie's first husband, Georgie's father, had been attorney for the Cherokee Nation and left a very generous insurance policy for his children. As soon as Georgie started receiving insurance payments shortly after his father died, first his own share and then Rosemary's share also, he left for Europe and a life as houseguest, pianist, companion, charmer, perhaps something even more intimate, perhaps entertaining both sexes, as I was told by his mother, who also told me he occasionally worked in clubs as a pianist but preferred not to work. I thought his life sounded very romantic and exciting. When he was forty his insurance payments finished, and he had to return to the United States, settling in New York.

I had met cousin Georgie when I was six years old and thought he was a star. Perhaps I developed a little crush on him. I didn't see him again until I was twenty-two and was disappointed to find him shallow, untruthful, and manipulative, telling elaborate lies to win my sympathy, such as telling me he was dying of tuberculosis. (He had had tuberculosis, but it had been treated in England and was arrested, and he was not about to go through the gates of death.) He found me snobbish, as he told my mother. We never rekindled our earlier good relationship. I heard nothing from him when my father died or when my mother (his aunt) died, nor have I heard from him in the forty years since then, although we live perhaps two miles apart. We don't choose our relatives.

From time to time the U.S. government would send substantial sums of cash to Nellie, Georgie, and Edwin. This was in restitution for stealing the Wea Indian tribal lands in the mid-nineteenth century.

One day years later, when I was a practicing physician, I received a call at my office from a Mr. Armstrong, who wanted to make an appointment to see me. Not recognizing the name, I assumed he was a new patient. He arrived punctually, and I showed him in and made my usual opening remarks: "The purpose of our meeting today is for me to learn something of your situation and what you consider your problems to be and for us to decide if we can what, if anything, you might want to do about them."

He gazed at me tranquilly for a while and then said calmly, "I'm your cousin."

This rather startled me. I wondered how to deal with it. Was he dangerous? But after a few questions from me, I understood he was telling the truth, and we began a pleasant, if not lengthy, relationship.

He told me he had just been released from a two-year term in naval prison, his punishment for trying to defect through Hong Kong to Communist China. China didn't want to keep him and sent him back, and the Navy put him in prison. Edwin was a gentle, soft-spoken, intelligent young man still looking for his path in life. I saw him a few times while he was staying in New York. We cast the *I Ching* a few times, with some interesting results, and had some good dinners, but then we lost touch.

A few years later I heard he had been seen sitting on the temple steps in the Hanuman Dhoka in Kathmandu and was said to be living on the last installment of his Wea Indian money. Years later, a common distant relative, Cousin Theda, died intestate, and we both inherited part of her estate. I heard he had changed his name to "Mr. O" and was living in Buffalo. He seemed a benign soul, and I hope he has had a happy life.

XXXXXXXXXXXXXXXXXXXXXXXXXXXXXXXXXXXXXXXXXXXXX

At any rate, back to Houston and the summer of 1941. After cooking for her husband, children, and grandchildren for many years, my grandmother had lost interest in cooking. I knew her cooking was not delicious, but I didn't care. She was, however, very interested in painting, mostly architectural scenes and still lifes.

She was an accomplished painter, working in oils, watercolors, and pastels and taking lessons occasionally at the Houston Museum of Fine Arts. Even as a child, I thought most of her works were beautiful, but now, as an adult, I like them a great deal and treasure the eight of her paintings which I have. She was a talented artist, and most of her works show fine design sense and wonderful, vivid, and unusual color usage.

By 1941, a number of her paintings were hanging in her house, more were stored away in closets, some were hanging in her children's houses, and two or three were usually in progress on easels.

I wanted to learn to paint too, and Granny was so kind and patient in her efforts to teach me, with explanations about colors and materials and a readiness to answer any questions I had. I loved the painting lessons she gave me, even though I didn't have her talent, which we both knew. Neither of us minded.

We spent most of one summer painting a watercolor of a magnificent peacock with an unbelievably brilliant tail. I suspect Granny was not too interested in this childishly exuberant project, but she never let on, and she eventually said I had done a very good job.

For many years I saw the peacock from time to time and was amused in a condescending way at my early attempt to create something beautiful. He was never framed; the sheet of paper on which he existed became mixed with other papers. Eventually he became misplaced. Sometimes I now think with sadness of my beautiful lost peacock and hope I will find him again someday.

Her last painting, done while she was dying of lung cancer, shows a group of horses staring out at the observer from a clump of bushes. The horses look wistful but serene. I feel melancholy when I look at this painting and wonder what she might have been thinking while she was working on it. I wish I could see her again.

XXXXXXXXXXXXXXXXXXXXXXXXXXXXXXXXXXXXXXXXXXXXX

After we had washed and put away the dinner dishes, we would sit in the backyard from about 7 PM until we got too uncomfortable from the mosquitoes, who got more lively and aggressive as the evening got darker. We sat in two big wooden Adirondack chairs, one white, one blue, in front of the large fig tree. My grandmother was never able to persuade me to eat any of the figs, which she said were delicious. In later years I became quite fond of figs and regretted never having eaten any of her homegrown ones.

Sometimes, if we had company, we would set up the croquet court in the backyard and play a game or two. We would leave this in place for a few days, and often my grandmother and I would play, just the two of us.

On rainy days we would sit in the living room talking and listening to the radio. In the evening we heard *The Shadow, Inner Sanctum, Jack Benny*, and *The Bell Telephone Hour.* Sometimes I would massage Granny's feet, always surprised by the odd corns on her toes, for which she went occasionally to the "foot doctor." She would say to me in a soft, pleading voice, "Rub my feet—they hurt," and I would be happy to rub her feet as long as she wanted.

Bedtime was at 9 PM. I slept in the dining room on a sofa next to two large windows. Air-conditioning was as yet unknown. The Houston climate was generally hot and humid, and the windows were wide open. One night soon after my arrival, I was awakened in the middle of the night by loud, terrifying screams coming from just outside my window. I ran to my grandmother's room in fright and awakened her.

After listening for a moment to further screams, she smiled and told me that it was only some of the neighborhood cats playing. From then on, the cats played under my window, sometimes two or three times in one night, and I eventually got used to their noisy play. It was only some years later that I realized the cats were really making love under the window—and those neighborhood cats were a very loving and playful bunch.

XXXXXXXXXXXXXXXXXXXXXXXXXXXXXXXXXXXXXXXXXXXXX

My grandmother was interested in various alternative religious groups, such as the Rosicrucians, Unity, and other New Thought groups, but especially in a group named The Great I AM. This group had been founded by Edna and Guy Ballard and their son, Jeffrey. They were usually called by their "spiritual" names: Godfrey Ray King, Lotus Ray King (who had been Joan of Arc in a previous lifetime), and their son, Jeffrey Ray King. After a few years, the son was no longer mentioned—perhaps he had turned into a black sheep.

The Ballard-Kings had written several books, all printed in vivid purple ink, which generally urged the members to live good lives. The books were dictated to the Ballard-Kings by various "Ascended Masters," such as St. Germain, Archangel Michael, and other beings of extremely high spiritual stature.

These great beings sometimes visited the earth, and when here they stayed mostly inside Mt. Shasta in California. Sometimes they came into the open on the surface of the earth, in the Panther Meadow on the slopes of Mt. Shasta, or elsewhere, as they chose, and they communicated frequently with the Ballard-Kings.

Even now, over sixty years later, members of the Mt. Shasta City branch of The Great I Am sometimes report seeing Ascended Masters standing in the Panther Meadow. I have been to Mt. Shasta several times and always try to have a look at the Panther Meadow, although sometimes there is too much snow to get close. So far I have not encountered any Ascended Masters or archangels there. But I will continue to keep my eyes open whenever I may be at Mt. Shasta. There's plenty that I don't know.

It was forbidden by The Great I Am to eat things that grew underground, such as potatoes, garlic, onions, and peanuts. Red food like tomatoes and strawberries was also forbidden, as were red or black clothes, and there were many other such rules.

The Book of Hymns, also printed in purple ink, contained music written by Lotus Ray King, and the songs, bland and of no particular musical merit, were sung at the regular services. The services also featured "Affirmations" rhythmically and repetitively chanted by the congregation: "I am a child of God and therefore perfect; I am a child of God and therefore perfect; I Am, I Am, I Am."

The Ascended Masters were portrayed as wearing golden clothes, and they had huge purple eyes, long brown hair like Jesus, and halos. The Ballard-Kings and some of the members also wore golden clothes. One of the leading Houston members, Mrs. Ray, an ancient woman who did healing, had extremely startling huge purple eyes (as I recall, bigger than Elizabeth

Taylor's), just as shown in the pictures of the Ascended Masters. All in all, the group was benign and apparently of benefit or comfort to the believers.

My grandmother usually took me to the I Am meetings once a week. They were held in a downtown hotel, which I thought was very impressive. Sometimes there was a lecture by one or both of the senior Ballard-Kings. I found the lectures of little interest, although I enjoyed reading the purple-printed books telling of interstellar travel and of wonderful supernatural doings of the Ascended Masters. The books were rather like lusterless descendants of Victorian supernatural novels by such writers as Marie Corelli (*The Sorrows of Satan)* and Edward Bulwer-Lytton (*Zanoni, The Last Days of Pompeii),* he of "It was a dark and stormy night."

Later, the FBI accused the Ballard-Kings of selling false information through the mail and threatened to send them to prison if they did not desist. The books were harmless; they couldn't even mislead an eight-year-old.

XXXXXXXXXXXXXXXXXXXXXXXXXXXXXXXXXXXXXXXXXXXX

Sometimes on Sundays my grandmother would get dressed up: she put on extra face powder and lipstick, one of her good dresses, her long string of pearls or sometimes the long string of pink glass beads instead, and her round, flat-topped hat covered with pink feathers. I would put on my best outfit, and we would wait on the corner until the trolley came along.

Wooden, painted dark green, with a yellow metal roof—it was magnificent! We climbed up the stairs, put our coins into the money box, and then took our places. There were ten rows of wooden benches with a central aisle, two seats on each side. The windows were kept raised and open except when it rained. I always wanted the window seat, for a better view, and my grandmother always let me sit there.

The trolley clanked along on its rails down Mandell Street, turned right on Richmond Avenue, turned left on Montrose Boulevard, and went past the T.P. Lee mansion, the grandest house in town. (Later, T. P. Lee, a rich Texas oilman, married the beautiful actress Hedy Lamarr. After they were divorced a few years later, partly due to ongoing troubles and embarrassment arising from her kleptomania, he married another beautiful and psychiatrically troubled actress, Gene Tierney, whom I occasionally saw years later at fashionable Houston restaurants.)

After passing the Lee mansion, the trolley turned right onto West Alabama and went as far as Main Street, then left to the center of town, where there were four big movie houses and two smaller theaters showing B movies. The candy store had in its window a fantastically complicated taffy-pulling machine kneading and pulling huge wads of pink taffy, or sometimes white or brown instead.

We would have lunch downtown, usually at Weldon's cafeteria. I needed help carrying my tray; Granny did not. Then we would go to a movie, but only the big movies, no B pictures. Afterward we would go to the candy store to buy taffy, which we would eat on the trolley going home. Sometimes, if we had plenty of time, we would visit the pet shop, where some friendly monkeys lived in the rear of the store. Since I couldn't have a twin, which I had always wanted, a monkey might do instead. I longed to have a monkey and had almost persuaded my grandmother to buy one for me. My mother got wind of it and said, "No No No," and that was the end of my monkey plan.

On the return trip home, the trolley passed Settegast-Kopf, the city's leading funeral home, with its white pillars and beveled glass doors. Frequently there were a crowd of people, limousines, and a giant hearse. Sometimes motorcycle policemen waited to accompany the procession to the cemetery. I looked with curiosity, knowing what a funeral home was for but knowing that it was only for other people, people I didn't know.

We were home by 4 PM, put on our regular house clothes, and got ready for dinner and for evening in the backyard: looking for the moon, watching the stars come out, watching the fireflies, and talking with each other and with any neighbors who might drop by.

XXXXXXXXXXXXXXXXXXXXXXXXXXXXXXXXXXXXXXXXX

On December 7, 1941, the Japanese bombed Pearl Harbor, America entered the war, and much was permanently changed.

My grandmother and I were able to preserve our cocoon of happiness for a while. For the next four years, through the summer of 1945, I was allowed to spend part of each summer with my grandmother. These were the most contented days of my life, and these summer months with my grandmother were the happiest times of my childhood.

Little Devils

The next year, 1942, before I turned nine, Sammy and Johnnie and I began to enjoy the early stages of a life of crime.

All the men in the apartment complex went to work every day. Sometimes we would see one of the neighbor ladies go out. Very few apartments or houses in McAllen would ever be locked, and if so, the windows were left open. We would occasionally decide to sneak into a temporarily vacant apartment. Once inside, we would look around for a while, opening some of the drawers and looking in the closets, particularly inspecting the female underwear. Usually we left everything almost as it was, perhaps just leaving one drawer slightly open or moving something so as to be noticed, such as moving a bathroom towel to the kitchen sink.

We never stole anything, or broke anything, or committed any vandalism. We did not think that the neighbors would be disturbed to see that there had been an intruder or that their things had been inspected or moved. We thought surely the neighbors would be amused and would enjoy the mystery of what could have happened. We were never caught at this. I still feel sorry about the distress we must have caused. My parents once discussed this at the dinner table, all the while staring at me, or so I thought. I tried my best to look innocent. They didn't ask if I were guilty; I didn't tell.

Sometimes we would pick the neighbors' flowers, making nice bouquets to take home. It wasn't too long before it was revealed who the flower stealers were. We were all scolded and actually almost quit doing it. I was the most incorrigible culprit and had the childlike idea that the bouquets would please my mother and that she wouldn't think I had stolen the flowers from the neighbors' gardens. I'm sure she was embarrassed.

XXXXXXXXXXXXXXXXXXXXXXXXXXXXXXXXXXXXXXXXXX

On Saturdays our parents would give us ten cents for a movie, plus five cents for some popcorn or candy. We would usually leave early for the movie. There were a few coin-operated telephones in the two drugstores on Main

Street. There were still operators who answered and said, "number puhleez," would request a five-cent deposit, and then would put the call through from their manual central switchboards at the telephone company office. Somehow I had discovered that if I put a dime, or even a penny, into a slot for a different denomination coin, that the clinking sound of the coin falling through the telephone would fool the operator into thinking that the right amount had been deposited. In other words, we could beat the system, and so the call was free.

We enjoyed calling up many of the local people, those who had what we thought of as "funny" names, like "Snodgrass" or "Fortenberry," or other names appealing to a ten-year-old's sense of humor. Once the victim answered, we would make fun of his name and would make obscene remarks. We eventually began to threaten bodily harm unless he bought us off, say by putting a million dollars under a specified rock. Some of the victims would become indignant and demand, "Who is this?" or make a threat that if they caught us, we would be sorry. We would laugh and hang up. It never occurred to us that the victims would not think it was all a funny joke. We never intended to actually get any money, nor did we do so. These were our "normal" childlike thought processes.

We asked one of them repeatedly, "Do you shit on your metal roof in the summer?" This was wordplay on his name and his occupation. He would gasp and stutter and then become abusive, and we would giggle and hang up. It turned out that he became seriously worried. He thought he was in danger and got a permit to carry a handgun. This man was one of my father's friends.

We sometimes called local stores and ordered huge amounts of merchandise to be delivered to a fake address. We thought this was a good joke too, until we found out that a florist shop had been financially damaged by sending masses of flowers to an unsuspecting recipient, who was as surprised as the florist was. The flower shop was owned by the parents of one of our classmates. We felt slightly guilty.

After we had amused ourselves sufficiently by defrauding the telephone company and upsetting our victims, we would visit the ten-cent stores (Woolworth's, Kress's, and Kresge's) and inspect the candy counters, which had open bins full of various kinds of candies. When nobody was looking, we would scoop up a handful of whatever we liked best. We didn't think we should be too greedy—it might be dangerous—so we took only two handfuls from each store. Six handfuls divided between the three of us quite nicely satisfied our sweet tooths for the afternoon.

We were then ready for the movies. Going upstairs to sit in the first row of the balcony, we would pull out our previously prepared small rocks. We had tied black threads around the rocks, each smaller than a grape. Looking over the edge of the balcony, we could see the people sitting directly below. Lowering a rock slowly, we would touch someone gently on the head. The person would feel his head, perhaps intending to brush away a fly. In a couple of minutes, we would touch his head again, and so it went. Most of the victims finally wised up and moved to different locations.

We thought this routine was hilarious and had a hard time not laughing too loudly. Once someone quickly reached up, seized the rock, and pulled it loose from its thread. Another afternoon an usher came up and asked us if we were annoying the customers. "Oh, no," we said almost in unison, and he went away. This was as close as we came to getting into trouble for the rock-on-a-thread trick.

Stealing candy and making weird, threatening, and obscene telephone calls went on for many months, perhaps up to a year. As time went on, our calls and candy stealing became more frequent, and almost every Saturday afternoon was spent making mischief. We thoroughly enjoyed our bad deeds.

However, one Saturday afternoon, just as we were about finished tormenting a victim, someone put his hand firmly on my shoulder and said, "You had better come with us." Startled, I turned around to see three uniformed policemen. One had his hand on Sammy's shoulder and the other on Johnnie's. Standing up, I staggered and almost fainted. "We're going to the police station," one of them said.

Separated from each other, we were told not to speak to each other as we walked the four blocks to the station. I was terrified, and my knees shook. I could see that Sammy and Johnnie both looked very solemn and very pale. People stared with curiosity at this unusual parade. When we got to the station, we were taken into separate rooms and told to sit down. The policemen went out of the rooms and locked us inside.

After about thirty minutes of stewing in my own juices and getting increasingly afraid and worried, a policeman came into my room, sat down, and began to ask me questions: "What is your name? What is your address? Age? What is your father's name? What work does he do? Where do you go to school? What grade are you in? How many people have you called up and threatened and used obscene language with? What are their names? Besides your two friends, how many others also do this calling? Why do you do it? How much money have you taken from the people you call? Do you call people in other towns? You may be going to jail or to reform school for years, so you had better tell the truth, or else you will be very sorry."

My inquisitor left the room and locked the door again. After about an hour, the door opened, and there were my parents. The policeman said, "You have been very bad; you are a criminal. Your parents are going to take you home for now. We will be coming around to ask you some more questions. You haven't told us the complete truth yet."

My mother was tearful and said, "How could you do this to us? I don't know if I can stand it." My father glared at me, but he didn't look any more hostile and disapproving than usual. I felt sorry for my mother and was afraid of my father. There was no talk while we drove the few blocks home, but I was sick with shame and fear that I would be going to reform school.

Two days later, two FBI men came to our apartment and spent the afternoon. They wanted to talk with me alone, so my mother had to go into the bedroom and close the door, while I was grilled sitting at the dinner table on the porch, which also served as the dining room. They asked me, "Have you kidnapped anybody? Have you hurt anybody as part of a plan to get money? Have you stabbed anyone? Or shot anyone? Have you killed anyone? Do you have a gun?" By that time I was almost nine years old, almost grown up, and therefore did not consider it strange that the police and FBI would think that my friends and I might actually be murderers or otherwise dangerous criminals.

They told me to write the letters of the alphabet several times, in capitals and in small letters. Then I had to write sample words they dictated to me, and finally I had to write phrases and sentences they dictated. These samples were to be sent to handwriting experts to see if they matched ransom notes, death threat notes, and extortion demands connected with crimes as yet unsolved. When they left, they said good-bye to my mother and also said they would be back for some more questions. My father had no comment when he heard what had happened with the FBI men.

In about ten days, they came back. There were more similar questions and more writing of sample phrases. They were very stern and said they would let me know what was going to happen to me. They repeated the threat of going to reform school "for a long time." We never revealed defrauding the telephone company, the candy stealing, or the rock-on-a-thread maneuvers. As soon as the FBI men left, my mother burst into tears, and I felt worse than ever. As usual, my father had no comment.

The same routine was going on at my friends' houses. We were all *scared*. After a couple weeks, the police told my parents that nothing further was going to be done and that our victims were not going to be told who we were, only that the culprits had been apprehended and that the mischief would not go on again—if it did, they were to let the police know, and they would deal with it. They said my parents should watch me carefully. They followed this advice for a long time, but I was so scared that I was good, good, good for two or three years. Sammy and Johnnie were also super-good-goodie for a long time.

We did not make any more mischief, and I guess we had learned our lessons. Our hilarious lives of crime had come to an abrupt finish. The man we had frightened so badly he had taken to carrying a handgun was very relieved. He told some of his friends, including my father, that he thought the threat had been disposed of. My father, thank goodness, did not reveal the identity of the culprits. The police must have been extremely closemouthed, as the rumor mill of the little town would have broadcast our crimes if anyone had known. Or maybe people did know.

My parents did not punish me in any way, but my mother talked seriously to me about trying to do the right thing in life. Perhaps they understood that the police had thrown a terrible fright into all of us and that was sufficient punishment and deterrence. Or perhaps they didn't know what action to take in this nasty situation.

XXXXXXXXXXXXXXXXXXXXXXXXXXXXXXXXXXXXXXXXXX

The next month, my parents and I were going to drive to San Antonio, a seven-hour trip in those days. I was looking forward to this adventure. The day before we were going to leave, I visited my friend Johnnie at his house. His parents were out. Johnnie had discovered bars of Ex-Lax, a powerful laxative, in the bathroom medicine cabinet.

He took a nibble and said it was very good. "There are six bars of this candy," he said. "We can eat some, and my folks won't ever notice." He offered me a bar of the Ex-Lax, which I believed was candy. It was quite good, and I gobbled up the whole bar. Johnnie decided not to eat any more of the candy, saying perhaps his parents would notice and be angry with him.

That night, I became violently ill, with explosive and often-repeated diarrhea. I was too sick to go on the trip to San Antonio, and it was cancelled, as my mother thought she should stay at home with me. After some careful questioning, I finally told about eating the candy the day before. My parents said, "Oh." They looked angry and later that day called up Johnnie's mother to discuss the situation. Johnnie later told me he got in trouble with his parents, even though he himself had eaten only a nibble of the candy. My parents thought Johnnie was a bad influence on me and didn't like me to play with him anymore.

I still feel guilty about the distress I caused our victims and my parents. However, over the course of many years, these sins died from lack of nourishment and were embalmed. I put them in my mausoleum of embalmed sins. When I visit the mausoleum now, the sins still look alive, but this is only an illusion.

XX

Neither of my parents had ever been members of a church and did not attend church services except on special occasions, like Easter. I had not been baptized or brought up attending a church. Most of my fellow students belonged to churchgoing Christian families. The Mexicans were all Catholics, of course, and the Anglos were of various Protestant denominations. One of my friends in the second grade, Betty-Jean Cottingham, a tiny, doll-like child, belonged to the First Baptist Church.

The Baptists were having a membership drive, and Betty-Jean was the church representative for the second grade. She issued an invitation to all those students not already members of a church to join the Baptist church. I thought this was a good idea and wanted to join so as to be better friends with Betty-Jean.

When I asked my mother if I could join the Baptist church, she said, "No, I don't want you to be taught wrong things." At school the next day, I reported what she had said and heard a gasp from some of the students. This further marked me as an outcast, a pariah, and revealed my mother as a wicked heathen.

I have been forever grateful to my mother for saving me from becoming a brainwashed religious bigot. H. L. Mencken once remarked about someone, "Oh, he's a real Christian—full of hate." This was a fairly accurate description of the fundamentalist "religious" outlook of the time, at least in that little Texas town so long ago.

XXXXXXXXXXXXXXXXXXXXXXXXXXXXXXXXXXXXXXXXXXX

In 1939 America began to build ships and munitions to send to England to help in the struggle against Nazi Germany. This helped the lingering problems of chronic large-scale unemployment and poverty caused by the Great Depression, which had started in 1929, hit bottom in 1933, and then only slightly and slowly improved.

The year I reached the end of the second grade, the Texas school system expanded from an eleven-year format to a twelve-year program. My whole second-grade class was promoted to the fourth grade, which began in September 1941. We skipped the third grade entirely, making up the third grade work during the next school year, 1941–1942.

XXXXXXXXXXXXXXXXXXXXXXXXXXXXXXXXXXXXXXXXXXX

Although I had gradually become aware that something dirty took place between boys and girls, I had no idea what it might be, but I knew that it was considered very interesting by most of my classmates. Perhaps there was some kind of manipulation of the lower abdominal area. I did not think that my parents did this dirty thing, and neither did any of the other adults that I knew. Only very depraved white-trash people did it, perhaps mostly in the changing rooms at the swimming pool, or in their trailer houses. I thought that probably Mexicans also did it, but they were too different—they didn't really count.

I knew better than to ask either of my parents for any information about it. Of course my attraction to my three crush objects was homoerotic, but nothing of a genital or overtly sexual nature occurred, even in fantasy, as I was totally ignorant about sex, and the three hug-boys were either also ignorant or not interested in physical contact (with me). But somehow I knew it was necessary to keep these desires hidden from all, but particularly from my parents.

When I was eight years old, Tom, one of my playmates, invited me to go with him into a children's playhouse in his backyard. We sat down, and he explained to me that by stroking our "weenies," they could be made to feel very good, and did I want to try it with him, right now? Or we could stroke each other's weenies, if I preferred.

I knew something dirty was closing in and so said to him, "No, I don't want to try—it would make my mother very mad," which I knew was a sissy answer, although accurate. It was the only answer I could think of at the moment, except for the true answer, of course, which was that I was terrified of what he proposed. I was also very curious and excited about this situation.

Well, he unbuttoned his pants and tried alone for a while. While pretending distaste or indifference, I carefully watched what Tom was doing. Nothing much seemed to happen, to my considerable relief. He told me that when we got older, if we stroked our weenies it would feel super good and milk would come out the end. This was called "coming," he said, and it was a sign of being grown up. I did not believe anything he said and was eager to escape from this filthy situation.

Naturally, I did not report any of this to my mother, or there would have been real, genuine hell to pay. Tom and I remained friends, but there was no repeat of the episode in the playhouse. This may have been one of the missed turning points in my life. Later I ruminated about what Tom had told me and wondered if I liked the idea. I was tempted to stroke my own weenie in the way that I had seen Tom do but refrained, as I thought it was something bad.

Another small piece of Eve's apple had been seen, if not tasted.

XXXXXXXXXXXXXXXXXXXXXXXXXXXXXXXXXXXXXXXXXXXXXX

America entered the Second World War in December of 1941, precipitated by the Japanese surprise bombing of Pearl Harbor. I was eight years old at the time and remember clearly the fear and dismay that the bombing produced.

In the small town of McAllen, only seven miles from the Mexican border, the rhythm of life continued more or less as before for a while, especially for many of the children. The mobilization of men and industry for the war effort put a rather sudden end to the lingering unemployment and poverty.

An air force base, Moore Field, was built about ten miles north of town. A military draft was instituted to call up men to serve in the armed forces. The fathers of some of my classmates were drafted or had volunteered to join the army, and some of them were eventually wounded or killed. I didn't know any of the men who were hurt or killed.

My father was slightly older than the age limit for joining the service or being drafted. He continued to work in his machine shop, building farm equipment and spare parts for a secret Navy project. His Navy work entitled him to an extra gasoline rationing book.

There were shortages of many items, including meat, butter, sugar, coffee, cigarettes, silk stockings, rubber bands, perfume, and chewing gum. We were encouraged to save the tinfoil from cigarette packages and gum wrappers. The government issued a large variety of rationing books, with stamps and little round cardboard discs, called "points," to use when purchasing any of the scarce items. These were proofs of entitlement to a certain amount of the items and were used in addition to money to pay for the items.

Whenever any of my uncles or aunts came to visit, we would drive the seven miles to Mexico, to the small Mexican border town of Reynosa. There we would have a big, delicious Mexican dinner, and I would usually be given a glass of beer, which I loved. My uncle Van would give me an entire bottle, all for me. I loved him. After the meal, we would go shopping. My mother and my aunts would buy silk stockings and perfume and would hide these items in their underwear so as to smuggle them back across the border into the United States. We would also buy a bag of sugar and some little square packages of rainbow-colored Chiclets chewing gum for me.

There was no shortage of anything in Mexico, which was neutral until the last day of the War, as I recall, as were a number of other neighboring countries. In the last day of the conflict they declared war on Japan and Germany. I suppose they were hoping for a cut of the victor's spoils or at least saw the value of being officially on the side of the winners, the United States and its allies.

We were all somewhat afraid that German U-boats (submarines) would unload Nazis and other monstrous types to invade, take us prisoner, and maybe kill us. Maybe these monsters would come across the river from Mexico, which was not yet on the side of the U.S. powers. Or maybe the Japanese U-boats would come to the Pacific Coast or to the Gulf of Mexico and would unload masses of sadistic little bucktoothed soldiers with thick horn-rimmed glasses, as the wartime propaganda portrayed the Japanese. They would try to torture us all for the glory of their emperor and Admiral Tojo, head of the Japanese armed services.

Many times we were told to keep our lights turned off at night so as not to be visible from the air, and specifically in Houston, so as not to make a lighted background against which our ships would be silhouetted and would be sitting ducks for Axis torpedoes.

Gasoline and automobile tires were also rationed and hard to obtain, so driving was very curtailed. Airplane tickets were not available to civilians, and train travel was very limited.

There was no television yet, and movies were not air-conditioned. Many people read on a regular basis and became very well-informed, very well educated. Some taught themselves Sanskrit, French, and other languages. This may have been the last gasp of literate America, or at least the last time reading was practiced on such a large scale.

XXXXXXXXXXXXXXXXXXXXXXXXXXXXXXXXXXXXXXXXXXXXXX

In 1943, when I was ten, my parents gave me a bicycle for my birthday. I was delighted and soon learned to ride. My father even helped me a little with this—I guess he was glad to see his sissy boy doing something butch. My mother wouldn't let me go off our block. I was disappointed I wasn't allowed to ride my bicycle down to the levee, two miles away, where my friends often went on Saturdays or Sundays. The spillways were dry 99 percent of the time, only filling with water when there were very heavy rains and the Rio Grande, five miles away, was flooded and overflowed into them. I think my mother was afraid that I might get hurt bicycling on the local highway.

However, she often sent me to the grocery store, which was two blocks away. I had a wicker basket strapped to the handlebars to carry home the items on her grocery list. This seemed like a little adventure to me, and I enjoyed going to the grocery store.

I also got to see and sometimes talk to one of my hug objects, handsome Harold, who worked at the store afternoons and Saturdays. We would go into the back of the store where the chickens were killed and plucked, and sometimes we lingered longer than we should have, just having a pleasant chat. I think Harold enjoyed the break from work, and I enjoyed Harold. It was quite innocent.

At about the same time, I discovered gardening and growing flowers. Our landlords, the Nelsons, allowed me to use a small plot of ground, about six by four feet, next to the garbage cans and close to the alley, one of the less desirable spots in the yard. It was okay with me, and I set to work to dig up the hard dirt and get the plot ready.

At the grocery store were racks of vegetable and flower seeds, with pictures of giant colorful flowers or huge vegetables on the front of the packets. For my first attempt, I picked out a package of Iceland poppy seeds, a very unlikely choice, but I insisted.

I planted the seeds carefully and lovingly, and in about ten days they began to come up. I watered them carefully every day and looked to see that no insects got on them and that the flower bed remained free of weeds or other garbage. The little plants looked at me and said, "Thank you for taking such good care of us. We are going to surprise you. We are going to make a lot of extra-beautiful flowers for you. Thank you, yes, yes." In about six weeks, buds began to form, and ten days later the first flower opened: a pale salmon-colored beauty. The plants bloomed prolifically. Several of the neighbors came to look at the Iceland poppies—no one had seen flowers like these before.

The McAllen Garden Club flower show was announced, and I decided to enter. My mother bought me a pink hobnail design glass vase, which I still have, and helped me make an attractive arrangement of the Iceland poppies. The ladies running the show were pleased and smiled at me. On the day of the judging, I was surprised and happy to see that my flowers had won a "Special First Prize for Iceland Poppies." The fact that mine were the only Iceland poppies entered in the show did not take away any of the glory of having won the special first prize. I was very proud.

Years later I wondered how these little flowers, so far from their native Iceland, had managed to thrive and bloom in the dry inferno of South Texas next to the garbage cans. I am sure that it was the love I had for my poppies that made them able to thrive and even win a prize.

I have tried several times since then to grow Iceland poppies in Connecticut and on my terrace in New York but have never persuaded them even to germinate. Perhaps they decided to spread their joy around to others. They had already done plenty for my happiness.

XXXXXXXXXXXXXXXXXXXXXXXXXXXXXXXXXXXXXXXXXXXX

There were attempts by my parents and teachers to persuade me to go out with some of the little girls. The idea terrified me. Our class went on a few group hayrides. There was some holding hands, even some kissing, but of course not by me or my "date," who was usually the ugliest girl in school, glad to be escorted to the hayride, even by a nonsexual, timid, four-eyed nerd like me. The hayrides were enormously uncomfortable for me. I hated them. Eve's apple was revolting.

I was also invited to most of the children's birthday, Halloween, and other parties. My mother made me go. These parties were attended by both boys and girls and were truly very bland and innocent events, always closely supervised by the parents of the birthday child.

Nevertheless, I was boiling with anxiety and almost paralyzed with confusion, having difficulty even speaking. The parties were horrible torments for me. I was filled with shame, not because I had done anything, but just because I existed. I felt it was shameful for me to exist and that I was a terrible person. After the party had started, sometimes I would hide under a bush in the yard and spend an hour crying inconsolably. Gradually, the parents and the other children came to accept that I was shy. Little did they know the extent of this handicap.

However, at the same time that I was struggling to make some place for myself with the other students, I was also capable of cruelty toward my best friend, Sammy, who was from one of the few Jewish families in town.

Each semester, the class voted on various officers and tasks, such as president, secretary, person in charge of the blackboard and the erasers, and flower girl, whose job was to arrange the flowers in vases and change the water when needed. One semester, the last term of the fifth-grade year, it suddenly occurred to me that it would be hilarious to nominate Sammy to be "flower girl." I had not discussed this idea with him previously. When I made the nomination, the class roared with laughter and unanimously voted him in as that semester's flower girl.

Sammy was mortified; I thought he was going to cry. Then I thought I was also going to cry when I realized what a mean thing I had done. The teacher did not intervene as she should have. Sammy and I were not such good friends after that.

Another day, when we were outside playing, he kept interfering with my attempt to blow a string of soap bubbles. He was laughing, but I was getting very angry. Suddenly I unloosed a nasty anti-Semitic curse at him. I have no idea where this came from, as my parents did not have anti-Semitic feelings and did not make anti-Semitic remarks. There were very few Jewish families in the neighboring towns, and there was no anti-Semitic sentiment or talk in that part of the country. As soon as I had said it, I felt terrible, but I hoped somehow my nasty remark would simply vanish.

The next day, Sammy's mother came to call on my mother, an unusual event. She told my mother what I had said to Sammy. My mother was horrified, called me in, and asked me if this were true. "Yes, Mother. I'm very sorry," I said in front of the two women. Later that night, my mother told me to apologize to Sammy and that I should never again say such nasty things to Sammy or to anyone else.

The next day I apologized and tried to tell Sammy how truly sorry I was to have said an ugly thing to him. I asked him to forgive me. He was a very kind and polite boy, and he said, "Oh, yes." The fact was that I had betrayed his friendship and viciously turned on him without cause. I had hurt him and had ruined our friendship. I have continued to feel terrible and ashamed about this wicked deed, and if there were one thing in my life that I could undo and erase, this would be it.

Besides Sammy's family, there was only one other Jewish family in McAllen. The two daughters were my schoolmates. The elder, Joann, was my age. Her little sister, Shirley, was two years younger. I liked them both, and they liked me. They didn't show scorn for me because I liked to read. I could see how nice their parents were to them. Their parents seemed to love them, an idea which was very painful for me and made me jealous.

There was a very pleasant, relaxed atmosphere in their home, so different from the brooding, tense, angry atmosphere in my own home. And there were always good cooking odors when I visited their house. The same was true of Sammy's parents and of his home. Both sets of parents were warm and cordial to me until the bad incident occurred. I am sure that Sammy's mother had told Joann's mother how bigoted and untrustworthy I was.

Neither of these families knew, nor did my own, of my jealousy of Sammy and Joann and Shirley or that I wished very much to be Jewish myself. Of course, it was not the religion that interested me; it was the kindliness and respect for learning that the children and their parents all showed. This was quite different from the attitudes of the Anglo and the Mexican families and children and from my own family.

In mid-1945 the war ended, first with Germany and its allies in Europe, and then a little later with Japan, after America had dropped the two terrifyingly destructive atomic bombs on Nagasaki and Hiroshima. The whole country was of course very relieved that the fighting had stopped, and soon the troops were demobilized and began to return home. Little by little life returned to a more normal condition.

I finished grammar school and graduated from the eighth grade in 1946, age twelve, and was ready to start McAllen High School the following September, more maladjusted than ever.

XXXXXXXXXXXXXXXXXXXXXXXXXXXXXXXXXXXXXXXXXXXXX

In August that summer I turned thirteen. My parents decided to surprise me with a "special birthday present," a six-week stay at Camp Rio Vista, a boys' summer camp in the Hill Country of central Texas. Perhaps they thought this would be a help in teaching me to socialize with other boys more easily, or perhaps help in the development of self-assurance, both of which I was woefully deficient in. I was not asked my opinion of the plan. I was skeptical, afraid, and unenthusiastic, which irritated both my parents, as the camp was quite expensive.

The first day came, and my parents drove me up to the camp. For once I was sorry to see them go and wondered how I was going to get through this ordeal by myself. I was assigned to a cabin with seven other boys. We were the "buffaloes" for purposes of team sports and general identification. I had an upper bunk, which I preferred. After unpacking and meeting the other boys, we all went to the mess hall for dinner, which was reasonably good. After that, there was an orientation session in the gym, where it was suggested that the campers were in for a good time. I didn't believe it.

The camp was on the banks of the Guadalupe River, the most beautiful river in Texas. About thirty feet wide, with clear water, a few minor rapids, and willows hanging over the edge, the river was as pretty as it was supposed to be. I enjoyed learning to use a canoe. Swimming was fun, as was archery. Horseback riding, canoeing, rifle practice, baseball, and a few other sports were also offered.

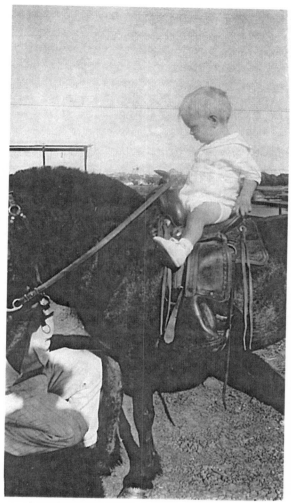

Author developing a fear of horses, Dallas, 1935

I had poor luck with horseback riding. The horses did not seem to like me. The first time I got on one of the beasts, it promptly scraped me off against the side of the corral. On my next attempt, it ducked under a low set of reins fastening the next horse to a post, so I was scraped backward and fell off the back end of the horse. Both times, as soon as the horse had succeeded in dislodging me, he ran off to his stable without looking back. I had the definite impression that the horses were practiced in getting rid of young and inexperienced riders. I decided that riding horses was not for me and refused to get on again or even to be around the disagreeable critters.

I remembered when a friend had invited me to ride his horse the previous summer. I got on without difficulty. As the horse started to walk a bit, the saddle, which had not been secured properly, slowly slipped to one side of the horse and then got lower until I was hanging off the horse sideways. The saddle then went further down, and I hung on until I was almost upside down, but finally I had to let go and fall to the ground. The horse stopped and stared at me, smiling to himself. My relationship with horses has not improved since then.

After the first two weeks at the camp, my mother, who had become too lonely for me, took me out of the camp to spend the weekend with her in San Antonio. I liked this much better than staying in the camp and was sorry when she took me back to Rio Vista on Sunday afternoon. My fellow campers looked at me as if I were a deserter and did not welcome me back. The next week, Mother took me out again. When I cam back after the weekend, the other campers had already divided up my belongings between them, including my clarinet, and were obviously disappointed that I had returned. They were reluctant to give my things back.

By the fourth week, I began to hear that some of the older campers performed a seriously dangerous test on the younger campers. This test was called the "Pederocious Test" and consisted of a heavy brick being tied by a four-foot string to a camper's penis and testicles. The camper stood on an upper bunk, and then the brick was dropped off the edge of the bunk. The test was to see if the camper was castrated. The rumor was that nobody so far this year had been castrated, but that this had happened to two boys the previous year.

The fifth weekend of the camp approached, and I was told that when I returned on Monday from my usual weekend out with my mother, I was going to have to undergo the Pederocious Test. I was terrified and was sure that I was going to be castrated, if not killed. When I tried to talk to the counselor assigned to our cabin, he just laughed. I told my mother that some of the other campers were planning to mutilate me and that I just could not go back to stay at the camp again.

My mother drove me back to the camp and complained to the head of the camp for allowing the campers to torture one another. We collected my belongings that afternoon, and so I escaped from the camp physically intact. I assumed I had escaped before permanent damage was done, but of course the real damage done to me was psychological. The next summer there was no talk about attending summer camp again. As an experiment, or as therapy, and certainly as a pleasant experience, summer camp was a ghastly failure. It confirmed for me again that I was unable to fit in with or be accepted by my peers.

XXX

There were two elementary schools in McAllen, each consisting of grades one through eight. In the ninth grade, both schools were combined for the four years of high school. One of the students from the other school joined my little group of yearned-for boys. Muscular, handsome, a basketball star, Bubba was popular with all. He looked irresistible in his basketball uniform, which revealed his best feature: strong and shapely legs covered with fuzzy blond hair.

I often imagined hugging Bubba's legs but didn't know what further to do with them, even in fantasy. Bubba was cordial to me and seemed to accept my admiration as something positive. By this time, I knew that the "wrestling" attempts were a no-no, so Bubba never experienced any of my octopus-like attempts to squeeze my admired classmates.

These four boys (Bubba, Harold, Charles, and Homer) remained objects of my interest, both open and secret, during all the years of grammar school and high school. We were classmates until we graduated together after finishing the twelfth grade in June of 1950.

I began to have a dim, nonverbal understanding that perhaps relationships could hold something of value and interest. This was contrary to my usual feeling that I would prefer to be permanently alone. Unfortunately, I lost track of all these shining boys and know nothing of their subsequent lives, but I hope all of them have fared well and are happy and getting plenty of affectionate hugs from those who love them.

XXXXXXXXXXXXXXXXXXXXXXXXXXXXXXXXXXXXXXXXXXX

My parents and I all read Richard Bucke's fascinating book, *Cosmic Consciousness*, a real modern classic, published in 1902. This is a description of more than one hundred historical figures who had spontaneous ecstasies, that is, ecstasies arising without the use of drugs, other physical or psychological maneuvers, or near-death experiences. Sometimes the ecstasies were associated with states of prayer or meditation. These ecstasies lasted varying times, differing from person to person.

The descriptions of these states were taken from eyewitness accounts, biographical and autobiographical accounts, and extracts from the teachings and writings of the ecstatics themselves. They included Jesus, Buddha, St. John of the Cross, St. Theresa of Avila, Baruch Spinoza, Walt Whitman, Edward Carpenter, and many others.

I was particularly heartened by these accounts and hoped that in my own life there might be some similar happy relief from the dreary and painful hopelessness of ordinary life.

Soon after, I was happy to have my first experience of ecstasy. It was late afternoon, and I was in the backyard watering the flowers. Suddenly the world began to glow, to shine, to glitter. I lost all uncomfortable feelings: fear, depression, anger, worry, guilt. These feelings were replaced by an utter conviction that all was well, all was perfect, that no matter what happened, it was the right thing, that nothing could hurt me in any meaningful way. Divinity was within me and was filling me. I had an expanded presence; I was everywhere in the yard, looking at the flowers and trees from all directions at once. I was everywhere in the universe, looking at all the stars from every location. This ecstatic experience lasted about ten minutes and then slowly faded over the next half hour, leaving me calm, serene, happy, and somewhat withdrawn, or turned inward.

It was the first of many such experiences, which have continued my entire life, usually occurring spontaneously two or three times a year. They have been a tremendous blessing and comfort. They always occur when I am alone, sometimes when I am listening to music or looking at a beautiful picture or landscape. I don't know any method to make them occur. For many years, I didn't tell anyone of these experiences, preferring to keep them as special secrets, and afraid of what others might think.

However, I eventually learned that many people have had similar experiences. Perhaps this is some evolution the human race is undergoing. I do not want to present myself as a saint or a holy man, which certainly is/ was not the case.

XXXXXXXXXXXXXXXXXXXXXXXXXXXXXXXXXXXXXXXXXXX

By the time of the senior prom, I was a confirmed serious social phobic, and I steadfastly refused to attend the prom, much less to take Miss Ugly as my date. She was another shy, bookish person. Her face was covered with freckles and pimples. She wore thick glasses (as I did also) and had buck teeth, bad breath, and body odor. We had both been in the senior class play, Oscar Wilde's *The Importance of Being Earnest*. Miss Ugly played Miss Prism, and I played Reverend Chasuble. We were told that both were perfect typecast roles for us. But I thought I was much uglier than she.

Because of the play, we were thought of as a "pair," an idea which pained me and perhaps displeased her too. There was a great deal of dating pressure on me from parents and teachers, but I was far too shy, anxious, and confused even to go through with the charade of a "date" to the senior prom. Miss

Ugly was quite disappointed and did not understand that it was not her, but I, who was the problem.

I was sorry that her feelings were hurt but did not know what to do about it or how to explain the true situation to her. I was struggling and being defeated by my own demons, not for the first or the last time.

My parents began to understand that there was some kind of a problem—perhaps the fact that I was "clean and pure" was not the whole story or even a desirable story. I knew that there was something very different and quite unacceptable about me but had no idea what it might be.

I only knew that my feelings were not like those the other children had, that I was a very bad person in some essential but mysterious and unspeakable way. Seeds of unrecognized homophobia had already begun to grow in me. Perhaps Eve's apple had no redeeming features.

XXXXXXXXXXXXXXXXXXXXXXXXXXXXXXXXXXXXXXXXXXXX

I wondered vaguely what might be coming next, of course not expecting anything good to happen.

High School (1946–1950)

Most Wednesday evenings my parents and I would drive from McAllen to the neighboring town of Pharr, Texas, two miles away, to hear a lecture at the Episcopal Church. The minister, Reverend Stewart, had a degree from Harvard Divinity School, knew Sanskrit, and gave courses in comparative religion at the church and at the local junior college.

Sometimes he would give a series of lectures solely on Buddhism, or solely on Hinduism, concentrating on the Upanishads, the Vedanta, or one of the other five classic schools of Hindu philosophy. These lectures would be considered outstanding anywhere, even today. They were usually inspiring.

Occasionally, perhaps every third time, I would see a halo form around Mr. Stewart's head. This was a shimmering light extending out five or six inches in all directions from his head and neck. The light seemed to move and would sometimes develop a protuberance rising upward perhaps eighteen to twenty-four inches. His face would begin to glow. The halo would last fifteen to twenty minutes during his lecture. It was not apparently caused by any lighting effect and would stay with him as he moved about the room.

I asked my parents if they had seen this light. "Yes," they said. It seemed that about one third of the congregation of nearly sixty people had seen it. The halo was visible on many occasions.

There was a family tradition, stronger on my mother's side, of various kinds of second sight. There had been many instances of visions of angelic beings, recently dead relatives, and other discarnate entities, generally but not always benign. There were many episodes of telepathy and a few of faith healing. I have had several of these experiences. The vision of Mr. Stewart's halo was an unusual, positive, and interesting event, but I did not consider it out of the realm of the normal.

Because of Mr. Stewart's Indian religious lectures, my parents and I began to read books on Hindu philosophy and to discuss the ideas presented. We became particularly interested in the philosophy of the Vedanta.

There are three classic schools of thought in this metaphysical philosophy: dualism, nondualism (the Advaita philosophy), and qualified nondualism.

The distinctions concern the apparent multiplicity of phenomena: Is it real (dualism)? Solely a misconception of our minds (nondualism)? Or something in between (qualified nondualism)? My father did not reveal which school he favored. My mother was a strong adherent of the nondualism school, but I thought the qualified nondualism school was more realistic and acceptable. My failure to agree with her thinking enraged her, and we had many heated, serious, and quite hostile arguments about this subject.

Looking back on that time, I realize how constricting, controlling, and insecure my mother was and what an abnormal and peculiar atmosphere existed at home. I was tormented by guilt about disagreeing and thereby hurting my mother but felt angry when I was forced into a corner by her. I was not permitted to have my own opinion about much of anything.

These arguments went on two or three times a week for over two years, and finally I capitulated and said I agreed with her that Advaita was the only correct school of Vedanta. I tried to lie convincingly, but she realized that something was not right, and she continued to pick at me about this subject until she died twenty years later.

XXXXXXXXXXXXXXXXXXXXXXXXXXXXXXXXXXXXXXXXXXXX

My mother had become an abusive shrew. She scolded my father almost incessantly all through breakfast, on those occasions when he returned home for lunch, and then all through dinner. Her complaints centered on his gross appearance and behavior, his generally morose and silent attitude, and his failure to make enough money. In later years, she added details of his sexual shortcomings and on many occasions, both at home and in public, yelled "Queer" at him, which I truly think he was not.

He usually didn't make any reply and never defended himself against her blasts. "What a sissy," I said to myself. Even though I did not like my father and usually felt contempt for him, I also sometimes felt sorry for him. But I wished he would defend himself, or even take a punch at my mother, to shut up her incessant strident tongue-lashing.

At that time, I didn't fully understand my mother's situation. Over the previous two years, she had been hospitalized several times, first for a ruptured tubal pregnancy. Then she developed intestinal obstructions due to adhesions and needed two more operations to relieve this condition. In the two years this was occurring, she spent a total of about twelve months in the hospital. My grandmother came down from Houston to take care of me, and this made me happy.

Finally, Mother's physical condition improved and she came home, but she was very weak for a long time, did not feel well, and needed a lot of rest.

Most importantly, she had become a secret morphine addict while in the hospital, a condition which persisted on and off for the rest of her life. I think the morphine made her life hellish. It certainly was hellish for those around her. Like many other addicts, she was able to keep the details and practice of her addiction hidden most of the time, even if the effects were flagrant. Within a few days of finally leaving the hospital, she resumed her heavy drinking. At first she tried to keep this secret, for instance, by keeping her scotch whiskey in a Listerine bottle. During her frequent drunken episodes she was ferociously angry, abusive, and assaultive toward my father. I can remember episodes in which she screamed curses at him, hitting him as hard as she could, at the same time vomiting and clutching her abdomen in pain.

After three months, my father couldn't hold up any longer. He told my mother that unless she completely stopped drinking, he would leave her and take me with him, as she was becoming an unfit mother. She immediately completely stopped her drinking.

When he told me of this episode years later, he implied that the threat of losing me was what really caused her to stop drinking. I was very moved when I heard this. She did not drink at all for about twelve years, until I left for college. Then she resumed her active alcoholism, which gradually became worse.

I promised myself that I would never marry, because no matter how pleasant and reasonable my wife-to-be might appear, how could I ever be sure that she would not become a tongue-lashing harpy like my mother? And then I would have ruined the rest of my life by taking a chance on marriage. Better to be alone forever. Needless to say, I did not discuss my resolution with anyone, including my father. It would have been like trying to discuss vegetarianism with an alligator.

My as yet unrecognized latent homosexuality no doubt contributed to this decision. It seemed to me that marriage was a condition of perpetual fierce fighting and hatred but one which both parties were prepared to endure until death.

Neither of my parents had had a happy childhood or good role models in their own parents. They were both unprepared to be parents. My mother wanted to have a child. My father did not. My arrival created increased stress between them. It never occurred to me that they had any love for one another. Perhaps they did not.

Author, age 16, 1950

They both had many points of immaturity and confusion and struggled to cope with their own lives as well as try to keep their marriage together. I am convinced that they both did their best to be good parents. In spite of the traumas I experienced at their hands while I was growing up, and even though they created some permanent damage and handicaps, I think of them with love and sorrow and wish I could have just five minutes to give them a hug, thank them for all the good things they gave me and did for me, and tell them that I love them. They were my only parents. Perhaps I am too forgiving.

XXXXXXXXXXXXXXXXXXXXXXXXXXXXXXXXXXXXXXXXXXX

Whichever school of Vedanta one believed in, all of them condemned sex in any form. It was a terrible mistake to be interested in sex, much less to do anything about it. Any sex was bad, wrong, and wasteful. Any sexual activity, including masturbation, wasted the vital energy in orgasm, so that the kundalini or serpent power could never be activated. The concept of evil was not stressed as it was in Christianity.

If you could not raise your kundalini, you could never become enlightened and would always remain a gross, coarse, low creature devoid of spiritual worth and doomed to endless degraded and painful rebirths, which I already suspected was my condition.

There was no differentiation made between various forms of sex; all were unfortunate dead ends. Perhaps some forms, like the so-far unnamed and unrecognized gay sex, were even more regrettable than others. This fit right in with my sexual views formed some years earlier at the swimming pool: dirty, low-class, bad, to be avoided.

I also came to view masturbation as a terrible mistake and vowed never to do it. Needless to say, this resolve crumbled on a regular basis, sometimes daily, and I felt for many years that I should commit suicide because I was doomed to be a wasteful and worthless impulse-ridden person who could never become enlightened.

Many times I promised myself that I would commit suicide if I ever masturbated again. Within twenty-four hours I had fallen again, failed myself again. I then carried the double shame that I had both masturbated and was too cowardly to kill myself.

I was unhappy, lonely, and afraid, with no one to turn to for help. I felt there was nothing pleasant to look forward to, no hope for any happiness. I was not able to imagine any help for my situation. I was doomed to be painfully unhappy and alone forever, I thought.

Some evenings I would go for a walk by myself. The route was always to the empty school football field two blocks away, where I climbed over the fence and then hid under the bleachers. When I felt adequately hidden, I would cry desperately for thirty minutes or so. I would then dry my eyes, wait a few minutes to let my red eyes clear up a little, and walk back home.

I did this a couple of times a week for a few years. I was never discovered in this activity and of course never revealed it to anyone, until now. My parents would have punished me severely if they had known.

XXXXXXXXXXXXXXXXXXXXXXXXXXXXXXXXXXXXXXXXXXX

From all the trips I had made with my mother to the beauty parlor, I knew my mother's hairdresser, Charles. He was a painter in his spare time. He talked about painting, and I knew that one of his works had won a prize in a local contest. I wanted to learn more about painting than my grandmother had taught me. I wondered if Charles would teach me about painting but somehow knew this was a dangerous thing to say to my mother.

One day, at about age twelve, I commented to my mother that I knew Charles was a painter and I would like to see his paintings. My mother looked startled and after a frozen silence said, "No. That is not a good idea. Charles is a *depraved man.*" That concluded the fourth and final part of my sex education received at home. (The first part was not to run water on my peepee, the second part was not to let adults know anything about peepee play, the third part was the knowledge of something ugly growing on my father, and the fourth part was to *avoid depraved men.*)

I did not know exactly what Charles's depravity was and wondered if something similar was also true of me. I assumed so. Eve's apple was assuming some strange shapes.

XXXXXXXXXXXXXXXXXXXXXXXXXXXXXXXXXXXXXXXXXXXXXXX

Toward the end of my sophomore year in high school, my old friend, Sammy, started to take piano lessons. We had become more friendly again in recent years. He told me how much he enjoyed the lessons and how good the teacher was. I asked my mother if I could also take piano lessons. Even though we did not have a piano at home, she agreed. I had a talk with Sammy's teacher, Esther Lee Blakemore, a kindly middle-aged widow who had recently moved to town from Long Beach, California, along with her elderly mother and three cats.

Mrs. Blakemore gave lessons in a ramshackle wooden building behind the Methodist church. At the far end of the building, away from her studio, there was a room with an old out-of-tune spare piano. Mrs. Blakemore told me I could practice there in the afternoons after school. I was delighted. It turned out that I had considerable talent and made rapid progress, playing fairly difficult concert pieces, such as Liszt's *Etude in D-flat* and Chopin's *Fantaisie-Impromptu* by the end of the first year of piano study.

Mrs. Blakemore was generous in pouring out her good spirits, kindness, and affection on me—it made a tremendous difference at the time. My memories of her are among the happiest of the time before I left home. I loved music and the piano from the start, and it has been perhaps the most valuable thing in my life. The fact that piano playing is a solitary activity also suited me perfectly.

Sometimes it seems that life is like a dungeon and that music is a magical window through which one can look out from the torture chamber and see a beautiful and always changing landscape.

XXXXXXXXXXXXXXXXXXXXXXXXXXXXXXXXXXXXXXXXXXXXXXX

One hour of the school day was called study hall. This was held every afternoon in the school library and was supposed to be used to study and prepare homework. My homework was always caught up; my grades were always excellent. I was always ahead of the assignments, so I used the time for reading subjects of interest to me.

One year I read a thirty-seven volume history of Turkey. It was fascinating—another world opened in those pages. What splendid depravity in the royal court of the Sultans! They rivaled and perhaps surpassed the debaucheries and excesses of the Roman Caesars as presented by Suetonius in his *Lives of the Twelve Caesars*, a book I discovered with delight in college a few years later.

There were references to physical and/or sexual practices which were mysterious to me, and I was curious to learn what these were. I had not yet heard of Oscar Wilde and his "love that dares not say its name." Neither did the Turkish Sultans name exactly what they were doing, but I knew that whatever they were doing, it was interesting and very, very *wrong*.

Meanwhile, back in the "real" world, my high school classmates were experimenting with dating and boy-girl relationships. This frightened me tremendously, and of course I did not make any pretense of wanting to participate in this scary activity. I had developed a practice of not talking about what I was, but neither did I pretend to be what I was not. This has been one of my guides in life.

My study hall reading continued. Like many small town schools with limited funds, the high school library accepted miscellaneous donations made by local people. Some of these gift horses were perhaps Trojan horses and were taken in without much critical inspection, so there was a considerable variety of reading material to explore.

I discovered a copy of Krafft-Ebing's *Psychopathia Sexualis*, a compendium of sexual variations and perversities which I read with great interest. The juicy parts were in Latin, which I did not know, but even so, I was able to puzzle out a little of the text. The book threw some light on my own situation. I realized that I had an erotic inclination toward boys, that I was a "sexual invert" according to Krafft-Ebing's terminology. I didn't see this as desiring sexual or genital behavior, as I had no knowledge of the mechanics of the sex act. Rather I wanted to hug, to be close to another boy.

Krafft-Ebing believed sexual inversion was a form of mental illness, an idea which did not shock me in the least, as I knew I was out of step with most of my classmates about so many other things. I wondered idly if perhaps I were insane. If so, I didn't much care.

Another early writer, Karl Ulrichs, was the first modern European to openly acknowledge his own man-loving nature. He called men who were attracted to other men *urnings*. I liked this name better, as the term *invert* suggested being upside down or standing on my head, and I wasn't sure if I might have to spend much of my life upside down, or at least on a slant, an unattractive idea. These scraps of information were very confusing to me.

I had not yet encountered the term *homosexual* or any other term in use at that time—fag, fairy, pansy, queer, cocksucker, queen, a friend of Dorothy, having a touch of the lavender. The term *gay* had not yet come into use.

I had read of Plato and Michelangelo and a few other famous urnings, but unfortunately for me they were all dead. I desperately needed some advice and guidance more personal than I could obtain from a book in the McAllen, Texas, high school library. There was no one to ask. Any reader who has grown up gay knows what this feels like.

A little later, I came across references to the French writer Andre Gide, who was a fellow urning. He had written several novels and was a well-known and apparently respected, although controversial, writer. He was at that time about eighty years old and lived in Paris. I thought Andre Gide was the sole living urning, other than myself, and was sorry he was unreachable. How could a young Texas boy with no money or connections manage to get to Paris and meet and talk with this famous writer? There was no way. I had no hope. Life was too confusing and ominous.

Somehow I had a nonverbal understanding that homosexuality was wrong, unacceptable, evil. I do not know how I had developed such an idea, as homosexuality was a truly taboo subject. The only thing I remember hearing about it was my mother's comment about Charles being a "*depraved man.*"

The time was the early 1950s, a puritanical and repressed era. It was, for instance, forbidden by the Movie Industry Production Code (formerly known as the Hays Code) for a movie to show a married couple lying in the same bed. This was some years before Kinsey's pioneering studies. Sex was simply not talked about; it was not a fit subject for decent people to mention. Perhaps this may explain how I came to finish high school with almost no knowledge of sex practices, much less any experience of them. After all, I was a "nice" boy.

Knowing I was different in some totally unacceptable and disgusting evil way, I was despondent and thought I should kill myself. A few years earlier, at age eight, after a particularly severe quarrel with both my parents, I had tried suicide by swallowing all the aspirin tablets left in an already open bottle, perhaps twenty tablets. I thought this would kill me, and I was very sorry that the only effect was a slight ringing in my ears for a few hours. Naturally, I didn't tell anyone. In my home, it was not acceptable for me to be upset about anything, particularly any action of my always perfect parents.

I have never entirely discarded the idea of suicide as a way of escape. I smile when I say, "Often, the idea of suicide is the only thing that keeps me alive." Those who have had the thought of suicide as a friendly companion through life will understand what this means.

XX

But there were many ordinary, practical concerns. Two years before I graduated from high school, my mother decided that something should be done about my crooked teeth. One upper canine tooth stuck straight out like a fang, and one lower front tooth was growing from left to right instead of straight up. I was ashamed of my teeth. Both jaws were overcrowded, in spite of the fact I had the good fortune to have congenital absence of all four wisdom teeth.

My parents (probably my mother) decided that I should have corrective orthodontic work, a considerable financial sacrifice. The closest good orthodontist, Dr. Dan Peavy, was in San Antonio, 180 miles north of McAllen. Once a month I would take the overnight train from McAllen to San Antonio, riding in an upper berth in the Pullman car. On one trip, Margaret Truman, the President's daughter, was also in the same Pullman car. I was thrilled and felt I was rising high in the world to be in such company. I was elegant and important by proxy.

When the train reached San Antonio the next morning, I would visit the orthodontist and have my braces tightened. I sometimes visited the music store if there was time, and then I took the bus home in the afternoon, arriving back in McAllen by 6 PM, in time for dinner.

One morning in San Antonio, while I was passing through downtown Travis Park on the way to Dr. Peavy's office, a well-dressed and pleasant-looking man approached me, fanned out a large number of twenty dollar bills, and asked me if I would like to have some. I was frightened, said no, and left immediately to run to the dentist's office.

This unusual incident surprised me. I didn't realize until later in the day that some kind of urning activity was probably implied. Another turning point avoided (or missed), I think. I didn't tell anyone about this.

After two years, the orthodontic work was mostly finished, but the braces stayed on for another two years for final adjustments. I had to continue to visit the orthodontist periodically for checkups. Then came a period of two more years during which I had to wear a retaining device at night to try to keep the teeth in their new positions.

The result was quite good. My mother and I were pleased. My grandmother thought it was a success. My father did not comment.

XXXXXXXXXXXXXXXXXXXXXXXXXXXXXXXXXXXXXXXX

Always hanging over me like a storm cloud was my father's hatred. I could feel his ever-present hostility, and when he was around the atmosphere was stifling and poisoned.

One evening my father was sitting in his favorite chair in the living room, reading the newspaper and waiting for dinner. I was standing barefooted in the same room; dinner was almost ready. My father glanced at me and said, "Look down by your right foot." When I looked down, I saw a large scorpion, a common insect in south Texas, about three inches from my foot. Startled, I jumped away.

My father chuckled and commented, "If you look where you are going, you will not get in so much trouble." This was good advice and was one of the few pieces of advice he ever gave me. He called my mother to kill the scorpion and then resumed his newspaper reading.

I assumed my father was disappointed that I had not stepped on the scorpion so that I might have learned his lesson better, and I wondered why he had warned me. This was the nature of our affection for one another.

He had hated me before I was born. Later on, he was embarrassed that people might think we had any connection. I was something of a sissy, and he was ashamed of me.

I do not remember ever looking forward to seeing my father or talking to him. I did not ask him more questions than were really necessary and generally did not speak to him spontaneously, other than a routine "hello" and "good-bye." He seldom spoke to me either. I do not recall his ever helping me with my homework or having any interest in what I was doing.

As a practical and polite man, he did not usually let his hostility show. I feel sure he was sometimes tempted to get rid of me. He must have realized that to do something which would result in my death might expose him to too much trouble, legal and otherwise.

Anyway, if he waited a few more years, I would be grown, out of the house, on my own, and perhaps living far away and having no further contact with him. Perhaps he enjoyed this daydream without any conscious realization that my mother would not so easily let me go.

Occasionally I would catch him looking at me with a grim expression which he had forgotten to veil. I took this to be the face of his murderous wishes, which I assumed were normal for him—nothing unusual in that.

XXXXXXXXXXXXXXXXXXXXXXXXXXXXXXXXXXXXXXXXXXX

1950 was my last year of high school, and the question of what to do after graduation concerned all the students. I wanted to go on to college, possibly to become a doctor. My parents agreed that I could go to college but told me they could not afford to send me away to college and that I could only attend the local two-year junior college in Edinburg, Texas, ten miles away from McAllen.

Years later I was saddened and somewhat surprised to find out that my father had made no financial contribution to my education after high school. He refused to do so. He had often said to me and my mother that he thought parents should contribute absolutely nothing to a child after he reached sixteen.

This frightened me, but as I passed my sixteenth birthday and was still going to school, I thought he had changed his mind. He had not, and my further education was entirely financed by my mother.

His dislike of me did not get any better until about thirty years later, when he became very slightly warmer at the end of his life. That was because my mother's alcoholism had become worse, and we commiserated about her daily terrible verbal abuse of him and sometimes of me too. This was our bond.

My mother, on the other hand, was overly interested in all my activities, thoughts, and studies. She was quite controlling and dominating. She had had to save me from destruction by my father before I was born, and she remained protective of me until the end of her life thirty years later. I am grateful to her for preserving me.

None of my classmates or any other children had ever been permitted to come into our apartment, as they might be too noisy or might track in dirt or break something. I was often not permitted to go outside to visit or play with my friends. My mother did not explain why, and I knew better than to ask.

I remained an only child and so was the focus of my parents' attention, for good and bad. Not permitted to have thoughts, feelings, or preferences not approved by my mother, I felt quite smothered by her and yearned to get away. At the same time, I felt grateful to her for shielding me from my father's hatred. Without her, I am sure he would have managed to get rid of me one way or another.

A family gathering, Houston, 1950

So, by the end of my high school years, I had become a shy, bookish, depressed, eccentric boy who knew there was something unusual and unacceptable and probably evil about his inner core. There was no one I could turn to for help. It was like being adrift alone in a small boat on an empty and menacing ocean. I sometimes thought it would be better if the boat sank.

XXXXXXXXXXXXXXXXXXXXXXXXXXXXXXXXXXXXXXXXXXXXXXX

I asked the high school placement counselor about the possibility of attending Rice Institute (now Rice University) in Houston. Rice was a very good college 350 miles north of McAllen. My grandmother lived only a mile away from the Rice campus, and perhaps I could live with her. And a wonderful feature of living with my grandmother would be that she had a piano, which I loved to play.

Rice had a massive endowment, so there was no tuition. There was great competition for places in the entering class. Most of the students were either first or second in their high school graduating classes. I was third in mine. But my high school placement counselor told me there was no chance that I would be accepted there.

On my own, I wrote to Rice anyway, requested an admission form, filled it out, and sent it in. This was over the unexplained opposition of my placement counselor and my mother, who did not want me to escape from home. Rice requested grade transcripts, and an interview by a local alumnus was arranged. After waiting two months, I was surprised and delighted to receive an acceptance.

My father was indifferent to my good news but was undoubtedly glad to be getting his embarrassing son out of town. My mother was opposed to her little birdie leaving home. Since I could live safely with my grandmother, and since the school was free, my mother's opposition was frustrated, but she still didn't approve of my defection.

I looked forward to living with my grandmother, to attending college, escaping McAllen, and escaping from home.

In September of 1950, at age seventeen, I entered the freshman class at Rice Institute.

Oh, Love, Where Are You?
College, 1950–1953

When I moved to Houston, I was happy to be living with Granny, but school was very challenging.

Psychologically I was in poor condition when I entered Rice: extremely anxious, depressed, sometimes suicidal, and socially phobic. I had made some progress with a conscious plan to make my dream life my primary reality and to make the external reality seem like an insubstantial dream. In other words, I was trying to exchange my inner and outer worlds. Eventually this produced unpleasant results. When the external world really began to become insubstantial, with buildings seemingly made of cardboard and the sky looking like a backdrop, (technically called *derealization*), I knew I had gone too far. I was fearful, ill at ease, and knew I had to stop trying to exchange inner and outer worlds.

My grandmother, 1950

A couple of years earlier, I had at last surrendered to the temptation to masturbate, which soon became a regular occurrence. Much to my surprise, each time I had an orgasm. I practiced this vice as often as I could, always imagining that I was holding on to one of my earlier hug objects. This behavior continued for the two years I lived with Granny and after that for two more years while I lived in the school dormitory.

At my grandmother's, I enjoyed the privacy to masturbate while taking a bath or when in my bedroom at night, with the door shut, supposedly asleep. My grandmother did not burst in on me several times a day, as my mother had done.

I was relieved not to be living at home and was never homesick.

XX

Rice still permitted and promoted annual hazing of the new freshman students, a revolting custom. All of us were issued beanie caps, which were to be worn at all times. It was forbidden to have a haircut until Thanksgiving. The second week of school, while I was on the sidewalk in front of Rice waiting for the bus, a carload of University of Houston students pulled up. They surrounded me, demanding my beanie.

"Give us your cap, you sissy queer, before we knock you out. We're going to kidnap you, and maybe we'll kill you." I tried to resist as two of them grabbed me and one grabbed my beanie. I held on so tightly that I got a very badly sprained finger and could only write with my left hand for the rest of the freshman year. I lost the beanie anyway.

Fortunately, they seemed to forget about the kidnap threat, and after a few more nasty remarks they drove away. I could not use my right hand for writing until almost the end of the school year, eight months later. I wasn't able to get a replacement cap; the absence of my beanie marked me as a nonconforming oddball.

Without the beanie, it was even more noticeable that my hair was becoming abnormally long. These were the Eisenhower years; all males wore their hair quite short, and middle-of-the-road conformity was the order of the day. Eventually I couldn't tolerate the way my long hair looked. I thought it marked me as a freak, a queer, an undesirable oddball.

I was unbearably ashamed to be seen on the street. Reluctantly, I made the decision to have a haircut a month before Thanksgiving. This was another obvious sign of my nonconformity, but I thought the other students didn't like me one way or the other and hoped they wouldn't notice.

Two weeks later, on coming out of a large class one morning, several of my classmates grabbed me and threw me onto the ground in front of about 150 other students. They held my head, pulled out a pair of scissors, and chopped off my hair almost to the scalp. I was told that this was my punishment for being an oddball.

Fortunately, in the struggle they avoided stabbing me in the eyes or elsewhere with their scissors. Maybe they were afraid they might be punished if they went that far. Many of my other classmates who were watching this scene expressed sympathy, but I was frantic with shame and slunk off to a remote part of the campus to hide under a bush.

I thought, "This is how it's going to be. I'm no good. I can't fit in. I can't live with people. They all hate me, and I hate them too. I can't even hide—they will hunt me down like they did today. Next time it will be much worse for me. Maybe they will torture and kill me. It's what I deserve anyway for being such a bad person." The situation seemed hopeless—immensely humiliating, crushing.

The last tiny shred of self-respect had been destroyed. There was no way I could stay alive. I began to cry, gasping for breath, but trying not to make any sound, so as to escape notice. After a couple of hours of crying and confusion, I decided to kill myself. I went to a local drugstore and bought some razor blades. I wrote a suicide note explaining that it was not possible to continue living after what my classmates had done to me.

For reasons not clear to me at the time (or now), I decided to visit Dr. George Richter, professor of chemistry and acting dean of the school, before killing myself. I wanted to tell him how awful I thought this kind of hazing was. This was to be my last good act, for the welfare of other potential victims. After that, I would be free to kill myself by using the razor blades to cut my wrists and neck, after dark, under one of the bushes on the campus. I planned to be found dead the next morning.

After going to the dean's office, his secretary called him and then very politely showed me into his office.

Of course I did not tell the dean of my plans to self-destruct, but I did tell him how cruel and unfair I thought the situation was. I intended to tell him the names of the attacking students but did not get a chance.

He looked at me coldly and asked, "What did you expect would happen when you chose to be out of step with the hazing regulations? Don't you agree with me that you fully deserve what has just happened to you?" He laughed with obvious scorn. I realized with a feeling of horror that Dr. Richter was just as sadistic as my scissoring classmates. Speechless with sadness and shame, I just looked at him. I felt like I had now been raped twice in one day.

"I'm very busy, and your time is up," he said. The three minutes he spent with me were horrible and unforgettable. Later I came to believe that he was a monster of cruelty to as many students as he could manage to torture, and I hope he is enjoying the proper rewards for his evil behavior.

But by then all the steam seemed to have gone out of me. I did not have the energy to carry out my plan for self-elimination. I was so ashamed of my cowardice. There was really no escape possible for me in any direction, even suicide. Crying, I lay down under a bush for a few hours. I kept fingering the razor blades but did not have the courage to use them.

I then crept home to my grandmother's house. I hurried into my room without stopping to talk with her, commenting that I had to study for a test tomorrow. She knew something was wrong but wisely didn't ask any questions.

For the rest of the four years I spent at Rice I felt that everyone knew what had happened to me, that I was disgraced, that all knew what a disgusting loser I was. I was now an official pariah and an outcast.

But being at college was still better than remaining at home with my parents.

XXXXXXXXXXXXXXXXXXXXXXXXXXXXXXXXXXXXXXXXXXXXXXX

Some years after graduation, I returned to Rice one day to have lunch with Dr. Andrew Louis, my favorite professor and chairman of the German department. Dr. Richter was also present in the faculty dining room. My host pointed him out and commented that he was a professor of chemistry and had once acted as dean of the college and that he was a very fine man.

I replied, "I knew him when I was a student here. I took an organic chemistry course from him. Once, when he was acting dean, I turned to him for help in a personal crisis. At that time, he seemed pleased to treat me with contempt and cruelty. I think he is a sadistic monster."

The subject of Dr. Richter was dropped immediately, like a dead rat, and the conversation turned to other matters. Neither of us commented further on Dr. Richter.

I was sorry to have been so accusatory in front of Dr. Louis, which probably made him uncomfortable. He had been a real friend and had helped me a great deal. Perhaps his kindness had saved my life.

When I enrolled for his first-year German course, I was surprised that the chairman of the department was teaching the course. I was interested, attentive, and asked many questions. I think Dr. Louis was pleased that a student was showing so much interest and initiative. He was a wonderful and much-needed counterbalance to the dreadful Dr. Radoslav Tsanoff, dragon and chairman of the philosophy department, whom I also encountered during my freshman year.

Dr. Louis gave me a good grade for the year, and I signed up for second- and then third-year German. I became proficient in reading, fair in verbal comprehension, poor in writing, and even poorer in speaking. I was better at the passive than at the active aspect of language study.

At the beginning of my senior year, Middle High German was offered, to be taught by Dr. Louis. Since it was a graduate-level class, Dr. Louis's approval to enroll was needed, which he readily gave. But he told me that I was the only student enrolled and that he hoped there would be some others. There were not. Dr. Louis decided to give the course anyway.

We were assigned a small room in the library, and for the entire year I had the great pleasure of having personal instruction by the head of the department. His fields of special interest were grammar, philology, and Middle High German literature. He was a very expert teacher.

Grammar was very important in Middle High and was not exactly the same as in modern German. I enjoyed learning the intricacies of this old language and as a side benefit learned to read Chaucer easily: English of the middle ages used much of the same grammar and some of the same vocabulary as did Middle High.

We spent the first semester reading *The Nibelungenlied*, the great German epic poem of the middle ages. The second semester was spent in the study of various poets of courtly love. Dr. Louis suggested that I write a long paper on the traditions of courtly love as embodied in *The Nibelungenlied*.

I worked very hard on the paper and produced a scholarly original contribution to the subject. He gave me a 1 Plus (Rice terminology for A Plus) for the paper and for the course.

At the end of the year, Dr. Louis invited me to stay at Rice and do some more work on my paper. It could serve as my MA thesis, and I would receive an MA in two years. I was very tempted to accept his kind, complimentary offer, as Dr. Louis had become my friend, and I was reluctant to move on to medical school.

My father told me that if I stayed on at Rice, acting like a "perpetual student," as he put it, he would refuse to pay anything toward my medical school expenses. This was a serious threat, as there were very few medical school scholarships or other student financial aid in those days.

I decided not to stay on at Rice for an MA, and when I told Dr. Louis, he was visibly disappointed. Perhaps this was the right decision, but it was ironic that my father had no intention of paying any medical school expenses for me in any event, and he did not, in spite of what he had implied earlier. He did not pay any college expenses for me either. All these expenses were fully paid for by my mother alone.

Over the course of my stay at Rice, Dr. Louis acted as a friend, mentor, and confidant. He occasionally invited me to have dinner with him, and I was very pleased and flattered. He had a brilliant intellect, and I enjoyed his stimulating conversation and his stories of studying in Germany. No other students were invited to join us, and I think that he didn't invite other students for one-on-one meetings either.

I considered applying for a Fulbright scholarship to go to Germany to study existential philosophy with Martin Heidegger. But due to my belief in my father's threat I decided to go right on to medical school.

After I left Rice and started medical school in New York, I went to visit Dr. Louis whenever I came home to Houston for a holiday. He was glad to see me, and we would meet for lunch or dinner. It was almost like the old days, but not quite. As two years went by, I could feel that Dr. Louis was not so interested to see me anymore. This hurt my feelings a little, but I realized that as a fine teacher, he was primarily interested in his current students.

Then he became too busy to see me, but we would have cordial phone conversations. Then he seemed to be impatient about spending any time on the phone, and so I gradually stopped calling. We exchanged Christmas cards with brief notes for a few years, and then the cards stopped coming from Dr. Louis. I sent cards to him for three more years but then stopped.

Twenty years later, when I had become more prosperous, I began to make annual contributions to the Fondren Library at Rice for purchase of books in the fields of Germanic grammar, philology, and Middle High German, to be marked as contributed anonymously in honor of Dr. Louis. I received an acknowledgment and receipt from the library. After two years, I received a letter of thanks from Mrs. Louis but no communication from Dr. Louis himself.

When I contacted an old friend who worked at the library and asked about Dr. Louis, Sophie told me she was aware of my annual contributions, and she thought this was a very nice memorial to Dr. Louis, who had killed himself some years earlier. I was shocked and saddened at this news. I have never found out anything further about the circumstances or causes of his suicide. He was a fine man, and his good influence is still with me more than fifty years later.

He sometimes spoke with high praise of the eighteenth century writer Lessing's drama "Nathan der Weise." When I was staying in London recently, I saw a notice that it was to be staged in London for the first time in forty years. I was able to attend and enjoyed the play immensely. I thought many times then, just as I had for years, of Dr. Louis's kindness and intellectual gifts to me.

Over the years, I have continued the contributions to the library. They have now accumulated and grown to a substantial sum, and many books are purchased each year in honor of Dr. Louis. I am told that the Fondren Library's collection of books in Dr. Louis's favorite fields has now come to be known as an outstanding collection. I am proud of my tribute to Dr. Louis and know he would be pleased.

XXXXXXXXXXXXXXXXXXXXXXXXXXXXXXXXXXXXXXXXXXXXXX

At the beginning of my Rice experience, there were some modest entrance fees and other charges. I had to pay in advance for daily lunches for the entire year. These were served in the student dining room on the campus. I was too anxious, too shy, too ashamed of myself, too afraid of the other students to ever enter the dining room. Not once that year did I go into the dining room to eat my paid-for lunch. I lost forty pounds, the silver lining to that dark cloud.

The idea of trying to be friendly, or to ingratiate myself with my fellow students, or of taking steps to become "one of the boys," never crossed my mind as a possibility. I felt destined to be an outcast, which perhaps at that time seemed better to me than to be an acceptable person with social responsibilities.

Also included in the entrance fees were charges for season tickets to all athletic events, including the football games. The students were expected to attend all the games, of whatever kind. My total attendance at athletic events in four years at Rice was one (boring) football game.

I was part of a group of students who were too arrogant and felt too intellectually superior to waste their time watching athletic events or to participate in any activity with a group of jocks and know-nothings. I had absolutely no interest in watching athletic events or participating in them. I tried to conceal this arrogance, but it made the situation with some of my classmates more difficult for me.

Even today I still strongly prefer not to attend or watch exhibitions of any kind of group athletic activities which feature brutalization of opponents. I much prefer swimming, diving, or tennis but even so have little interest. I had enjoyed playing a bit of tennis for two years in high school but did not care to continue it in college.

In my opinion, the emphasis on competitive sports as commercial exhibitions is a strong contributing factor in the declining morality of the United States and in the general dumbing down of the population. The Roman Caesars knew a great deal about this. Mindless, passive watching of brutal scenes featuring very large men, obscenely overpaid and bulging with muscles, while our teachers are paid minimal wages and not accorded much respect—this seems a bizarre reversal of proper social values. Tremendous publicity, noise, drinking, screaming, and cheering add to the tawdry nature of the sports presentations.

XXXXXXXXXXXXXXXXXXXXXXXXXXXXXXXXXXXXXXXXXXXXX

Rice offered many advantages, opportunities, and positive experiences. The fine new library had open stacks, so we were free to wander around the collection, looking at whatever interested us. Naturally, I made an immediate search for and discovery of the works of Andre Gide. He described the absolute separation of love and lust in his own life: he loved his wife and was devoted to her but never had sex with her; he had sex with adolescent Arab boys in North Africa but never fell in love with them. I believed what he said but was puzzled.

Soon I found my way to Marquis de Sade and Ritter von Sacher-Masoch, along with D.H. Lawrence, Marcel Proust, Oscar Wilde, Algernon Swinburne, and other "evil" writers, as I admiringly thought them to be. The library was really a treasury of information and made me feel less isolated. At least I had some kindred books, if not any kindred people. Later on I met some real human friends.

I realized that I was depressed and that my continual suicidal ruminations were not normal. The condition was quite painful. One of my friends, a younger classmate from a wealthy family, offered to pay for me to see a psychiatrist. I didn't feel I could accept his kind offer, but I appreciated his gesture very much, and it was one of the factors which caused me to fall seriously in love with him. This made my situation even more painful, as Perry did not want to develop a homoerotic side. At that time I still knew nothing about gay sex or its mechanics.

Perry was a year behind me in college. He was a freshman, and I was a sophomore when we met. He was brilliant, and we shared interests in reading and music. I was tremendously attracted to him. The following summer, we wrote long letters back and forth discussing Shakespeare's "Coriolanus." We exchanged several pictures of ourselves.

After school resumed in the fall, he suggested that we get tickets for the Houston Symphony. I remember riding downtown on the bus with him. The bus was crowded, and we had to stand close together. I was aware of and excited by standing inside his aura.

We attended my first symphonic concert. The soloist was the great English pianist Clifford Curzon, who performed the Brahms Second Piano Concerto. The conductor was Efrem Kurtz. The music was moving and impressive, and afterward we both floated back to Rice on what seemed a cloud of happiness.

A note on the career of Efrem Kurtz, the conductor: the Houston Symphony at that time was largely supported and completely controlled by Miss Ima Hogg, Governor Hogg's daughter and a generous philanthropist in Houston. Suddenly Efrem Kurtz was no longer the conductor; he was no longer in Houston. What had happened?

The story went around that Conductor Kurtz had a romantic relationship with the (female) harp player. Miss Ima was certainly not going to put up with immorality of this sort. Both the harpist and the conductor were summarily expelled. Perhaps the story isn't true, but they both suddenly disappeared from the orchestra.

Perry obviously liked me and wanted to be my friend, which was a very unusual experience for me. I was tremendously moved. I obsessed constantly about him. He seemed incredibly attractive to me, with even features, blond hair, blue eyes, warm kindness, and a beautiful smile.

Back at Rice in the fall, we talked of sexual inversion and noticed that some obviously homosexual students turned their heads to watch attractive men. We developed a code name for them: men with revolving heads. I knew I was in love with Perry, but I had no sexual ideas about him, except I realized I yearned to hug him and hold him. I did not know anything about sexual activities. Like Gide, I was developing a split between love and sexual desire.

When I eventually told Perry that I suspected that I might have a revolving head myself, and that I was in love with him, he was surprised, shocked, and disappointed. He promptly and firmly distanced himself from me. He left Rice at the end of the year and transferred to a leading Eastern university. I was heartbroken.

I visited him at his new school once, and he visited me at medical school in New York once. The visits were tense with what was unspoken between us. Perhaps he was fleeing the possible lure of the homoerotic life more than he was fleeing me. Apparently he did not want to experiment or to visit my gay world.

He went on to a prestigious medical school. We gradually lost touch, as I chose not to contact him. Contact with him was very painful for me. I did not want to impinge on his life. Later he married, had children, and has had a distinguished medical career.

The loss of Perry as my best friend was my first tragedy. I yearned for him for years and have never forgotten my intense feelings of love and then sorrow and abandonment after he left. At that time, I wished I were not an invert, and I hoped to see him again before life finished.

Perry joined Chencha, my loving Mexican nursemaid, in my pantheon of lost beloved beings, always visible in my mind's eye but never reachable. The pantheon still exists, but now, years later, it's only painful when I think about it.

Note: In the summer of 2007 I planned to attend a medical meeting in his city. With a sudden inspiration, I wrote to Perry to invite him to lunch while I was there, and we arranged a meeting. It felt like a happy reunion. It was as if fifty years had passed in a flash, but our relationship had remained as close and loving as it had ever been. We were both surprised and happy. This was a great gift for me, and I look forward to more visits with my re-found friend Perry.

XXX

I begged my mother for money to get treatment for my depression. She was not sympathetic and refused to help. She said, "Psychiatrists teach their patients to hate their parents. I would rather see you dead." I was not surprised at her reaction. Although the probability of my committing suicide was moderate, I did not make an attempt.

It was about this time that my mother began to turn her ferocious blasts of anger toward me. Often I did not know what had enraged her or what I might have said or done to provoke her rage. She would be totally implacable and tirelessly and very effectively critical and condemnatory. It is a terribly painful and confusing situation to be afraid of a person you love.

In the concentration camp that my relationship with my parents was becoming, my mother had begun to practice soul murder on me, repeatedly cutting off and destroying parts of my initiative and individuality, my right to exist as an independent person. She was unstable and inconsistent; she could rapidly change from angry belligerence to a sunny, laughing mood, without any apparent explanation, and then unpredictably change back again.

I never knew how to act to try to avoid her violent attacks. It is injurious to the psyche to have to turn for comfort to the person who hurts you. Sometimes the torturer is quite skilled at consoling his victim, and this increases his control.

However, I believe my depression had started years before, at about age eight, and was primarily an inborn biochemical abnormality, perhaps made worse by childhood and later traumas. Many years of treatment by orthodox Freudian analysis, Jungian analysis, group therapy, and meditation therapy helped only slightly.

Much later, I was lucky to find an excellent psychopharmacologist, and medicines definitely helped but did not totally eliminate the depression. Now when I become depressed, I feel a floor under me, usually preventing me from falling into hell.

XXXXXXXXXXXXXXXXXXXXXXXXXXXXXXXXXXXXXXXXXXX

All the Rice students had to choose a major field of study. For me, it was premedical studies, which aimed at eventually going on to medical school and included introductory courses in biology, chemistry, physics, calculus, English composition, philosophy, and other subjects.

My introductory philosophy class was taught by the head of the philosophy department, Dr. Radoslav A. Tsanoff (notice his initials), who had a PhD from the University of Constantinople, 1900. He had written a basic ethics text,

The Moral Ideals of Our Civilization, in which he wrote of homosexuality as the "slime which oozed out of Sparta and engulfed the rest of Greece." In other words, he was what would now be called homophobic. He had been teaching at Rice since the school opened in 1912 and was extremely learned, closed-minded, and cruel.

One day he was discussing Aristotle's definition of "space": "Space is the boundary of the contained body with the containing body." Puzzled, I raised my hand and said I did not understand what this meant. Dr. RAT looked down his long pointed nose, snorted, and roared at me. In a condescending and hostile tone he said, "The reason you do not understand Aristotle's definition is that you have *great* poverty of intellect." I shriveled up, and I could hear a strange shrinking and shifting sound as the rest of the students slid down in their chairs.

Another day he was presenting St. Anselm's ontological proof of God's existence, a syllogism in which St. Anselm changed the meaning of one of the words halfway through, thereby making the "proof" come out the way he desired. At the end of the class, I asked Dr. RAT if St. Anselm were not confusing two meanings of one word.

Snorting loudly, he replied in stentorian tones, "There is indeed a confusion here, but it is not in the mind of St. Anselm. SNORT, SNORT, SNORT." And waggle waggle of his enormous bushy eyebrows. The other students all ran away. But just as with my Aristotle question, he gave no answer.

I learned that to ask Dr. RAT a question was an opening, an invitation, to be insulted and pulverized.

Later I was told that this paragon of moral ideals was known for humiliating and tormenting his students. Apparently he was a sadist. He was usually officially described as "beloved," due to his long tenure and advanced age, but I wondered who believed that crap.

In my last two years at Rice, I became a philosophy major, because of my interest in the subject and in spite of the presence of Dr. RAT. So I had to learn to cope with Dr. R. until eventually I escaped, graduating with honors and Phi Beta Kappa. The president of the Rice chapter of Phi Beta Kappa was my friend and mentor Dr. Louis.

As for the definition of space, Aristotle meant that there was no vacuum or emptiness, that everything was bordered by something else. I still think Aristotle's terminology, at least in my English translation, is very unclear. Perhaps Dr. RAT himself did not know what Aristotle meant, but that seems unlikely.

I found the classwork stimulating. For the first time, I was in a setting in which students were not ashamed of their intelligence or knowledge. Serious conversations were common and acceptable. For the first time, I found a place where talk was not restricted to football, other sports, and sex. An interest in classical music was almost taken for granted. It was a joyful revelation to me that such a place and such people existed.

XXXXXXXXXXXXXXXXXXXXXXXXXXXXXXXXXXXXXXXXXXX

Early in my freshman year, I inquired at a downtown music store for a piano teacher and was referred to Mme. Elizabeth Morosoff, head of the piano department at the Southern College of Fine Arts. She asked me to play for her, and so I started to play Chopin's *Berceuse*. As I was very nervous about playing for this eminent teacher, and because I was poorly prepared and hadn't practiced for two weeks, I trembled and made many mistakes.

About two thirds of the way through the piece, Mme. Morosoff exclaimed, "Stop, stop!! That's the kind of playing that makes me sick!!" I agreed with her. She wanted to hand me over to her assistant, but I was firm and persistent about wanting to study with her, and so she accepted me as a student, with the proviso that I must practice at least two hours a day.

"You must start all over again," she said, and so for the next month there were only five-finger exercises on the white keys, C-D-E-F-G and down again, with extreme emphasis on what Madame said was proper finger and hand position. She turned out to be a real martinet, was very serious about piano playing, but was an excellent teacher and eventually revealed a kinder and more pleasant side.

She suggested that I practice the Etudes of Pischna, which are as difficult and ugly as they are boring, but they are useful for the fingers. No pianist would ever perform one of these in a concert—they were not created to be heard.

She directed me to number the measures of each piece I studied and then to memorize each measure by number, each hand alone and then together. She would say, "Play measure 173 with the left hand alone," and I would do so. It was a grueling way to study but gave a very reliable result.

Fortunately the two hours of daily practice easily became a habit. It was always a pleasure to me to sit at the keyboard and practice and play. It was a small holiday and visit to a better world.

Eventually I found out something of Madame's history. Her family was originally Russian, had been quite wealthy, and had to flee Moscow after the revolution of 1917. They settled in Prague and again became affluent. She showed me a photo of the family's factory, which was a giant establishment with many buildings and smokestacks.

She had attended the conservatory in Prague and was a student of Vilem Kurtz (brother of Efrem Kurtz, conductor of the Houston Symphony) and a fellow pupil of the great pianist Rudolph Firkusny. She told me that Gershwin's *Rhapsody in Blue* had swept through Europe about then and that all the students at the conservatory had eagerly learned it.

At the end of World War II, the Germans were on the point of withdrawing from Prague as the Russians advanced. They offered Madame and her family a ride in one of their trucks over to the U.S. lines, as they preferred to surrender to the Allies rather than to the Russians. The Morosoffs were given one hour to get ready and were allowed to bring one suitcase of belongings each. They eventually reached Houston and were in the process of again becoming affluent.

Madame introduced herself to the Houston musical community by giving a highly successful solo piano recital. She accepted a teaching post at the Southern College of Fine Arts. But health problems caused her to retire temporarily from public performance.

One day, in the middle of my piano lesson, Firkusny came to call on his old friend. I was introduced to him, and that was the conclusion of my lesson. I was not invited to play for him and was disappointed that he did not play for me, but I was thrilled to meet the great pianist.

Mme. Morosoff, Dr. Louis, and Dr. RAT were all extremely knowledgeable about their specialties. Madame was stern and demanding but was devoted to her art and had a real desire that her students should share her serious interest and joy in music, and she tried her best to teach them to play really well. Dr. Louis was kindly and encouraging and wanted to pass on his knowledge and enthusiasm to his students. Dr. RAT, on the other hand, was also stern and demanding, but he had contempt for his students, was sadistic to those who could not defend or protect themselves, and it seemed that his teaching activities were mostly designed to keep his arrogance inflated as much as possible.

The contrasts between my three principal teachers, Mme. Morosoff, Dr. Louis, and Dr. RAT, were striking. I have always tried to follow Dr. Louis's and Madame's examples and to avoid Dr. RAT's.

XXXXXXXXXXXXXXXXXXXXXXXXXXXXXXXXXXXXXXXXXXX

Within a few months of entering Rice, I met a number of the more intelligent and sophisticated Rice students, some of whom revealed themselves to me as gay.

My first real college friend, Fred Hagen, a third-year philosophy major, recognized me as gay and took me under his wing, not only as a fellow student, but also as a neophyte in the gay world. Fred was a brilliant student, taking graduate mathematics courses while he was still a freshman. I found his ability to quote verbatim long passages from many philosophers and other writers tremendously impressive. In retrospect, I realize Fred's most unusual ability was to lay out or explain with crystalline clarity any philosophical system or any points within the system.

Fred lived with his parents in Houston, had a large late model high-powered Chrysler convertible, plenty of spending money, and knew his way around the Houston gay community. Good-looking, charming, and amusing, he was much courted. I heard that he also had other spectacular working assets, but I never experienced them firsthand.

He was a philosophy major and was Professor RAT's best student, even if he might have been tainted by the slime that apparently was still oozing out of Sparta. He had great self-assurance, well-justified, and an arrogant impatience much like RAT's own.

Fred was rattlesnake fast with his quips and retorts. I sometimes thought they would get him into trouble, but he always avoided the repercussions. Once a group of us was sitting in the second floor library lobby when two of the school's leading football players came up the stairway.

Although many suspected Fred was gay, they didn't know for certain. The football players were very sure of themselves and thought that Fred would naturally be physically attracted to them. In fact, he was attracted to delicate and effeminate men, not burly behemoth athletes.

One of the football players asked Fred, "Do you have the time?" Fred smiled sweetly at him and replied, "Sorry, not now. Later." The football players did a double take, scowled, and went on their way.

Houston had many fried chicken restaurants. One, Bill Williams, across the street from the school, was a favorite with the students. The menu offered fried chicken in various combinations, such as all white meat dinner, all chicken livers dinner, and other assortments. One Sunday evening, a group of us decided to walk over for dinner. The surly, gum-chewing waitress came to take our order. "Yeah?" she said, and we began to give our orders.

Fred was last, and when she looked at him and growled, "Yeah?" he looked at her coolly, leered, and said, "I'm going to try your thighs tonight." Her face turned red and she looked as if she might explode. Fred said, "That's dinner number five on your menu." It was listed as "all-thigh dinner." She was both enraged and speechless.

Another time, there was considerable interest in a debate to be held on the Rice campus between Fred and a Jesuit priest from a local college. The subject to be debated was the existence of God. After about thirty minutes of orderly debate, the priest said, "The existence of God is a social necessity. If people did not believe in God, there would be widespread raping, looting, riots, and murder."

Fred, who was an avowed agnostic, fixed the priest with an eagle glare and said, "Speak for yourself, Father." Some in the audience gasped at the rudeness; some laughed at the sharpness of Fred's rejoinder. The Jesuit seemed irritated.

I enjoyed and appreciated Fred's interest in me. He introduced me to the Houston gay bars, which were also the first gay bars I had ever seen. The experiences were both scary and thrilling. I was nervous and excited and knew that I was on the right road to my goal of finding someone to love, even if I didn't see the way ahead clearly.

Fred introduced me to many of his friends, who were cordial, but none of them made a pass at me, as they considered me Fred's boyfriend, which was not the case.

One of his friends, Jimmy, told me an amusing story about a pickup in one of the bars. Jimmy and the man went to the man's house, where Jimmy was led into the bedroom and asked to sit patiently and fully clothed on the bed. After a few minutes the man came out from the next room. He was naked, except for a number of long peacock feathers, which he had put up his rectum; they were held in place with a sort of girdle. As the man pranced and jumped around the room, Jimmy was supposed to repeat, "Pretty peacock. Pretty peacock," over and over. After a short while the man had an orgasm, even without any genital manipulation. There was nothing in the event for Jimmy, except his amusement at the situation. This was the first in a long series of strange and interesting sexual stories which I have enjoyed hearing over the years.

It was against the law to operate a gathering place for homosexuals or to serve them liquor or beer, so the bars were all illegal. But the grass was very green in all of them. I never had a legal drink while at Rice, being under legal drinking age until I moved out of Houston after graduation.

Fred and I did not have sex or a romance, but he kept an eye on me to steer me away from trouble. He knew I had never had sex and that I was really a baby in the gay woods. I feel that Fred, by befriending me, perhaps also saved me from suicide, as I was very alone, depressed, and adrift. I feel a great debt of gratitude to him.

When I heard from him in 2002 that he had advanced esophageal cancer, I went to visit him in Tucson, where he lived after retiring from a career teaching philosophy at the University of Utah. I wanted to thank him for his help so many years before. I had not seen Freddy for forty years and was shocked, horrified, and heartbroken to see his wretched condition: emaciated, sallow, feeble. We began to talk just as if we had seen each other yesterday, and I realized how much I had missed seeing Freddy all these years past.

His mind, however, was as brilliantly sharp as ever. I met his partner, a composer, with whom he had lived for over thirty years. I told Fred of my gratitude and love for what he had done for me. I think this brought him some gratification.

He was in considerable pain and died a few months later, lovingly cared for by his partner.

XXXXXXXXXXXXXXXXXXXXXXXXXXXXXXXXXXXXXXXXXX

While I was first finding my way in the gay world, under Fred's careful supervision, I developed minor but thrilling crushes on some of my fellow students, all male of course. I never revealed myself directly to any of them, which was probably wise. By the time we graduated four years later, some of my favorites knew I had strongly positive feelings for them but also that I was not going to embarrass them or be sexually aggressive, so they relaxed and enjoyed their roles as friends.

However, there was an episode in which I made inappropriate approaches to one of the other students. I thought he was irresistibly attractive in every way, and I desperately wanted to hug him. Over a period of three months I left perhaps ten anonymous, short, mild love notes under his car's windshield wiper. I heard that he found these notes and was puzzled. I never told anyone what I had done, and perhaps he never knew who his secret admirer was.

This fantasy hug affair was slightly painful for me but fortunately did not lead me into any trouble. It never occurred to me just to go up to him, say hello, and invite him for a cup of coffee. I hadn't learned of such ordinary social niceties but didn't have sufficient self-confidence to try such a ploy anyway.

More serious was the trouble I inflicted unwittingly on a gay man whom I saw at the bars and on whom I developed a crush. He had black hair and dark eyes, was intelligent, graceful, handsome, and radiated a kind of animal magnetism. A few years older than I, he had an office job in downtown Houston. Fred introduced us one evening in a gay bar. We spoke briefly, pleasantly, and casually several times in the bars.

I looked him up in the telephone book, wanting to find out his address. Over the course of six months, I wrote him ten or twelve anonymous, passionate but nonerotic love letters. I still knew nothing about sexual practices, so I did not make any sexual comments or suggestions in the letters. Again I did not tell anyone what I had done. As before, it did not occur to me just to go up to him and start a friendly conversation. I was too shy and felt too inadequate.

The following year, I was horrified to find that he had been living at home with his parents, and that his father, who had the same name, but was

Senior, had received, opened, and read all my letters. These letters strongly hinted at my crush object's homosexuality, and his father was enraged. The father demanded to know who was writing these letters and why, and my acquaintance truly could not tell him. The father soon kicked him out of the house, and they were no longer on speaking terms.

I heard about this from mutual friends. Needless to say, I did not reveal myself, nor did I ask many questions, as I did not want to appear too interested. Two years later, we met by chance at a gay bar and went to bed. Perhaps I was too guilty and anxious about what I had done, but the sexual encounter was not satisfactory for either of us, and we never tried it again. A few years later, I heard that the rupture between father and son had become permanent and apparently irretrievable. I felt very guilty about what I had done and still feel guilty and regretful fifty-five years after this episode. Should I have confessed my misdeeds to my victim and asked for his forgiveness? The answer is not clear.

XXXXXXXXXXXXXXXXXXXXXXXXXXXXXXXXXXXXXXXXXXX

At the beginning of my third year at Rice, my piano playing had become annoying to my grandmother's tenants, who lived in her upstairs apartment. I had to leave and moved into the college dormitory. There was a piano in the student center, which was sometimes available, and I continued my piano lesson as best I could. Mme. Morosoff tried to be understanding about my practice difficulties. My junior year was the year my relationship with Perry crashed, and I was very distressed about it almost constantly.

In spite of, and in addition to, all the painful events, there were many happy times. For the first time, I felt a member of a congenial group. We often met in the library's music room for elaborate conversations and/or to listen to classical music recordings. As seriously bookish students, we all had been issued keys to the library and enjoyed coming and going as we pleased.

We all had been assigned carrels on the third floor of the library and often were there late at night. We would sometimes walk across Main Street to the Medical Center, where several of the hospitals had all-night cafeterias. These were open to the public, and we could have a snack and a cup of coffee.

I never attended any of the official school social events, such as dances, pep rallies, or other gatherings. I was too shy—I anticipated nothing but trouble should I show up at an event. It was not so much that I expected any particular bad result, but I had tremendous reluctance to participate in the event. It wasn't the result that scared me; it was the beginning that was terrifying. My social phobia was alive and well, perhaps getting stronger.

The era of casual drug use had not yet started. None of us used marijuana, cocaine, speed, narcotics, poppers, or any of the other hard drugs that became widely available some years later. Most of us smoked cigarettes; most of us drank a little when there was appropriate occasion. Occasionally we went to some of the local bars for a beer; hard liquor was still illegal in Texas. I loved the lively, bright, casual, laughing conversations, completely without the edge of smoldering rage and danger I knew from home.

Occasionally I would be invited, usually through Freddy or one of his friends, to a gay party. This would consist of gathering at some gay person's apartment or house, listening to show tunes brought back by the host from his recent trip to New York, where he had seen some Broadway musicals.

Many of the parties I attended were put on by Houston's so-called "A Group," made up of men with perhaps good jobs, some or a lot of money, perhaps social connections, but all with social pretensions and dripping with scorn for anyone they thought their social or financial inferior. Being naïve at the time, I thought this was an acceptable if unpleasant way to behave; it was just the way things were. At their parties there would be a bar at which the guests usually mixed their own drinks; there were also coolers full of bottles of beer. Recently I learned that several of these men purchased a large burial plot in one of the Houston cemeteries and were in the process of being buried in proximity to one another. Some of them are still living.

I drank a great deal at these parties and sometimes had a hangover the next day. I didn't feel drunk and was told that I didn't misbehave. After a sufficient number of drinks, I would enter a more pleasant state of consciousness, which I judged to be the normal result of drinking: the result everyone had or was aiming at.

This was the classic "hollow leg" symptom, which I didn't recognize then or for many years to come. Sometimes, if a friend would ask, "Don't you think you've had enough to drink?" I would answer firmly but without anger, "No, I don't." I thought the friend was a wet blanket and made a mental note to avoid him in the future.

Now that I lived in the dormitory, my grandmother no longer watched my activities, including when I came home in the evening and who brought me home. I became bolder and more adventuresome. I had still not experienced sex, and although I disapproved of it as strongly as ever, I was intensely curious and determined to explore further.

I continued to have occasional spontaneous ecstasies but never discussed these with anyone. These experiences sustained my belief that there was a great deal more to life than we could see or know.

XXXXXXXXXXXXXXXXXXXXXXXXXXXXXXXXXXXXXXXXXXXX

Oh, Love, Where Are You? Meeting Cupid, 1953

One evening I caught the bus on Main Street and went on my first excursion alone to a gay bar, one of the downtown places. I was very excited to be taking a further step alone and noticed that my hands and knees were shaking slightly.

Effie's Pink Elephant was an old established dive. Maybe notorious would be a better word; it was dirty, smelling of stale beer and cigarette smoke. The "P.E." was dimly lit. It was better not to see the place or the customers too clearly. The clientele was a drunken, dilapidated, low-life bunch, but all presumably were gay.

That evening most of the seats at the bar were occupied, and perhaps twenty men were standing around the room, leaning against the walls. There was very little conversation, as most men were there alone, with the intention of cruising and picking up someone for sex. It was not a social occasion. We were all staring into space, trying to look friendly and approachable but at the same time tough and unconcerned.

I had been leaning against the bar for about ten minutes, drinking a Lone Star beer out of a tall-necked bottle, when I noticed a short, heavyset man staring at me. After a few minutes, he shuffled over and stood closer. I could see he was middle-aged, poorly dressed, slovenly, and seemed unsteady on his feet, from drinking I supposed.

I knew he was interested to pick me up, and I was very excited by the situation, if not by the person. He moved around in front, directly facing me, put his face close to mine and smiled. I saw that he was unshaven, had red eyes, missing teeth, and foul breath.

I looked at him and smiled politely. Taking this as an encouraging sign, he said, "How about it?"

I was shocked at the dilapidation of the man and the directness of his approach. I murmured feebly, "Pardon me?"

Then he said in a much louder voice, "Well, how about it? Right now!" He put his face even closer, gave me what he thought was an inviting leer, and licked his lips, as if I had not already understood his message.

Suddenly, I was too repelled to continue this contact. I said, "No. I have to go. Right now!" and fled out the door, walked to Main Street, and caught the bus back to Rice.

This was my first attempt at making a sexual connection. I was delighted and knew I was making progress. I had hoped for something slightly more tasteful, perhaps even with a touch of romance, but this was better than the nothingness of the previous years, or so it seemed to me then. It was the first step. I was full of hope, expecting to find a wonderful new world through sex.

XXXXXXXXXXXXXXXXXXXXXXXXXXXXXXXXXXXXXXXXXXX

Fred, his friends, and others I met in the gay bars sometimes mentioned and made jokes about cars cruising Main Street, picking up men who were waiting at bus stops. This was somewhat risky for the drivers.

Most of the waiting men were waiting for the bus. A few were hustlers or were waiting to prey on the drivers who might pick them up. But some were hoping to be picked up for consensual sex. It was risky for the waiting men too, as some of the drivers were unpredictable, drunk, or dangerous.

Some of the drivers or the pickups liked to follow sex by beating up their sex partners and dumping them out of the car. Some of the Rice football players liked to cruise Main Street, pick up a "queer," enjoy sex with him, and then rob him, beat him up, and dump him in a deserted location. They sometimes bragged to the other students about doing this. I believed them, as there was an occasional confirmation from some of our gay friends or acquaintances.

In May of my junior year, I went to San Antonio for one of my regular orthodontic checkups. I made the two-hundred-mile bus trip in the morning and returned to Houston the same afternoon. The bus arrived about 8 PM at the downtown bus station.

I walked over to Main Street and waited for one of the buses going out South Main Street to Rice. In about five minutes, a baby blue four-door late-model Ford passed by. The driver looked back at me. He turned the corner, and I knew he was going to circle the block. Perhaps the long-awaited sexy knight on his baby blue stallion had appeared.

Soon the blue car turned on to Main Street again. It slowly pulled up in front of the bus stop. The driver leaned over and spoke to me through the open window. "Where are you going?"

"Rice," I said.

"Would you like a ride?"

"Yes, thank you."

He said, "Get in," and pushed the door open for me. I got in the car, tremendously excited, said hello, and glanced cautiously at the driver. He looked about fifty, overweight, balding, with spectacles and two double chins. He had an open, somewhat worn, kindly face, and I knew right away that this was to be my Cupid, my first teacher in the wonderful New World of Sex.

"Are you a student there?" he asked.

"Yes. I'm a junior this year."

"Are you enjoying it? What are you studying?"

"Well, I like it most of the time. I'm a philosophy major, but I hope to go on to medical school after graduation."

"I'm an accountant myself, and I've been in practice a few years. I have my own office downtown. By the way, my name is Artie."

"And I'm John."

We continued driving in silence for a couple of minutes, heading south on Main Street toward Rice. Artie put his right hand on my left thigh and gave a slight squeeze, then let his hand rest there. In a moment he moved his hand between my legs and began to feel around. He did not seem timid or unsure of himself.

"Does that feel good?" he asked.

"Oh, yes."

"Good. Well, why don't you put your hand between my legs too?"

I put my hand in his crotch and felt that he had an erection. Hallelujah!! I knew I had crossed the border into the New World and was determined to press on past the frontier. As we drove on, playing with each other, I looked out the window nervously, worried that someone would see us, would catch us. Gay sex was a criminal activity according to the laws of Texas.

"Would you like to see my office?"

"Oh, yes."

He turned his car around and drove about ten minutes back to the center of town. We turned onto one of the more nondescript downtown streets, pulled up and parked before a small two-story office building. He unlocked the front door, and we went up a flight of worn wooden stairs. Upstairs was a poorly lit musty-smelling corridor, doors with frosted glass panels opening off on both sides. We stopped before one that announced "Arthur J. Fielding, Accountant, CPA."

"Well, this one is mine," he said, unlocking the door and flipping on the light. "Come on in."

A combined light and wooden-bladed ceiling fan shed a dull yellowish glow. The office had the same musty smell as the corridor. An old green leatherette sofa with a hole in one of the cushions stood against the wall, along with a couple of straight wooden armchairs, a well-used wooden desk with a scarred top and a pile of papers on one corner, a desk lamp, a swiveling desk chair, and a little table with a few dog-eared magazines. A door was open into a small clothes closet. The floor was covered with stained and buckled linoleum.

We stood there for a few seconds. I wondered what was coming next.

Artie suddenly grabbed me. In spite of being about six inches shorter than I, he pressed his mouth forcibly against mine and stuck his firm, rubbery tongue into my mouth. I was startled and immediately jumped away. In spite of being so excited that I could hardly stand up, I noticed that he had a very strong smell of garlic.

"Didn't you know what we were going to do tonight?" he asked. "What's wrong? Haven't you ever been picked up on Main Street before?"

"No," I whispered, embarrassed at my naïveté.

He looked at me for a while, smiling with narrowed eyes, then took a chance and asked a delicate question. "Have you ever been with a man before?"

"No."

He took another chance. "Have you ever had sex before?"

"No."

"Would you like to have sex with me now?"

"Yes."

He squinted at me, then relaxed and smiled again. I think it was very hard for him to believe that he had trolled in a nineteen-year-old virginal chickie, a Rice student to boot. He decided to believe me, and the atmosphere suddenly became less tense. He stroked my head and gave me some gentle kisses on the cheeks and some benign hugs.

After a few moments, he suggested that we both take off our clothes.

"Okay," I said, and he took off all his clothes.

Maybe forty pounds overweight, he had strong muscular legs, spindly arms, and a sagging fat stomach. His body and back were heavily covered with coarse wiry black hair. I didn't care what he looked like. He was going to be an important teacher and guide for me. No one studies with an important teacher because of his good looks.

I took off most of my clothes, but Artie suggested that what we were going to do would be better accomplished without any clothes at all, so I discarded the remnants of my modesty. Even though I was young, slim, and in good shape, I was ashamed of my body and felt ugly, inadequate, and unacceptable, as usual. I still had no idea of the basic mechanics of the sex act, so I was grateful that Artie had invited me to this lesson.

"We have to lie down on the floor," he said.

I took off my glasses and so did he. Without my glasses, I felt really naked. I hoped that the action was about to start. As I lay down on the linoleum floor, I had a close look at the pattern: yellowish background with faded green stripes in a checkerboard arrangement, with many little pits in the linoleum, souvenirs of years of hard use. The coolness of the floor felt good in the heat of the May evening, but it was too hard to be comfortable.

"Lie on your left side," he said. In spite of all my library research, I had no idea what this position was designed to accomplish. Artie lay down on the floor too. On his left side facing me, he put his head down by my knees.

I heard an unfamiliar sucking and clicking sound, and when I looked over at him, I could see he was taking out a complete set of dentures. He was trying to do this surreptitiously, so I didn't make any comment and pretended not to notice.

"This is called sixty-nine," he said. He proceeded to show me the purpose of this odd position. He suggested that I should reciprocate, and I did, without enthusiasm, feeling it was the polite thing to do in the circumstance. After a while, we both came. We rolled onto our backs on the linoleum and looked up at the ceiling for a while. We puffed a little as we caught our breaths.

"How did you like that?" he asked.

"Fine. It felt very good," I said, exaggerating my positive feeling about the event.

"Well, let's put our clothes back on, and I'll drive you back to Rice," he said.

We made small talk as we drove out to Rice. Just before Artie let me out of the car, he asked, "Would you like to get together again?"

I said, "Well, I don't know my schedule yet." He gave me his business card and suggested I should call him.

"Okay," I said, having no intention of ever calling him.

As he drove off, I was relieved. I was also proud of myself for having persevered in my drive to enter the Land of Sex. I had a curiously flat feeling. All the premonitory excitement had evaporated. There was absolutely no personal attraction, sexual excitement, or romance involved. It had been a purely physical act, not a very interesting one at that, but educational all the same.

Artie had been considerate and gentle with a neophyte, but the act seemed abrupt and purely physical on his part also. Perhaps I might have liked it better if we had been lying on a bed, or at least on a rug, instead of on the cold, hard, ugly linoleum. Or if we had had any personal interest in one another.

XXX

Three weeks later, feeling a revival of my curiosity, and wanting to make further progress in exploring my new world, I went downtown one evening and stood at a bus stop. Soon the baby blue Ford pulled up. Artie opened the door and asked, "Would you like a ride?"

"Sure," I said and climbed in.

After a few pleasantries, he asked if I would like to go to his office again.

"Okay," I said. In a few minutes we were in his office again, and the clothes were all off again.

He grabbed me again and tried his rubber tongue routine on me again. This time I was not startled and so waited a while, curious to see what the tongue stuff was about. It wasn't very interesting.

Taking his tongue out of my mouth, he asked, "Would you like me to show you another way to have sex?" he asked.

"Yes, I guess so." I wondered what was coming next, as this time he was not taking out his false teeth.

"Lie down on the floor on your stomach."

Still a willing pupil, I did as suggested and was soon closely eyeing the faded linoleum again. He brought me a smelly sofa cushion for my head. Climbing on top of me, that is, his front to my back, he showed me another way to have sex. I found this new way somewhat uncomfortable and not really erotic, and I didn't like this fat man with garlic breath lying on top of me humping and huffing for what seemed like a very long time.

After some minutes of pounding away, he began to gasp. "Oh—Oh— Gawd amighty," he said. Then he yelled out, "Oh—*fuck—fuck—shit amighty*!!" After this uproar which accompanied his orgasm, he climbed off.

There was no gratification for me in the activity. I thought the whole thing was about as interesting as pulling weeds in the garden, but I appreciated the lesson all the same. As we were getting dressed, he began to scold me.

"That's called 'going up the dirt road,'" he said, "and it was a really dirty thing you just did. You shouldn't ever do that again. You will ruin yourself. Don't tell anyone what you did. It's too disgusting, too dirty. Everyone will think you are a degenerate.

"You're like all the rest of them. Dirty! No self-control. No standards. You don't know how to behave!!" He went on in this disorganized, scolding vein as he was driving me home. He must have been feeling guilty. I thought he was tedious but tried to show appropriate interest in his remarks. We reached Rice.

"Bye-bye," I said and ran through the gate into the campus.

This concluded my first instructions in the arts of love.

After that, I saw him from time to time at a gay bar, and we would smile and nod, but I was not interested in any more lessons. Not from him. Farewell, my plump Cupid.

XXXXXXXXXXXXXXXXXXXXXXXXXXXXXXXXXXXXXXXXXX

Soon after, I had a strange dream. Eve, on an excursion out of her garden, appeared, dressed in a short golden gown and wearing a golden crown and many large jewels. Her upper body was human, but her legs and feet were like those of an eagle, with huge talons. She was masquerading as the Whore of Babylon, riding in her golden chariot drawn by a dragon with seven heads, and was carrying a golden cup brimming over with the disgusting filth of her fornication, as the Bible so intriguingly tells us.

The dragon stopped in front of me. Eve dismounted and approached me. "I have three gifts for you," she said. Suddenly she stuck her left hand into my skull, and with a razor-sharp fingernail she cut a deep gash in my brain. This lobotomy disconnected my love center from my prudence and judgment centers. If it had not been for this lobotomy, love might never have come to me.

She then thrust her right hand into my chest and into my heart. In that hand she was holding a small worm with sharp teeth, a stinger, and abrasive skin, and she let this worm loose inside my heart as a souvenir. Since then, the worm has stung me and chewed on the inside of my heart. The pain has been terrible, and no treatment could help. This gift helps me to feel alive, reminds me of why I am alive, and gives me hope I might someday meet someone who could take away the pain.

Eve climbed back in her chariot, smiled at me, and held out a golden box. "Here is your third present," she said, handing me the casket. She clicked her tongue at her dragon, who roared and then flew into the sky, drawing the golden chariot behind him. They disappeared over the horizon.

I opened the box and looked inside. Lying on a small white silk cushion was a brilliant red magic apple. Feeling curious, I took a bite. A sensation of sweetness filled my mouth and my soul, so strong I almost fainted. The sweetness completely faded away within two seconds. I took another bite, with the same results.

The apple had the magic property of becoming whole again within a minute or two. No matter how many bites I took, it was still brilliant red, complete, and perfect, and I kept it in its golden box. The love apple Eve gave me is glowingly beautiful, immensely alluring, and its sweetness never lasts for more than an instant.

When I woke from the dream, I found the golden box with Eve's magic gift on my bedside table.

So, now I have Eve's apple. It is what I wanted all along.

The next morning, the steaming summer sun came up. My springtime was over. I wondered if I would ever find a hug lover to satisfy my yearning and loneliness. Perhaps I should look for a new and better Cupid. Fortunately I did not know how many years of always wanting love but never finding it lay ahead.

XXXXXXXXXXXXXXXXXXXXXXXXXXXXXXXXXXXXXXXXXXXX

The great pianist and composer-transcriber Leopold Godowsky wrote on the title page of one of his piano compositions, *The Gardens of Buitenzorg*:

"Painful yearnings for past happenings irrevocably gone—those memories which the ocean of time gradually submerges and finally buries in oblivion."

But our sweet and poisonous memories sometimes rise up out of the ocean of memory, and we can feel our pain again.

Summer of 1953

I: Working in New Iberia

As the end of my junior year in college approached, I needed to find a summer job. Several previous summers I had worked for my father in his machine shop in McAllen. We were not friendly, and I did not like the work, although I learned to weld and to use the lathe, the milling machine, the drill press, and the other large machines. I was afraid of the milling machine, as I always felt a strong impulse to stick my hands into the cutting section so as to grind them up and mutilate them, as my father had threatened to do to me years before. I didn't want to work in his machine shop this summer or ever again.

The only job I could find was making cold calls trying to sell cemetery lots over the telephone, which did not seem promising to me. My father offered me a job working for his oil field service company in New Iberia, Louisiana. I accepted.

In the early 1950s, my father had invented a tool, the first of its kind, to detect leaks in pipe being installed in oil and gas wells as they were completed. This was an important technological innovation and spread rapidly through the drilling industry. As he needed funds to start up his company, he had to turn to some local businessmen for financing. They agreed to invest $10,000 and in return received half the stock of the new business. The company created to use the tool grew rapidly. This was a fantastically profitable deal for them, although they never said thanks or expressed any gratitude, according to my father.

High-pressure, low-volume pumps invented and manufactured by my father were mounted on trucks which could drive to the drilling sites, often located in swamps. The truck also carried the testing tools, which were connected to the pump by a long rubber hose running from the pump to the top of the derrick, over a pulley, and then down to the rig floor, a distance of almost two hundred feet. The tool was placed inside the pipe. When pressure was applied and held, the rubber hose expanded and shortened by about

119

twenty feet. A leak could either be seen (water would shoot out through the leak) or could be detected if the pressure gauge began to drop. When the pressure was released at the end of the test, the hose relaxed and again lengthened to its original dimension. Unless the rubber hose were pulled vigorously, it would knot up and jam inside the pipe. My job was to pull the hose. I did this all summer.

Being the boss's son is usually problematic. I was paid half the going hourly rate and had to work twice as much as anyone else. There were five three-man crews in New Iberia (the operator, the assistant, and the hose-puller). When crew number one was called on a job, they would drive to the location. It was always uncertain how long the job would take, but it was usually between ten and thirty-six hours. When the next job called in, crew number two would be dispatched, et cetera. When a crew returned from a job, it went to the bottom of the list and became number five. The men could rest until they were called again.

Except I was always first up—when my crew came in, the supervisor immediately sent me to the head of the line to join the next crew to be dispatched. I got almost no rest or time off. Unlike the other men, I wasn't paid any overtime. My salary was half the going rate. All this courtesy of my father.

Working conditions in the swamp locations were hard: extremely hot, clouds of mosquitoes, nowhere to rest during breaks, noisy, and dangerous— hard physical labor twenty-four hours a day or until the job was finished. The surrounding swampy area was crawling with poisonous snakes. Sometimes if there was a problem with the drilling process, we all had to sit around until the problem was solved, maybe up to twenty-four hours. I would lie down close to one of the boilers—it was so hot next to the boiler that the mosquitoes wouldn't bite me on that side. After a while, I would turn over and let the other side get boiled but relieved of mosquito bites. As I had been very sedentary and studious, this hard work was probably good for me, but I didn't like it and felt resentful at the half pay, always up routine.

I complained to the boss of the New Iberia office, but he just laughed at me.

XXXXXXXXXXXXXXXXXXXXXXXXXXXXXXXXXXXXXXXXXXXXXXX

II: Shadows on the Teche

I had rented an upstairs bedroom in the house of two old ladies on St. Peter Street. Sisters, one a widow, the other a spinster, both were retired schoolteachers. They were sweet to me, occasionally giving me cake or ice cream. Sometimes they even let me play their piano.

At the end of St. Peter Street was a holy rollers church, and did they get going! The whole church vibrated with tremendously loud joyful racket—singing, shouting, screaming, stomping. I think they were having great fun.

Two blocks away, on Main Street, stood the lovely antebellum plantation house, Shadows on the Teche, with white pillars, verandas, azaleas, oak trees festooned with Spanish moss, and the beautiful Bayou Teche flowing slowly along at the bottom of the backyard. The place was a local tourist attraction but badly in need of restoration. Curious, I went inside on a tour. The atmosphere was eerie and unwelcoming, as if unhappy ghosts were hovering. The bouffant-headed tour guide told us that the owner was in residence; his rooms were not included in the tour.

Across Main Street from the Shadows was a simple white wooden structure, a fruit and vegetable stand. One day I went in to buy a banana and chatted for a few minutes with the owner, who was about forty, slim, energetic, handsome, and obviously gay.

In spite of his jocularity, he had the look of those who spend much time crying privately, perhaps only inwardly.

He said, "Well, we're neighbors. Let's get acquainted. My day name is Ray-Bob, but you can call me by my real name, Gwendolyn, honey. What's your name?"

"John. Glad to meet you."

"That's your day name. But what's your real name? Mine's Gwendolyn, like I told you. G-W-E-N-D-O-L-Y-N."

"Well, I guess I only have a day name; I don't have a real name yet. I'm sorry."

"Never mind, sweet. Goodie me, I get to give you your real name." His eyes crinkled as he smiled broadly.

"Oh," I said, smiling in return.

"From now on, your real name will be Rosie. It suits you. You're a real rosebud."

As I was six feet two, 180 pounds, slender, with blond hair, and blue eyes behind fairly thick glasses, I didn't think of myself as resembling a rosebud, but I decided to play along.

"Why, thank you, Gwendolyn. That's a nice name. I have to go on home now. Bye-Bye." I left, taking my banana for a midnight snack.

"Bye, little sweet Rosie," he said as I walked away. "See y'all real soon."

I wondered what all that was about. I liked odd people, as long as they were not dangerous or threatening. Ray-Bob seemed a kindred soul, sort of.

For the rest of the summer, I went to visit Gwendolyn Ray-Bob two or three times a week for a chat. He told me about the Weeks family, who had lived in the Shadows for over a hundred years. William Weeks Hall, the last surviving member of the family, was still in the house. Gwendolyn told me the recent history of the house. Perhaps his story was partly true.

"Master Billie was the last of the Weeks family," Ray-Bob said, "a big man, six feet tall, two hundred pounds. He had been much feared for his sexual predations. He was a bachelor and earlier in life had liked to whip black women, but later on, in his forties, he turned to men, also preferably black. He whipped them too, and sometimes you could hear the screams coming from the mansion. He gave his partners generous rewards, so there was never a shortage of willing whippees."

Gwendolyn rolled her eyes and sucked in her breath, as if terribly shocked, which was a pretty good performance.

"About fifteen or twenty years ago," he continued, "when he was in his forties, he met Absalom and fell in love. Absalom, whose nickname was Boss, was six feet five, two hundred seventy-five pounds, lumpy-faced, black, and built like a brick shithouse. He couldn't read or write but must have been a very good lover. Eventually he took Master Billie's whip away and turned it on him, towering over him as Billie groveled on the floor and begged for mercy. 'Mercy, mercy,' he pleaded. Then Boss would pick Billie up, throw him in the bed, and give him some hot, steamy mercy. MERCY—you get it?"

"MERCY, MERCY," Ray-Bob squealed as he pranced around the room pretending to be Master Billie. "Of course, everyone in town was scandalized, not by the screams, the whips, and the weird gay sex, but by the fact that the lord of the manor had taken a black man as his lover. Some of the local ladies refused to say mornin' to him anymore, and he was cryin' hurt.

"Gradually Billie and Boss were seen less and less in public. The servants all gradually wandered away, and the house fell into decay.

"The yard got overgrown, and sometimes moccasins sunned themselves in the garden—they crawled up from the bayou, only a hundred feet away. Billie and Boss lived on in the Shadows, all alone.

"Occasionally Boss was seen tidying up the garden or doing necessary repairs. Sometimes passers by could hear Master Billie playing Chopin in the drawing room, but no one saw him anymore, and eventually some even wondered if he were still alive.

"One night, Boss threw Billie onto the bed with more than usual force. Billie twisted his neck, and the next morning he couldn't move any part of his body below his neck. The doctor was called, and for a few months he tried to fix Master Billie, but the damage was permanent.

"Everyone knew it was an accident, and no charges were filed against Boss.

"Billie could eat and speak, and Boss took delicate care of his lover for several years. Even with Billie paralyzed, from time to time they could still whip up a mess of hot steamy MERCY—get it?

"Groceries were delivered, occasional repair men would be let in, and Billie's aunt Leticia visited twice a year from New Orleans, just to make sure he was being well cared for.

"After about fifteen years, Boss suddenly died, of a heart attack, I s'pose. Billie tried to call for help, but his voice wasn't strong enough, and nobody heard him. He almost died of starvation as Boss was rotting beside his bed. Neighbors noticed a foul smell coming from the dark, silent house, rang the bell, and then called the police. They broke through the front door, entered, and found the gruesome and tragic scene.

"This happened about two years ago. I already owned this place, and your auntie Gwendolyn saw Boss's body being carried out—what was left of it. When they picked him up, he was so rotten his head fell off."

I was open-mouthed, enthralled by Ray-Bob's lurid tale.

He continued, "A caretaker was hired, and now Master Billie just lies there, never speaking, patiently waiting to become a ghost and rejoin his Boss." He sighed and rolled his eyes. "Lordy! Lordy!" Ray-Bob concluded the story.

"Swanny," I said, trying to talk Southern.

Some of the story might have been true. This was the Deep South, of course, but maybe some of the details had been colorfully and elaborately embroidered.

My unfair treatment at work continued.

The chats with Gwendolyn Ray-Bob were among the few pleasant moments of the week. He was my guide in flying through lurid clouds of sexual fantasies. He really knew how to do it, how to operate in the gay world.

One day he said, "I met the most divine young stud yesterday. I was out cruising in my white Cadillac with the top down when I saw this hot number hitching. I often meet young guys this way. I'm very careful and haven't never had no trouble. When he got in, we jawed for a while, and then I asked him if he wanted a blow job. He did and pulled out his wang, bare and plain, right there in the open air. I was embarrassed and put the top up in a hurry. No use to push things too far, I always say.

"Well, your auntie Gwendolyn knows a dirty wang when she sees one, so I parked next to the bayou and told him to wash himself off good. He did, and then we went and parked out of sight in a sugarcane field. He came twice. He said he would stop by to see me at the fruit stand next week. Lordy, I sure hope he does."

Fascinated, I listened carefully to Ray-Bob's scintillating stories. His carefree and adventurous approach to life filled me with envy, terror, and admiration.

Auntie Gwendolyn fortunately never made a pass at me, as she was not exactly my type. Nor I hers, I guess.

XXXXXXXXXXXXXXXXXXXXXXXXXXXXXXXXXXXXXXXXXXXXX

III: New Orleans—Meeting the Froglets

The overwork continued at dear old Daddy's testing tool company. I was getting more irritable and resentful at what I thought was unfair treatment at work, so I decided to run away—to hitchhike to New Orleans. Although I had had very little practical experience of sex, I had heard from my gay friends in Houston that New Orleans was a center of sinful fun, drinking, gay sex, and whatever else you might like. All the rituals of Aphrodite were offered. I wanted to continue my sexual exploration and education and maybe meet some new gay friends.

I knew that if I told my boss I needed to take a short break, he would forbid it. So I just left early on a Friday morning, leaving a note saying I was taking the weekend off and would be back Sunday evening. A first for me, I hitchhiked to New Orleans. It took about seven hours, and I only had to change rides once. I enjoyed chatting with the drivers, who were both straight but entertaining talkers anyway, full of stories about New Orleans.

I had no idea where to stay. The French Quarter was supposed to be the center of the action. All the hotels in the Quarter were expensive, but I was lucky to find a comfortable, cheap room at the St. Charles Hotel, an ancient and fading establishment on St. Charles Avenue just a couple of blocks outside the Quarter. I left my little suitcase in my room and took off to look for sin central. It was late Friday afternoon, and the place was gearing up for the usual wild, dissipated orgy which took place each night, double on the weekends.

I started the evening in the Carousel Bar at the Monteleone Hotel, an old building covered in shiny white tiles, on Royal Street. After having one Singapore Sling, I decided to have another. They were both heavenly. The bar, which revolved once every fifteen minutes, was ever so elegant and worldly. The customers were smoking and drinking cocktails as they chattered and laughed. I knew I was on the right track. Deciding to move on, I wandered down Royal Street and ventured into several other bars featuring loud jazz music. After a couple of martinis, sloe gin fizzes, and sidecars, I switched to beer for the rest of the evening.

The barkers outside the stripper clubs tried to lure me in, but I was not really vulnerable to their temptations. A female impersonator club had a big sign hanging in front: "Boys Will Be Girls," it said. "More like it," I thought.

Wandering around the Quarter, I went into bars looking for a gay encounter. Tony Bacino's, a famous place just off Royal Street, drew me in. The chubby bartender, Candy, was a local celebrity. Behind the bar hung a life-sized painting of Candy lying on a chaise, dressed in what appeared to be several feather boas. From time to time, he shot a stream of seltzer water at the crotch of the painting and screamed, "Oooh, that douche feels so good. More, more." The customers of the bar roared and clapped. I had never been anywhere so sophisticated—I was thrilled.

Someone at Tony Bacino's told me of another bar, Lafitte's in Exile, farther down Bourbon Street toward Esplanade. It was said to be the oldest gay bar in the United States and was "in exile" because it had moved from its previous French Quarter location a few years before, when its original building was demolished.

Lafitte's large main room had a fireplace in one corner. There was a square bar at which maybe forty men were standing, and men were also leaning around the walls. Conversation, laughter, and loud music from the jukebox playing "Up a Lazy River" mingled in a beautiful din. A steep stairway led to a large second-floor room, where more men stood around drinking. This was long before the disco era; men never danced together in public, but they knew how to use their eyes.

The clientele was obviously more excitingly dissipated than I could comprehend. Through the evening, a few men talked to me, and some invited me to go home with them. None were up to my standards, whatever that meant. In other words, they didn't turn me on. And besides, by that time, twenty-seven beers had gone down the hatch, in addition to the bouquet of drinks which started the evening. I was developing the "hollow leg" which was so convenient and so dangerous.

By now it was past 2:00 AM and time for me to turn in. I wobbled the ten blocks back to the St. Charles Hotel. Too tired to undress fully, I went to bed with my underwear on. As soon as I turned out the light, I sensed something moving on the other side of the room. Looking carefully, I could see small emerald-green fluorescent froglets with long silky green hair and tall pointed ears jumping out of the walls, from the corners of the room, and from the woodwork. There were thousands of the cute little froglet rabbits. Fortunately, they didn't attack or come to pester me. Instead, they looked at me silently and then vanished just before they landed on the floor.

"How interesting," I thought, "maybe this is alcoholic hallucinosis," a temporary condition I had read about, caused by over-drinking, too much alcohol flooding the brain. "Nothing to be frightened of here," I thought. It didn't occur to me for many years that this was seriously abnormal, a warning sign which I chose to ignore. I knew what it was but not what it meant, just as years later I ignored the significance of daily blackouts and hangovers.

As I continued to watch the amusing froglets, or frabbits, I suddenly vomited all over myself and the bed—I had unloaded some of the evening's booze. Not wanting to spend the rest of the night lying in vomit, I called the hotel operator and told her I had had an accident and had made a mess. Could she send someone to help me, please?

Within two or three minutes, there was a knock. Surprisingly, I was able to stand and walk to the door. The night manager came into the room. "I drank too much and got sick," I said.

He sized up the situation, probably familiar to him. "Just sit down over there and rest. I'll have someone come to clean up and give you some fresh linens. Don't worry. I hope you feel better."

Within five minutes, a morose and silent maid came in carrying some sheets. She rapidly tidied, cleaned, and changed the sheets. "Thank you," I said, as I gave her a dollar tip. Compared to her weekly salary of about thirty dollars, it was worth much more in 1953 than it is now in 2008. She grunted as she left. I think we were both disgusted by the situation.

XXXXXXXXXXXXXXXXXXXXXXXXXXXXXXXXXXXXXXXXXXX

IV: New Orleans—Paul

The next day I slept until noon, then dressed and went out for an excellent lunch at Antoine's. I wandered around the Quarter for a while, and after going back to the hotel for a nap, it was time to start my search for love again.

I stopped at the French Market for coffee and beignets, admiring the beautiful St. Louis Cathedral across Jackson Square. Then I strolled back into the Quarter and looked for Lafitte's in Exile again, thinking I would retrace the more interesting parts of last night's bar crawl. I talked to a few mildly interesting men there and then decided to go on to Tony Bacino's.

It was about 7 PM, and the place was not yet crowded. I took a seat at the bar. Candy was whooping and douching her portrait. It wasn't so funny the second time.

The young man sitting to my right immediately attracted my interest. He looked to be in his mid-twenties and was tall, well-built, and handsome. Enticingly well-muscled arms declared themselves even when draped in a long-sleeved shirt. Smoking a cigarette in a white ivory cigarette holder, he looked over at me with a charming smile and raised his right eyebrow. He had light brown hair cut a little longer than I thought attractive, but he also had beautiful green eyes with long eyelashes, even features, and glowing skin.

Soon I opened the conversation, "Hi—I'm John. I just got to New Orleans yesterday for the first time. What I've seen so far is interesting, but I don't really know my way around."

With a rather flexible wrist, he waved his ivory holder for emphasis. "Oh, honey, I'm Paul. I'm so happy to make yuah acquaintance. You're a guest in mah city, and I would just love to show you around." He peered at me through his gold-rimmed lorgnette.

"Why, thank you," I said. "I would like that very much."

"Good. I live just two blocks from here. Darlin', why don't we start our tour at my house?"

Shortly, we were at the front door of an impressive old four-story house in the Quarter. He used his key, and we went into the grand mansion. A curving mahogany stairway led to the second floor, where there was a magnificent parlor with a grand piano and Victorian carved rosewood furniture covered with embroidered upholstery and colorful shawls with long silk fringes. Large potted ferns, gardenia plants, books scattered around, even a harp standing by the piano added to the overly rich atmosphere. The very high ceilings accommodated four or five fine full-length portrait paintings of aristocratic figures dressed in formal nineteenth-century clothing.

He again stared at me through his lorgnette. Smiling, he said, "Please pardon me for looking at you this way. My eyesight is unfortunately rather dim just now."

"But of course, think nothing of it," I said, brimming over with feelings of unaccustomed elegance. I suspected the lorgnette was an affectation, but it was an interesting touch. In my short gay history, I had not previously encountered anyone who used a lorgnette. Nor since then, either.

"I see you looking at my paintings," Paul said. "They are all by Thomas Sully, the English painter, and were collected by dear old Daddy. I worry about them sometimes and think we should donate them to the museum. Would you like to see more of the house?"

We paused at the top of the stairway to the third floor, and an intense physical attraction suddenly boiled over. We had been holding ourselves back politely for the past hour, and pent-up emotion and lust abruptly broke through our reserve. I could feel surges of physical energy trying to escape my body. After a long hug, with much stroking and passionate kissing and increasingly excited groping, he led me by my hand into a large bedroom. There was a fine four-poster bed with a lace canopy and two more Sullys on the wall. He had a fortune hanging on his walls.

Taking off our shoes and socks, we sat on the edge of the bed, kissing mouths, eyes, ears, necks. Our lips and tongues were having a fiesta. We removed each other's pants, then shirts, then underwear. I was pleased to see he had a powerful athletic figure, although he was gentle and delicate in his movements, perhaps even somewhat effeminate. His magnificent sexual equipment was in full bloom, as was mine. Mutual excitement and curiosity lost no time in asserting itself.

After we were satisfied, we lay in the bed, talking, smoking, and gently stroking each other. Soon we were ready for more.

"I want you, if you might find that agreeable?" he said.

Remembering the fat and hairy Houston Cupid who had begun my sexual initiation a few months before, I replied, "Oh—I don't know."

"Honey, I'm going to send you to heaven." Laughing, he tried to turn me onto my stomach. We struggled for a while. I was surprised how very strong he was. As he used more and more force, I finally couldn't resist him any longer and gave in. He easily turned me over and jumped on top of me, holding me down; then we lay absolutely still for a long time, with his tongue in my ear. He began to kiss my neck and back and cheeks.

"Relax, darlin', just relax. Feel my kisses warmin' you up." He was very skilled in this persuasion, and soon I felt him gently begin. He then became more passionate and made sure that I fully participated in the pleasure, although it was slightly painful at the same time. This was miles beyond my first sexual experience with Mr. Cupid on the linoleum in Houston. After a while, we rolled apart and lay on our backs.

Eventually he said, "Let's go down to the kitchen and have some tea."

"Okay, I'll put my clothes on." I reached for my clothes.

"Oh, no, you won't." He grabbed my clothes, threw them into a closet, and laughed. "Let's go down just like this. It's more entertainin'."

Feeling cheerily depraved, I followed him down the stairs. We sat nude in the kitchen, drinking jasmine tea from Limoges cups and eating delicate butterscotch éclairs. It was my first naked tea party. I wondered if this was a usual occurrence.

He talked of his family. "This house doesn't really belong to me. It was my parents', but dear old Daddy died most tragically two years ago in a hunting accident, and now the house belongs to my mother. She's been away for three weeks, and I really miss her. I love her so much. She spends most of her time at our plantation on the Mississippi; that's where she is right now. The last time I saw dear old Mama, she was on the front veranda of our plantation house, lyin' on the chaise longue, wrapped in yards and yards of black tulle, grieving for poor ole dead Daddy, and sippin' a julep."

Overcome by his own sad description, he began to cry. I put my arms around his fine broad shoulders in sympathy and concupiscence and murmured, "There, there, dear, I can feel how sad you are." I felt like a fraud, as I was more interested in the nude skin contact and feeling him up than in comforting my new friend. He sighed deeply.

Slowly and suggestively inserting another cigarette into his holder, he had a sudden change of mood and growled, "John, let's do it again. I want to have sex with you again right now."

"Oh, Paul, that would be wonderful, but I really have to go to the hotel and get some rest before I head back to New Iberia in the morning."

"Please, please—just stay here with me tonight. I'll wake you at six to go to your hotel. Is that early enough? Please stay, Johnny. I'm afraid, all alone in this big old house. There's a ghost here too, and he scares me. And I like you so much."

Between his hot desire for my presence, his magnificent body (body, body, *body*), his beautiful house, the Sully paintings, the ghost, his sexual vigor and enthusiasm, and his strong arms (arms, arms, *arms*), how could I resist? I struggled slightly, like a fly stuck in honey.

We went back upstairs to his bedroom and spent the rest of the night tightly entwined. Sometimes we moved enough to have more sexual glory, and as the sun rose, we had a sweet sunrise morning glory, too.

In the morning, after many kisses and hugs, I reluctantly left to go back to the hotel. At the last minute, Paul decided to come with me, and he even went with me later, after a final glory, to the bus station. As my bus pulled away, we waved good-bye. I will always remember the look of smiling, melancholy lust on the handsome face of this wistful champion. He sniffed and licked his lips as he winked goodbye through a few tears.

We neglected to exchange addresses or phone numbers—one of those oversights of careless youth.

In my gay experience so far, I had already had sex with two previous partners, but this was the first time someone had seemed really interested in me, and it felt wonderful. But I didn't consider what a fine opportunity I was thoughtlessly and stupidly discarding. I didn't have the experience to even imagine having a lover or a love affair. This was perhaps one of those missed turning points: a crossroad in life. It was not clear then or now where that other road might have led. Maybe to much joy, but at least to lots of hot sex, a prospect never to be scorned.

Later on, I learned he was well-known in the French Quarter for his good looks, his lorgnette, his wealth, and his startling sexual equipment and vigor. Three years later, I encountered him again while visiting New Orleans, and we had a repeat of our first night together. The romantic and captivating ardor of this encounter was almost as exciting as before, and the physical contact was still outstandingly steamy and invigorating. And again we parted without exchanging contact information. Fate prevented us.

The meeting with Paul was one of the most exciting and captivating meetings of my life. Over the years, I occasionally heard something about him, but then I lost all touch. Sometimes I feel a sharp pang of longing to return to Paul's house to pursue the love I so frivolously discarded there. But at least he now lives quite obligingly in my bedroom of favorite memories, as loving, beautiful, and forceful as ever.

XXXXXXXXXXXXXXXXXXXXXXXXXXXXXXXXXXXXXXXXXX

V: The Cozy Corner

As the Trailways bus heading back to New Iberia bounced along, I wondered what adventures my final weeks might offer. After my New Orleans weekend, I was feeling slightly more comfortable in my new gay identity and hoped that another meeting with someone as exciting as Paul would happen. Was it possible?

When I reached New Iberia that afternoon, my landladies told me everyone had been worried about me. They didn't smile when they told me this, but their eyes twinkled. They didn't ask me any questions but said my boss wanted me to call as soon as I came in. I called him, and he said, "I'm glad you're okay. Come to work tomorrow morning." I was glad he had no questions for me.

My disappearance had caused a furor. My mother had been furious with my father, my father had been scolding my boss, and my boss got in a fight with his wife. I felt a little embarrassed when I heard of these clashes. I telephoned my mother. I explained the unfairness of my job schedule and said I had needed a little time off, and so had gone to New Orleans to see the architecture and to have dinner at Antoine's. Naturally I omitted the interesting parts of the story, including Paul and the froglets.

Mother said she understood. "Please try to stick it out. It's only three more weeks," she said. Sometimes she could act as a prudent peacemaker.

And so the work began again, but this time I rotated with the crews on a regular basis, not the always-first-up crap which had been put on me before. Now maybe I could have a little more time off.

Auntie Gwendolyn Ray-Bob was curious about my New Orleans adventure and quizzed me about all that had happened there. He looked a little concerned when he heard about the froglets but smiled and nodded when he heard about my meeting with Paul.

"I think you missed out on something good there by not getting his number and making another date," he said.

I agreed.

Late the next Saturday afternoon, I went to the movies. It was a good bargain: children five cents, adults eleven cents, popcorn four cents. The new Tyrone Power film, *Pony Soldier*, was playing. Tyrone Power had never looked better.

There were a few bars within walking distance of my room on St. Peter Street. I wondered if any were like the gay bars in New Orleans. There were many good-looking Cajun men in New Iberia, and I thought a few of them had given me inviting looks.

That Saturday evening after the movie, I felt like exploring so went into one of the downtown bars, the Cozy Corner. It was crowded, but there was one seat at the bar. I sat down between a woman on one side and a man on the other. The woman on my right was there with a date and was concentrating on him.

The man on my left was there alone. He said, "Howdy, stranger. My name's Teddy. You new in town?"

"Yeah," I said, "I'm here for the summer—doin' some work in the oil field. My name's John. Glad to meet you."

He was dark and handsome, well-built, strong and rough appearing, with an aura of violence and anger. He seemed slightly intoxicated. I knew I was on unfamiliar territory, so I didn't have any particular plan. That is, I was not planning to try to seduce him.

"Me, I'm a roughneck," Teddy offered. He had large dark shining eyes, soft and flirtatious. His wide smile showed fine white teeth, and his perfect skin had a light tan. One strand of curly black hair fell across his forehead. A straight nose and full pink lips completed this luscious picture. He was a real beauty, just as good as Tyrone Power or any other pony soldier.

After about five more minutes of casual conversation, he suddenly said, "I have something that'll make your mouth water."

Surprised and a little wary, I said, "Oh, what's that?"

"You know." He motioned toward his crotch, then became silent and stared at the bar. "Maybe it's too big for you, but I bet you'd go for that."

I was too inexperienced to know what to do with his comment. Falling silent again, he stared into space. He seemed to be getting fidgety.

Not knowing how to turn this conversation to something more neutral, I stupidly said to him, "A penny for your thoughts." I hoped this little piece of effete jocularity might brighten the atmosphere.

As soon as I had spoken, a quiet voice in my head said, "Hope again, sissy boy."

"What's that you said?" he asked, glaring. Perhaps Teddy had never heard this phrase before.

"A penny for your thoughts," I repeated, smiling winsomely at him.

He sat up straighter on his barstool and yelled, "This is what I'll give you for talking to me like that, you goddamn queer." There was a hush in the bar as all heads turned. He hauled off and punched me in the face. It hurt, and my nose began to bleed. I was paralyzed by shock. Naturally, I didn't hit him back.

He stood up. "When I come back, I'm going to take you outside and make you suck me off, like you want to. I see your mouth watering, you faggot. And then I'm going to beat the shit out of you. Here, look at this." His back was to the crowd, and he was holding something concealed under his denim shirttail. He had pulled a knife out of his pocket. He pushed a button on its side and flipped open the blade. After pointing it at me and moving it slowly back and forth, he closed the knife and went off to the restroom.

I didn't know what had gone so wrong so fast. Perhaps he was drunker than I thought, or crazy, or perhaps he was showing off. I was plenty scared.

During Teddy's attack, he had knocked my glasses off and they had fallen on the floor. I was bending over looking for them but couldn't find them in the dim light. Some of the customers laughed, but finally a kind woman picked up my glasses and handed them to me. "Be careful," she said.

"Thanks," I said, putting on my glasses.

The bartender looked worried. He was the only person besides me who had seen the switchblade. "Hey, buddy, maybe you'd better leave before Teddy comes back. He's a pretty rough fighter, and I don't want no trouble in here."

"Okay," I said. I headed for the door. The customers resumed talking and laughing. Embarrassed and ashamed, I left and walked home rapidly, afraid that Mr. Stud-Thug might be right behind me. My right eye was beginning to swell shut.

This was definitely a defeat and a humiliation, and I knew it. My psyche would have a shriveled-up spell. The failed attempt to make a connection with a new and attractive stranger was to be a many-times-repeated defeat and disappointment through the coming years. Sometimes my fragile self-regard suffered serious and heavy blows. This time it was my nose and eye that were suffering.

The next day, Sunday, was my twentieth birthday. I have always liked my birthdays and was feeling cheerful, in spite of the trouble the night before. Somehow not ashamed of my black eye, I had a gala Sunday lunch alone downtown at the hotel. After I got home, my landladies surprised me by baking a cake and serving ice cream too. Very politely they avoided asking about my black eye. The three of us had a cheerful little birthday party.

I didn't mention the incident at the bar to anyone at work, but a few days later one of my fellow workers asked, "Have you ever been to the Cozy Corner? You might like it." He winked at me and scratched his crotch. News and rumors travel in a small town.

"Maybe," I said, feigning ignorance. "I've been to several bars, but I don't remember their names. Do you like to spend time at the Cozy Corner?"

He didn't answer, but he stared at me as he pointedly wiped down the long round testing tools. *A little too obvious*, I thought.

This wasn't a friendly interchange. I was now completely ready to leave New Iberia and hoped I could endure the five more days until it was time to go.

I survived, carefully.

XXXXXXXXXXXXXXXXXXXXXXXXXXXXXXXXXXXXXXXXXXXX

VI: Good-Bye to Louisiana

The final day came, and I felt sad and glad at the same time.

I said goodbye to my sweet landladies, to my boss and his wife, to my fellow workers, and to Auntie Gwendolyn Ray-Bob, who came with me to the bus station to see me off. He hugged me in plain sight of the other passengers and said, "Good-bye, sweet little Rosie." He gave me an RC Cola and a MoonPie as farewell gifts. I boarded the Trailways bus to Houston and sighed with relief as we rolled out of town.

After a couple of weeks recuperating at home in McAllen, I returned to Houston to start my senior year at Rice.

Two years later I heard that Auntie Gwendolyn had been found dead in his fruit stand, stabbed and with his throat cut. I was horrified; this was the first time I had experienced the murder of a gay friend. I hoped his death was quick. The police thought the motive was robbery. The murderer was never caught.

XXXXXXXXXXXXXXXXXXXXXXXXXXXXXXXXXXXXXXXXXXXX

Thinking about this eventful, successful, dangerous, sometimes dissipated, and very educational summer, I am surprised that I so quickly learned how to survive those odd lessons in living.

Now, fifty-five years later, I look back and can see these lonely and eager souls standing in the mists of memory. I hear them speaking and see them looking at me with tender eyes, holding out their arms to me. We look at one another with love, sorrow, and yearning. I speak to them in greeting and reach out my arms to them, but we are not yet able to touch across the decades which still separate us.

A Narrow Escape

The last few months of my junior year at Rice passed quietly, except for Freddy's crisis. This happened early in January of 1953, just after we all returned from our Christmas vacations. This was about two months before I met Mr. Cupid, who taught me how to have sex.

Freddy, a brilliant student, was the grader for a special mathematics class taken only by the football players and other athletes, most of whom were at Rice on athletic scholarships, not expected to do fine academic work, but expected to brutally kick the asses of opposing football players and other teams. Fred was occasionally hired to do some tutoring for these behemoths.

He was widely suspected of practicing the love that dare not speak its name, but no one outside our inner circle knew for sure. Occasionally Fred would make an off-color remark to some of the students, but he really had no interest in making sexual liaisons with them, not even casual ones, nor did he ever do so. He was most definitely not attracted to or interested in the behemoths.

He knew that some of the footballers were not prepared for their midterm math tests, in spite of extensive tutoring. If they did not pass, they might lose their scholarships, but they would at least be forbidden to play their sports until they improved their grades. Not believing this penalty could apply to them, they thought they were so special, so swaggeringly indispensable, that they did not have to do even the minimal schoolwork expected and required of them.

About a month before the first semester final exam, Fred warned them they must study more if they wanted to pass the exam. Three of the leaders of this group told Fred they expected him to pass them, and if he did not, they would tell the dean he had demanded sex with them as the price of a passing grade. Of course, as hyper-masculinoid he-men they wouldn't dream of cooperating with such a perverted, although hypothetical, act. Fred was concerned about this threat but said he would give them whatever grade they actually made on the test.

The day of the exam came, and most of them failed emphatically, including the bully triad. The next week, they carried out their threat.

They went to talk to the dean, Dr. George Richter. This was the man who had been so brutally unkind to me two years before when I had had my hair cut off by some of my classmates as a hazing prank.

Feigning indignant innocence, the jocks recounted that a few weeks earlier they just happened to wander into a bar, Eadie's Desert Room, for a drink and were surprised to see all the customers were male. They surmised it must be a queer bar.

They said they were shocked to see Freddy there talking and laughing with some of the other queers. He was acting as if he were on friendly terms with them. It was then that he threatened to fail them unless they let him give them a blow job or let him have other unspecified sex acts with them. Of course, they indignantly refused; what nerve the little fag had!

They structured this story to portray themselves as naively and innocently going into the bar. The truth was they had gone there several times before to pick up gay men, take them for a ride, rob them, beat them up, and dump them out of their own cars. We heard this from some of our friends who had been the victims of the jocks.

Occasionally, in a more honorable mood, some of them practiced honest prostitution. That is, they did not beat up and rob their customers. They accepted money and then leaned back. So we heard.

There was a thin and wavering line between being a customer and being a victim of these thugs. Being clean-cut, red-blooded American football heroes, nobody would believe what they were actually doing. Nobody would believe their victims either. We all knew the police would be of no help.

Whom to believe? The studly campus heroes who upheld the school's honor on the gridiron, or the fey, limp-wristed, pansy eggheads? Homophobic attitudes prevailed at Rice, as in the general society at that time. Intellectual ability, then perhaps even more than now, was scorned as unmanly and unnatural, certainly far less important than the ability to pass, catch, and tackle. Grunt, fuck, and fart, as we put it, just as scornful of the jocks as they were of us.

In fairness, one of my most outstanding classmates was a football player; he made All-American as well as Phi Beta Kappa and was polite, kind, handsome, and charming. He tried to get his teammates to refrain from their tawdry extortions but couldn't turn them from their purpose. Many of the other athletes were also fine young men, but the rotten apples among them made the whole barrel stink.

XXXXXXXXXXXXXXXXXXXXXXXXXXXXXXXXXXXXXXXXXXX

Fred was called in to Dean Richter, who sternly questioned him. He berated him for being in a queer bar. We had our coordinated stories ready. Fred explained that a group of us had gone to the art cinema on McGowan Street, and afterward we went into a bar across the street to have a beer and discuss the movie. We saw it was a gay bar but finished our beers anyway and then left. We were there for maybe fifteen minutes. But while there we saw three Rice football players come in and mingle with the crowd, talking with some of the customers. When the football players saw us, they grinned and waved and then left the place. We didn't talk with them.

We said we were most definitely not gay—oh, no, no, no, never. We had never been in the Desert Room before (a big lie) and would of course never go there again now that we knew what kind of a place it was (also a big lie).

I was also called in and questioned individually by bigot sadist Richter, as were several others of our circle, including Tom Smith, a giant athlete who was a philosophy major and was not gay. His girlfriend Mary, later to become his wife, was also questioned. She had been kind enough to offer to marry Fred if that were needed to provide a convincing mask of heterosexuality.

We all had consistent stories, but we were suspect because we were all scholarly students, eggheads, odd, and not devoted to athletic team events. Fred's major professor, Dr. RATsanoff, homophobe of long standing, was appalled. He didn't want to believe what he was hearing, and he didn't want some of his best students expelled.

This had become a very awkward situation.

Finally, we were all called in together—that is, the egghead fag group was called in. The jocks were not called in: they didn't need a lecture about the dangers of going to queer bars; naturally they were immune to that kind of perversion. The sadist bigot dean and assistant dean were present, along with Dr. RATsanoff and two police officers with gold bars on their shoulders.

Apparently it had been decided to accept our stories as a face-saving convenience for all, even though we were obviously not believed. It was made plain to us that the footballers were believed, which rankled us. The homophobic authorities had chosen to accept the little lamb disguises of these truly evil wolf-men.

The police read out a list of gay bars and asked us if we had ever visited any of them. "Oh, no, no, no," we said. Of course we had all been numerous times to all the bars which were still open. Some of the places on the list had been closed for years, but the police weren't current with their information. They warned us *never* to go into such places. "Oh, no, we *never* will. Thank you for telling us," we said, rolling our eyes as seriously and innocently as we could manage.

If the school authorities had decided we were homosexuals, even if we had never had any actual sex, we would be instantaneously expelled from college, and our careers would have been ruined.

But the danger subsided over the course of several weeks. Learning on the job left a mark on all of us. The lessons were: 1) bigots and sadists always side with the jocks against the nerds, and 2) gays were worth nothing.

Later we encountered the same football players several times in the same gay bar. We were all there for our usual purposes. They waved and winked at us. We did not wave back.

XXXXXXXXXXXXXXXXXXXXXXXXXXXXXXXXXXXXXXXXXXXX

Today it may be hard to realize that the mere admission that one was gay, even if no physical acts had ever taken place, was quite enough to warrant being expelled from college, medical school, and some jobs.

In many cities, the police drove the paddy wagons up to gay bars, took all the customers to jail, booked them, and possibly extorted some money from them. The next morning they would be released, but their names would appear on the front page of the local newspaper, often resulting in loss of jobs, breakup of marriages, ruined reputations, and occasionally a suicide.

To be caught in a homosexual act, perhaps at night in a parked car, or in a secluded area of a park, or even inside a private home, was a felony punishable by several years in prison. The punishment was actually meted out from time to time, usually with considerable publicity about how politician X was keeping the city safe from sex criminals and deviants.

This personal destruction masqueraded as official efforts to protect the community from depraved and dangerous perverts, as all homosexuals were believed to be.

In those days, and up until perhaps five to ten years ago, if a gay person were murdered, a sufficient defense was that the gay person had made a pass at a straight man. The straight man was of course justified in killing the gay man in self-defense, no matter how grisly and violent the murder. Even if the gay person had not made a pass at the straight man or was old, weak, or frail, it was sometimes still okay to murder him, using the self-protection pretense. Killing a queer was okay, like killing a cockroach.

It could be worse: I am told that even today, to be gay is punishable in Yemen by being thrown from an airplane.

Those who were not present at that time, or who were unaffected by such events or persecution, may wonder why some are still so very concerned about the gay rights movement.

We all knew we were in constant serious danger from the bigots. We all stayed closeted but tried to go on with our lives as carefully and prudently as possible. At the same time we continued to search for the kind of sex, friendship, and love we needed.

XXXXXXXXXXXXXXXXXXXXXXXXXXXXXXXXXXXXXXXXXXXXX

The Last Year at College, <u>1953–1954</u>

After the roller coaster summer of 1953, I was glad to return to the relative shelter of college life at Rice. In our senior year we had more options for our studies. I enrolled in seminars in American philosophy, Greek philosophy (Plato and Aristotle), pessimism, mediaeval history, parasitology, and Middle High German.

The first semester in Middle High we studied the Minnesingers, poets of courtly love, and the second semester was devoted to the great Middle High German epic, *The Nibelungenlied*, and related epics in Middle High German (*Parsifal, Tristan*), Old English, and Icelandic, with a sideways look at what Richard Wagner did in simplifying this material for the librettos of his Ring operas. I was surprised to find how much less interesting and profound Wagner's librettos were than the original works.

The Minnesingers wrote of passionate, devoted, extravagant, over-the-top, and often chaste and/or hopeless love. This is what I was looking for, and so these poets appealed strongly to my blossoming romantic nature. I memorized a number of their short, exquisite lyric poems and would sometimes recite them to myself as I walked or daydreamed. I was happy to have discovered some kindred souls, even if they existed hundreds of years ago.

During the second semester, I enjoyed the many lusty parts of *The Nibelungenlied* and also the intricate grammatical structures and problems which filled the work. For instance, the double and triple negatives sometimes reinforced each other, sometimes cancelled each other—a mechanism which foreshadowed the vacillating and ambiguous and ambivalent nature of our modern reality.

I wrote a long and carefully researched paper on the roots of the tradition of courtly love in Middle High German poetry. A second similar scholarly paper followed, on a comparison of traditions of courtly love in *The Nibelungenlied*, the Icelandic Eddas, and the opera librettos of Richard Wagner. I found both papers fascinating to research and write.

Dr. Louis was pleased with both and gave me an A plus for both semesters. He repeated his invitation that if I would stay at Rice one more year and do some more work to expand my papers, I would be granted an MA in German. I was very honored by his offer but had to decline.

A few months earlier, my father had again told me seriously that if I did anything to delay my entrance into medical school, he would refuse to do anything further to help me financially. "Everyone should be self-supporting after they reach sixteen," he said.

XXXXXXXXXXXXXXXXXXXXXXXXXXXXXXXXXXXXXXXXXXXX

The last year at Rice started with less anxiety than the previous ones. Perhaps the adventures of the summer in Louisiana had improved my self-confidence. All my classes were small and specialized, and I was able to insulate myself from other students who disturbed or frightened me.

I found parasitology fascinating and admired all the various parasites, flatworms, roundworms, insects, amoebas, and arthropods because of the tremendously complicated life cycles they had worked out for themselves. They seemed much more clever and sophisticated than our primitive human maneuvers. This course was taught by the head of the biology department, Dr. Asa Chandler, a brilliant scholar and teacher and a fine man.

He enjoyed occasionally telling us startling stories. He recounted the time an eminent scientist was giving a speech before a distinguished audience. Something about his nose seemed to be irritating him, and then a long green ascaris worm slowly crawled down and out from his nose, dangling in full view of the audience.

We all laughed uproariously, which was perhaps not the reaction Dr. Chandler was expecting.

I also enjoyed American philosophy class and was surprised by the subtlety and elegance of early writers like Jonathan Edwards and Cotton Mather, as well as the profound insights of more recent thinkers like C. S. Peirce, George Santayana, and Alfred North Whitehead.

The course in pessimism covered mostly the nineteenth-century German pessimists. It is always startling to read their writings, particularly Eduard von Hartmann, who wrote *The Philosophy of the Unconscious.*

Von Hartmann postulated that God, as the greatest being, is also the greatest sufferer. Naturally, when we realized the inexorable grimness and painfulness of life, we would all kill ourselves immediately. However, it is our moral duty to stay alive in order to help God out of His horribly painful existence.

The instructions for how to accomplish this supremely kind act by a simultaneous worldwide negation of our wills were a little difficult to understand. We would know we were succeeding when we saw the stars and all the universe fading out of existence. I thought this idea was charming.

That fall I was elected to Phi Beta Kappa, the scholastic honor society. It was a greater honor to be chosen for Phi Beta Kappa during the spring semester of the junior year, and I had been disappointed when that had not happened. When I told my parents, my mother seemed pleased. My father didn't comment.

For the eight semesters I was at Rice, I made the honor roll seven times. My parents said nothing. The first semester of my junior year, I made a C in organic chemistry, and this disqualified me from the honor roll for that semester. The class was taught by the noxious Dr. George Richter, with whom I had had an unpleasant contact.

I had a mishap a few minutes before the final exam: my glasses broke in half at the nosepiece. I am extremely myopic and can't see clearly more than eight inches in front of my face. The exam questions were written on the blackboard at the front of the room. I asked Dr. Richter if I could take the exam later. "Of course not," he said. "Just sit close enough to the blackboard to see the questions."

Seated with my knees against the front wall, I still could not see the board clearly, so I had to rise up many times to look at the questions from a distance of no more than eight inches. I had to repeatedly and gradually move my chair from the left side of the board to the right side, a distance of about thirty feet. I was blocking the view of the other students, who kept yelling at me to sit down and move out of the way.

I wasn't very well prepared for the test and was very rattled by what felt to me a weird public shaming. No matter how well I might have been prepared, this stress would have impacted greatly on my performance. However, it was clearly my fault that I did so poorly on the test.

I failed the test, and this ruined my grade that semester in organic chemistry. Both my parents disapproved and scolded me. I suppose they were concerned for my welfare or something like that. I despised Dr. Richter more than ever—not that he knew or cared, of course.

However, the laboratory in organic chemistry was interesting. We synthesized aspirin, oil of wintergreen, and some other easy-to-make compounds. There was some talk of synthesizing putrescine or cadaverine, which is what makes decomposing flesh smell so awful, but Dr. Richter decided against this. Fortunately that year the synthesis of isovaleric acid had been eliminated—the essence of B.O. I was told that in previous years clothes were ruined and that the students were shunned on the bus ride home.

The following year, as a senior, I had priority in choosing a room in the dormitory, and I was able to get a single room. I liked the privacy and the feeling I could hide away.

That year, my favorite uncle, Van, divorced Matt, his wife of many years. Perhaps over the years of marriage her virtues had ceased to hold charm for Van. He had started an affair with his secretary, Sadie Mae, who was brusque, businesslike, aggressive, and had a startlingly full figure. Matt was devastated but moved to a new apartment and tried to pull herself together. Van and Sadie soon moved in together in a new place.

Because of our loyalty to Van, we had all tried to welcome Sadie into the family, even though we much preferred Matt and missed her. But Sadie, through her aggressive insults and emotional hardness and coarseness, alienated all of us.

Van and Sadie remained married until his death after almost forty years of marriage. Sadie will appear again in this narrative.

Bill Holke, a childhood friend, offered Van a position in his company, William A. Smith, which built railroads. This was the premier railroad-building firm in the United States. Uncle Van and his friend Bill eventually bought the company, developed it, and then sold it to the Halliburton Company at a substantial price and profit.

Van's brother Edmund had worked most of his life as a civil engineer for the Union Pacific Railroad. His other brother, Murray, had likewise worked for the Southern Pacific Railroad for a time, and their father, Edmund Henry Doyle, had spent his working career with the Southern Pacific. Railroad building and maintenance had occupied all the males of the family for more than a half century.

After my grandfather E.H. died, my grandmother enjoyed using her free pass for the rest of her life on any routes of the Southern Pacific.

XXXXXXXXXXXXXXXXXXXXXXXXXXXXXXXXXXXXXXXXXXX

During the final college year, all my regular activities continued, with a slightly calmer atmosphere. The classes were mostly interesting and not taxing. I continued to go to the gay bars on a regular basis, often with Fred, who had a car. Oddly, I was not aware of my serious need for love.

A few mild and transitory romances developed. The most promising was with Clifford, an extremely handsome, intelligent, and charming young man three years my senior. He had already finished college and had a car and a good job downtown. Although he lived with his parents, he did not seem to be restricted or controlled by them. Sex was good, and we liked each other, but the relationship never caught fire.

XXXXXXXXXXXXXXXXXXXXXXXXXXXXXXXXXXXXXXXXXXXX

I continued my piano lessons with Mme. Morosoff and occasionally attended concerts. I was excited to hear Arthur Rubinstein play the Tchaikovsky piano concerto with the Houston Symphony. His recordings were magnificent, but I had not seen him play in person before. The piano part of the concerto begins with three crashing chords. The first one was fine, as was the second, but the third was a mass of wrong notes. From then on, even though the performance was grand and expressive, the large number of wrong notes was startling. A debut artist would have been ruined by a performance so inaccurate. Later I heard that sometimes Rubinstein had a seriously off night. It was obvious, in spite of all the wrong notes, that a great artist was performing.

Some years later, my parents bought the concert grand piano he played that evening. The Steinway dealer in Houston sent this wonderful piano to the music hall whenever a major artist appeared in Houston. After the concert, the piano would be taken back to the piano company. The company decided to get a new concert grand and so wanted to sell their old one.

I heard many important concert pianists play a concert on this piano. Among them were Byron Janis, Clifford Curzon, Leonard Pennario, Gina Bachauer, Leon Fleischer, and Rudolph Firkusny. It is one of my treasures and is still a magnificent instrument. I say it already knows how to play: it learned from the masters.

The next year, I heard Rubinstein play an all-Chopin program on this piano, and it was the most beautiful piano recital I have ever heard. His playing was exquisite, breathtaking.

I also heard Vladimir Horowitz perform in Houston on the same piano. His recital was shocking. He started with a Bach-Busoni piece—grand, sonorous, stately, impressive, a beautiful performance. He continued with some Rachmaninoff and Schumann pieces, played possibly a little too fast. As the evening went on, he played faster and faster, and louder, with an increasing number of mistakes. After intermission he played a Liszt group and finished with a Chopin group.

The concluding number, Chopin's great A-flat Polonaise, started at a blinding speed and then got faster. The octave section was a blur, visually and acoustically. The number of mistakes was astonishing. It was as if a gorilla were pounding the keyboard as fast and as loudly as possible.

The last page of the piece was a complete smear, incredibly fast, loud, and almost entirely wrong notes. At the end, Horowitz threw his hands high in the air, burst out in loud laughter, and ran off the stage. Obviously something was wrong. Later that year, he retired from further public performance due to a severe mental illness.

After an absence from the concert platform of twelve years, he resumed public performances in 1965 with a famous Carnegie Hall recital. The tickets were almost impossible to obtain. The day the tickets went on sale, I stood in line from 4 AM until 9 AM, when it was announced that the concert was sold out. I was disappointed not to get a ticket.

Later it became known that his wife, Wanda Toscanini Horowitz, had personally cornered more than half the tickets and had sold them at scalper's prices. There was a small scandal, and her reputation as a dragon-woman was further established.

I didn't hear him play again until years later, in London, at a Royal Command Performance. My friend Bert was with me then. We both recognized his playing was magnificent.

I admired Horowitz for his stunning virtuosity and his ability to make the piano sound orchestral. But I preferred Rubinstein's playing for his floating tone and tremendously expressive and moving presentation of all he played, especially Chopin. No one knows how he produced his glowing, lingering tone—I personally suspect it was a case of telekinesis, that he was mentally causing the piano strings to continue vibrating longer than usual.

In later years, I heard Rubinstein perform perhaps six more times, the last time when he was ninety-two years old and performed two piano concertos with the New York Philharmonic. His last performances were as beautiful as those of seventy years earlier, which of course I knew only from recordings.

My own piano studies were making slow but steady progress under the expert direction of Mme. Morosoff. Some of the pieces I studied with Madame over fifty years ago are still mostly stored in my memory, although I haven't played them for decades.

She twice invited me to visit her home, when she had parties for some of her students and her family too. I didn't realize at the time that I was seeing a pale reflection of Imperial Russia from her family's time in St. Petersburg before the Revolution.

XXXXXXXXXXXXXXXXXXXXXXXXXXXXXXXXXXXXXXXXXX

At Thanksgiving that year, my mother wanted to take a trip to San Antonio and invited me to join her there for a few days, as I had ten days off from school. We stayed at the St. Anthony Hotel, then the best hotel in San Antonio.

One evening after dinner, I went for a walk. San Antonio was ringed by military bases, and many off-duty servicemen came downtown in search of entertainment. Soon I saw a well-built, attractive young man, perhaps two or three years older than I. His excellent body was not much concealed by his tight clothes. Short sleeves revealed his large muscular arms. A handsome face and a blond crew-cut added to his charms. Smiling and loitering, he looked at me and said hello.

"Hi. I'm Tom."

"And I'm John. How ya doin'?"

We began to chat, and it was soon obvious that we both wanted closer contact.

He suggested going down to the River Walk, where there were many secluded corners. As soon as we found a suitably dark nook, we embraced and began to kiss and fondle one another. Tom unzipped his fly and exposed himself. In spite of being highly excited, I had no idea as to how to proceed, being relatively naïve about sex and never having done it standing up in a public place.

"Use your mouth. Give me a blow job," he said. I knelt down and proceeded to satisfy him. I found the whole situation very intense, even though there was no sexual satisfaction for me. Afterward, we talked for a few minutes, but the atmosphere between us had changed.

"I have to go on home," I said.

"Just a minute. Do you have any money?"

"Well, maybe five or six dollars."

He pulled out a knife and opened the blade. "Give me all your money."

Frightened, I handed over the money, and he counted it.

"That's not enough. I should get more than that for letting you blow me. Show me what's in your pockets."

I did, and when he saw there was no more money, he said, "Give me your watch."

"It was a gift, and I'll get in a lot of trouble if I lose it."

"I don't care. Give it to me."

I was reluctant but felt I had no choice. I handed it over, and he started examining the watch. He put his knife away.

"I have an idea. How much more money did you want?"

"Twenty dollars more was what I was looking for."

"I can go back to my hotel. I think I have that much money in my room."

"I want to go to your room with you."

I wasn't sure what he had in mind. Beating me up and then robbing me? A night of intense sex?? Both???

"Oh, no. It's the St. Anthony. They wouldn't let a stranger come in. There would be trouble, maybe a commotion. If I have the money in my room, I'll come back here and meet you in thirty minutes. Then I can give you the money, and you can give me my watch back."

"Okay."

He was taking a chance in agreeing to this arrangement but probably felt he could trust me and that the likelihood I would call the police was minimal. He had nothing much to lose by waiting an hour for my return. I walked the three blocks back to the hotel and found the money in my room. I was very anxious and wasn't sure I should go back to meet Tom again, but I was eager to get my watch back and to forestall questions from my mother about its disappearance.

I walked back to the river and stood on the bridge. Looking down, I saw Tom standing below in the shadows.

"Come on down. We can talk a little."

Despite my premonition of danger, I went down the stairs and joined him in the dark recess.

"Do you have the money?"

"Yes. Do you have my watch?"

I had the money in my right hand; he had the watch in his right hand. We went through the exchange without hesitation or difficulty. He put the money in his pocket, and I put the watch on my wrist.

"Well, thanks," he said. "You're a pretty nice guy." He put his arms around me, pulled me to him, and began to kiss and fondle me. "I really would like it if you gave me another blow job. This time it would be free, just as a favor to you." He again pulled out his equipment and showed a full erection. Dawn was coming; it was just beginning to get light.

The whole experience was unsettling for me, and I wanted to get away from the scene, but I was afraid if I turned down his "offer" that he would get angry and rob me again. I remembered his big knife.

"I would like that, but we have to do it fast. I have to be back at the hotel in a couple of minutes," I lied. And so I completed the act, gave him a long hug, and said goodbye.

He said, "Would you like to get together again tonight? Here? This time I want you to have a good time too."

"I'm sorry—I'm going back to Houston today. Good luck to you. Bye-bye." In spite of what had happened, I felt he was basically an affectionate and decent person, and he was certainly in fine physical shape. If I had been staying on in San Antonio, I might have agreed to see him again.

"Bye," he said. There was a dismal expression on his handsome face.

Back in the hotel, I was trembling as I went to bed.

The next morning I had breakfast with my mother. Afterward, she wanted to take a stroll, as San Antonio is a scenic and interesting city. We went to visit the Alamo, and then Mother wanted to take a walk by the river. The San Antonio River is about twenty feet below street level and has been beautifully landscaped, with a sidewalk on each bank, arching bridges over the river, and stairs leading to the street.

As we walked past the nook where I had been adventuring a few hours earlier, I exhaled a sigh and checked my wristwatch. After lunch we took a drive to Breckenridge Park to visit the Reptile Garden, where on Sundays rattlesnakes were killed, cornmeal-breaded, fried, and passed around to the audience to sample.

Thinking over the experience with Tom later, I felt he was confused about his role, basically gay, but perhaps he had not accepted his sexual orientation yet. Obviously he wanted the money, the male sex, and an excuse for his own behavior. Probably he was trying to be affectionate to another man as much as he could permit himself. I couldn't judge how much danger I was in with him but thought if I had tried to resist or had become aggressive, a fight or a knifing might have occurred.

My survival was connected to a careful effort not to escalate the situation. Tom appeared in better shape and much stronger than I. In addition, I was completely aware that I had enjoyed the situation, that the danger and unpredictability were spice for the occasion. Danger did not become something I tried to search out, but if it were attached to a situation I wanted, or if it arose in the course of some action, then I tried to make the best of it.

After that, whenever I visited San Antonio, I thought of this handsome mixed-up stud and wondered if I would encounter him again. I wondered what life might hold for him. I hope he has been happy and that he has made others happy too, which I intuitively suspected was part of his nature.

XXXXXXXXXXXXXXXXXXXXXXXXXXXXXXXXXXXXXXXXXXX

On returning to Rice after Thanksgiving, it was time to begin the application process for medical school admission.

My father's business had greatly prospered and expanded and now had offices across the Gulf Coast, in California, in Venezuela, and Mexico, and did some work in the Philippines, Norway, and England. Although the partners objected to moving the headquarters from McAllen to Houston, they realized my father's work would be more effective if it were based in Houston, a central location. But they insisted that the books, bank accounts, and company headquarters should remain in McAllen under their control and watchful eyes. They also refused to pay for the purchase and construction of the new Houston office. My father bought the land and paid for the new building himself. Later he charged the company a reasonable monthly rental.

He parked a small trailer on the property and used it for his personal office and drafting studio. He drew plans for his new inventions and improvements there. Years later, on the day he died, his partners changed the locks on his little studio, and I was never permitted access to it.

I have always wondered what he might have been working on, whether it might have been valuable, and how much I might have been cheated by the partners. Perhaps not at all—perhaps a great deal.

My parents had been planning to move to Houston in the near future and were talking of putting their McAllen house on the market. I realized that if they moved to Houston, I would be forced to live at home, that my mother would increase her tyrannical and drunken behavior, and I would not be able to stand up under her abuse.

My father would have been absolutely no help, as he would have preferred for me to disappear one way or another, whatever the reason.

MMMMMMMMMMMMMMMMMMMMMMMMMMMMMMMMMM

There was constant conversation among the premedical students as to where to apply to medical schools. There was more demand than there were places available in the med schools, so many students had to go to foreign schools for their training.

The Second World War had ended in the summer of 1945, and many of the returning veterans wanted to pursue medical training. They were somewhat older than my generation of students and much more studious, hardworking, and serious too, having been in a war. They also had government scholarships to help them continue their education. The competition was strenuous and intense.

By 1954, when I graduated from Rice, most of the veterans had already moved ahead, leaving the field more or less clear for us youngsters. All the students from the previous two classes at Rice had found places in U.S. medical schools.

There were two excellent schools close by, Baylor in Houston and the University of Texas in Galveston, fifty miles from Houston. My parents had warned me they couldn't afford to send me away to medical school, but perhaps Baylor or Galveston would be possible if I could live cheaply at home. Most of my fellow Rice students applied to these two schools, and so did I.

Completely disregarding my parents' warnings, I also applied to Tulane in New Orleans, the University of Pennsylvania in Philadelphia, Cornell in New York City, and Harvard in Boston. I did not really know much about any of these schools, but perhaps Harvard was the best known. The application process was said to be difficult. It was a common occurrence for a student to apply to many medical schools and receive no acceptances.

I sent off six sets of my transcripts to the various schools, and soon the personal interviews began. The high academic standing of Rice and my good grades were in my favor. Also, I learned later that many of the schools found it desirable to have students from other parts of the country.

Through the late winter and early spring the replies came in. I was accepted at Baylor, the University of Texas at Galveston, Tulane in New Orleans, the University of Pennsylvania in Philadelphia, and Cornell in New York City. Baylor was the least desirable to me, closely followed by Galveston, due entirely to the dreadful prospect of having to live at home.

Remembering my New Orleans adventures of the previous summer, I decided that Tulane, which was in the center of New Orleans, had too many close-by temptations and that I might not be able to study enough to get through what was always described as a tough course.

However, Paul, my blazing-hot erotic contact of last summer, lived in New Orleans, and he seemed a big plus. But I might not survive in the overheated sexual and alcoholic carnival of New Orleans.

I was pleased with the acceptances from Philadelphia and New York. The last school to reply was Harvard, and I was disappointed to be rejected there, as it had been my first choice because of its fine reputation.

All the accepting institutions wanted a prompt reply. My mother was again adamant that they could not afford to send me away. My father was present at this discussion; he looked on indifferently but said nothing. In those days, there was very little financial aid available, no student loans, and all the medical schools advised against tying to attend school and work at the same time.

I thought again about applying for a Fulbright scholarship, or accepting Dr. Louis's fine offer to work toward an MA in German, or to apply to Juilliard, as my love for music and the piano had grown very strong, but I felt shadowed and threatened by my father's attitude and decided to proceed on to medical school as soon as possible. He reinforced his viewpoint by repeating his warning again just before graduation, that in case of any deviation from a straight-ahead course on my part, he would do nothing further to help me, again giving me the impression he would be helping me, when, in fact, he hadn't given me any help since I was sixteen. What a fake!

I wrote to both the University of Pennsylvania and to Cornell to explain that I would like to attend but was constrained by severe financial problems. I asked them if they had any advice for me. A week later, I received a sorry/decline letter from the University of Pennsylvania, inviting me to apply again next year if my financial situation improved. I was dejected and felt the prospect of escaping from home was slipping away.

Two days later I received a letter from Cornell, informing me that I had been awarded a thousand-dollar scholarship for my first year there, given by the Joseph Collins Foundation of New York. This was more than adequate to pay the first-year tuition and fees, with some funds left over for housing, books, clothes, and food. I found out later that this was the only scholarship awarded to an entering student. It was a significant honor.

Although my mother did not want me to leave home, she knew how much I wanted to go east to school. She didn't realize of course that I was terrified by the prospect of living at home. She was pleased that I had been accepted at such a prestigious school as Cornell, and the scholarship award did sway her, so she gave a grudging assent to my going there.

In fairness to my mother, I now realize that her life was constricted and becoming emptier, due to her alcoholism, as well as her increasing age, and the natural result of years of misanthropy and self-imposed social isolation. She looked to my continuing presence to help relieve her burden of melancholy and loneliness. I felt very sorry for her sadness.

But I knew I couldn't survive the lethal situation of living at home. If I were going to continue living, I would have to escape my mother's demands. I am convinced that staying at home would have led to my suicide.

Unbeknownst to me, my father's business had become quite profitable by then, and my mother knew that she could visit me in New York as often as she chose, so our separation was not so drastic as she had previously feared. I was shocked twelve years later, after both my parents had died, to examine their bank accounts and to find that they both had an ample income, much more than enough to send me to Cornell. The talk about not being able to afford to send me to school was just an excuse to try to keep me at home, firmly tied to Mother's apron chains.

Their plans for moving to Houston were definite. I felt I was escaping just ahead of an advancing army. The balance of the senior year was relatively carefree. There were no disappointed loves, no hallucinations, no stickups with knives. My friends and I knew we were existing in a sort of twilight condition, but finally, in early June, graduation day arrived.

The late afternoon ceremony was held outdoors in front of the administration building at Rice. There were about four hundred undergraduate and fifty graduate students receiving degrees. Elgar's *Pomp and Circumstance* was played, and I felt a lump in my throat. There were some speeches, and then the students were all called, one by one, to receive their degrees. My name was read out as graduating "with honors in philosophy," and I walked across the platform, shook hands with William Vermillion Houston, the President of Rice, and received the coveted B.A. degree.

Graduation from Rice Institute, Houston, 1954

My parents, my grandmother, and my uncle Van and his new wife, Sadie, attended the ceremony. Everyone was pleasant and polite, and we all went out to dinner afterward. My father looked less angry and sullen than usual. He even gave me a slight smile after the ceremony, perhaps only for public appearances.

My parents gave me a beautiful new wristwatch for a graduation present. Before I went to bed that night, I had a moment of anxiety and disorientation. I realized that a major chapter of my life was closing, and a more adult life, with unknown responsibilities, stresses, and dangers, was waiting for me. But

I wanted to go forward and had no inclination to try to delay my life or turn back in any way.

The day after graduation Dr. Louis called me to repeat his kind offer to stay on at Rice in the graduate department to work on an MA in German. I was very pleased and thanked him sincerely, but I politely declined and said my family was pressing me to continue straight on to medical school and that I didn't feel I could evade their pressure, which was the truth. He knew I had been awarded a scholarship to go to Cornell, and he wished me good luck in my career.

Dr. RATsanoff, head of the philosophy department and my major professor, had never inquired about my plans, even though I was one of only three students majoring in philosophy. I didn't know whether in his arrogance he saw almost everyone as so inferior to himself that they were not deserving of even minimal politeness, if he specifically didn't like me, or both.

There was no hint that I would be welcome to stay on at Rice to work on an MA in philosophy. I had enjoyed my studies in philosophy, but Dr. RATsanoff was far too intimidating for me. I didn't consider even for a moment staying on to study philosophy under him. "The slime that oozed out of Sparta," indeed!! God protect us from such bellicose and learned bigots.

After graduation, I continued to live in the Rice dormitory for the rest of the summer. I found a pleasant job typing surgical reports in the record room at Hermann Hospital, one of the main Houston hospitals, which was just a ten-minute walk across Main Street from the Rice campus.

I had become a speed typist in high school and found that with the Dictaphone earphones on, I could short-circuit my consciousness. That is, I could doze, and the reports would flow automatically through my ears to my brain and on to my fingers. If I were stumped by a difficult passage, the other three secretary-typists were very kind and helped me. I was pleased to learn some of the medical language. And besides, the job kept me from having to go back to McAllen for another summer working in my father's machine shop or to the Louisiana swamps to work in his oil field testing business.

XXXXXXXXXXXXXXXXXXXXXXXXXXXXXXXXXXXXXXXXXXXX

Summer life in the dormitory was relaxed and pleasant. A number of my more interesting classmates were staying around until they left for various graduate schools in the fall. We got together for informal talks, sometimes went together across the street to the medical center to have dinner, went to the movies, and shared a sense of adventure and anticipation of what the next year would hold for all of us.

I had been interested in the decadent artistic movements of the turn of the nineteenth and twentieth centuries. I had read Oscar Wilde, Algernon Swinburne, Sacher-Masoch, Arthur Schnitzler, Marie Corelli, Bulwer-Lytton, and Madame Blavatsky, and had looked at the Yellow Book, the drawings of Aubrey Beardsley, and the paintings of the Pre-Raphaelites.

Trying in my modest way to be more decadent myself, I kept a bottle of sloe gin in my room and every morning before going to work drank about two ounces of the syrupy stuff. I didn't like the taste or the consistency much but persisted anyway, thinking that to become dissipated, one had to be resolute. The facts that I was on a relatively straitlaced career path and living a rather straightlaced life were only slight obstacles.

The Hermann Park zoo was across the street from the Rice campus, and I enjoyed hearing the lions and elephants roaring at night. I wondered what they were thinking of and if they enjoyed their lives. Sometimes in the daytime I would stroll over to the zoo and visit some of the animals, particularly Hugo the gorilla, whom I had known earlier in his life. He always looked sad, and I reflected that it seemed unlikely for any creature, including me, to have a happy life.

His owners had acquired him in Africa when he was an orphaned infant. They lived around the corner from my grandmother and welcomed visits from the neighbors. One evening I went to see Hugo. The owners brought him out dressed in a diaper. Crawling on the floor, he was quite docile and looked at me with as much interest as I had in looking at him. He climbed into my lap for a few minutes. Even though he was only a young child, he was quite large and probably very strong.

I was a little afraid of him but thrilled that I lived so close to such an exotic being. After that, whenever I passed Hugo's house, especially at night, I was slightly apprehensive when I had to go through the narrow passage between the tall oleander bushes, just right for a gorilla to hide in before he pounced on some innocent passer-by, like me. I thought of Edgar Allan Poe's "The Murders in the Rue Morgue," which features a homicidal gorilla.

A few more years of Hugo's life passed uneventfully, but then one day his owners took him for a ride to the grocery store, a common event for him. He was used to going for rides in the car and was said to enjoy them. But they left him alone in the car while they went in to do their shopping. The window was down slightly, and some unlucky woman with extremely poor judgment approached the car and stuck her arm in through the window to pet Hugo. He grabbed her arm, pulled on it, and gave her a nasty bite.

Of course, with his strength, he could have pulled her arm off if he had wanted, so perhaps he was just "playing." He was a Houston celebrity, and there were many articles in the newspaper about him, what to do with him, and where he should live. Perhaps he was too dangerous to remain at home.

It was decided that he should live in the zoo. He was upset, his owners were upset, the neighbors were upset, and the whole city knew every detail. After he went to the zoo and was installed in a nice large cage, he became depressed, moping about and eating poorly. He was in mourning.

His owners arranged to go, usually one at a time, to sit with him in his cage for a few hours every day. They could be seen sitting in rocking chairs and reading (the owners, that is). This cheered Hugo up somewhat. Many years passed, his owners died, and Hugo mourned. He continued living in his zoo cage until he died only a few years ago, having lived about forty years. A sad story.

XXXXXXXXXXXXXXXXXXXXXXXXXXXXXXXXXXXXXXXXXXXX

Freddy was still in Houston for the summer before leaving for graduate studies at the University of Oregon in the fall. We went to the gay bars several times a week. This was an idle pursuit, as nothing of interest happened. No sex, no romance, no new friends. All was in suspension.

We went to Hermann Park for the open-air summer concerts, sitting on the grass and listening to the Houston Symphony. One evening a more or less unknown young pianist played Rachmaninoff's "Rhapsody on a Theme of Paganini," and I realized that the sixteen-year-old was already a fine artist. I think it was his debut playing with an orchestra. He was Van Cliburn, and this was years before he won the Tchaikovsky Prize in Moscow and became famous.

Our little group of students was excited about the prospect of going on to further and different studies, but we were all apprehensive too, like tadpoles in a mud puddle which was drying up. I assumed we would all remain in contact by letter and by visits during school vacations, and this was partially correct, at least for the first few years.

At the end of the summer, Bill Agosta, one of the brightest students in my graduating class, drove his own car to Harvard to start a graduate degree in chemistry, and he invited me to ride with him.

When we reached New York, I was shocked that so many of the locals were walking around at high speed in the middle of the street, jaywalking in all directions. *Lawless and improper*, I thought, *not at all like Houston*.

Cornell University Medical College was located at Sixty-Ninth Street and York Avenue, a good east-side New York neighborhood. Olin Hall, the brand new school dormitory, was just across York Avenue from the medical school. I thought the buildings in the neighborhood looked soiled and grimy and assumed I was in a dangerous slum. I feared Cornell had turned out to be a slum school, whatever that meant.

I felt I had made a mistake in coming to Cornell and would have to transfer elsewhere as soon as possible, to a more decent place, although it would probably take at least a year. It was true the neighborhood didn't look brand new and shiny like Houston, but otherwise my assessment was totally wrong, as I shortly discovered.

Bill let me and my suitcases out at Olin Hall and drove off to his own new life at Harvard. We had been friendly classmates at Rice, but not close, and I never heard from him or saw him again, but neither did I make any efforts to contact him other than a ritual thank you letter for driving me to New York.

The casual nature of many of the relationships of youth seemed only natural at the time. I wish I had known better, as fine and intelligent people do not continue to arrive in endless supply all through life. I think none of us knew this.

I moved into Olin Hall, unpacked my suitcases, took a little walk in my new "slum" neighborhood, went to bed, and had a good night's sleep. The next day I walked across the street to start the registration process.

By persistence and good luck I had survived grammar school, high school, college, McAllen, and Houston, and now looked forward to a life with perhaps fewer restrictions and fears. I wanted to learn medicine and be of use to my fellow man. And I still hoped to find love.

Medical School—Beginning

The First Year, 1954–1955

My self-confidence had not improved much during my college years. I was still timid and reluctant to socialize with others or even speak to them. But in the excitement of starting a new life, the students all looked one another over and began to get acquainted, to exchange information about our new neighborhood, and to speculate about our coming classes. I was anxious and felt somewhat lost—new school, new big city. I knew no one in New York and no one in the medical school except for a fellow student from Texas.

He was also enrolled in the freshman class at Cornell, but he was no help to me, or I to him. We had taken different classes in college and did not socialize there but had known each other only enough to say hello in passing. I learned later that he told a number of the other medical students that I was a notorious homosexual in college, perhaps assuming they would be as homophobic as he was. He was actually giving me credit for more flair than I possessed. He kept a haughty and contemptuous attitude through the four years of medical school. Tall, good-looking, and something of a jock, he assumed an easy friendliness with some selected other students, but as the four years passed, he lost most of these presumed friends.

I saw him at the fiftieth reunion of our graduating class, and the relationship was only slightly warmer than before.

Olin Hall, a nine-story building, had been completed just a few weeks before we arrived. It was a modern, comfortable, pleasant place to live. Every student had his own room, adequately large, simply and functionally furnished. Each pair of rooms connected through a common shared bathroom, so we all had a "roommate."

I soon met my roommate, Dick Roberts, from Huntington on Long Island. He was a tall, blond, good-looking, pleasant man. Intelligent, low-key, hardworking, conscientious, friendly, and sociable, he was well-liked by most of our classmates. If he had heard the rumors about me, he didn't seem to be affected by them. We soon became friends and have remained so for over fifty years.

We explored the hospital cafeterias at mealtimes and talked some about our backgrounds and interests. Dick eventually came to view me as somewhat unusual in my interests and activities, slightly bizarre, but amusing, friendly, and nonthreatening. He did not seem anxious about starting medical school, but I assume it must have been at least somewhat stressful for him, as it was for the rest of us. Dick and I hung together for moral support during the beginning days.

The first day of school we found our way to various classrooms and amphitheaters. We met our new teachers and heard what we could expect in our courses and what was expected of us.

At the first biochemistry class several teachers in white coats stood at the front of the room. One of the professors, a pompous, middle-aged man, began to strut as he told us what we would learn in his course. A fellow student raised his hand and asked the professor his name. He looked startled, his face turned red, and he began to speak loudly. Angry and scolding, he said, "Before you come to a class, young man, you should know who your teacher is." Finally he told us his name: Dr. Vincent du Vigneaud. It was expected that he would win the Nobel Prize the next year, which he did. He was incensed that we did not know his name, even though none of us had ever seen him before. Later I learned that he was full of himself to the bursting point and it was better to avoid contact with him if possible.

We had a lecture from the cordial and welcoming dean of students, who told us that we were now on our own in the big city, with a variety of temptations and resources, and he hoped we would not get ourselves into trouble, which was good advice.

Next was anatomy class. One of the professors modestly and politely introduced himself as Dr. George Papanicolau, soon to be famous for his test for cervical or uterine cancer, which has since saved many lives. He spoke to us briefly. Then our chief anatomy teacher began to talk. A gurney was rolled in with a body covered by a sheet. He pulled the sheet back, and there was our first cadaver.

The class was totally silent as the teacher picked up a scalpel. There was a quiet collective sigh as he made the first cut in the cadaver and began to demonstrate dissection. We had all dissected worms, catfish, dogfish, and frogs in college, but this was *the real thing*. I felt queasy and looked around at the blanched faces of my classmates.

Later, in anatomy lab, Dick and I paired off to be dissection partners. We were introduced to our cadaver, an elderly man, who waited for us on a table in the dissection room. His head, hands, feet, and genitalia were wrapped in

158

Vaseline gauze. We named him Yorick. The three of us would be together for the entire school year.

I felt pleased and proud of myself for surviving the beginning of medical school. My anxiety level was high and stayed that way for many months.

XXXXXXXXXXXXXXXXXXXXXXXXXXXXXXXXXXXXXXXXXXXXX

Our class had ninety-six students, almost all of whom graduated together four years later. The school had been accused of discrimination in a national magazine some years before. Now the composition of each class was identical: one third of the students were Jewish, one third Catholic, and one third Protestant. There were five women and one black student in each class.

From my point of view, the students were divided into those from New York and those from other places. The New York students, perhaps because they had faced such cutthroat competition in college, were secretive and very unhelpful. For instance, if you missed a class, the New York students would not lend their class notes or otherwise tell what had been discussed in class. The students from other parts of the East Coast were not much better. As I was still quite shy, I did not readily turn to others for help if I could avoid it. Sometimes I preferred to miss out on something rather than ask for help.

The students from the South, the Midwest, and the West were usually helpful. I had not realized until then how refreshingly polite, cordial, helpful, and open the students at Rice had been.

There were about 1,100 instructors for the approximately 400 regular students and 50 graduate or other special students. We encountered most of the instructors once or twice, when they lectured on their special subjects; some of them we never saw. The professors and department heads were quite active in lecturing and teaching, and most were gracious and generous with their knowledge.

There were a few notable exceptions, vicious prima donnas who humiliated and belittled their students. None of these were notable in their fields, with the exception of Dr. du Vigneaud, who was as brilliantly talented in his research as he was disagreeable.

The first year courses covered basic sciences: anatomy, histology, biochemistry, physiology, embryology, neuroanatomy, and bacteriology. Each instructor was a specialist in his own field, and we were expected to have a burning interest in every subject, no matter how minute and specialized. This was of course not possible, but some of us could fake it well enough to get a good grade.

There was an enormous amount of memorization required. Some of the material was very specific and detailed, such as how to concoct the culture media used to grow various types of bacteria. I soon realized that I was never going to need to know these recipes by memory, and the same for a good deal of the other information we were required to cram into our minds. Everything presented was necessary for one or another of the numerous branches of medicine, but no student would need more than a small fraction of the memorized material pertinent to his own chosen field.

It seemed to me that this rote memorization was a big waste of time, like having to memorize the telephone directory before being permitted to make a telephone call. Coming from a liberal arts background, where reading and then evaluating information was the main feature of education, this attention to irrelevant and unusable details seemed not only a waste of time, but boring too.

By midway through the first semester, I was thinking of specializing in either psychiatry or dermatology and was inclining away from surgery, pediatrics, obstetrics, or other specialties.

XXXXXXXXXXXXXXXXXXXXXXXXXXXXXXXXXXXXXXXXXXX

Our dissection of Yorick, our cadaver, continued for the entire school year. After the end of the year, the remaining parts of Yorick were gathered up and sent off for a decent burial. It was in the anatomy lab, trying to find and demonstrate tiny details of anatomy, that we all became acquainted, generally working closely together. Even the New York students eventually became a little more helpful and freer with their information.

In biochemistry lab we used up an enormous number of little animals—rabbits, cats, mice, and others—in various experiments. We always knew the expected outcome of the "experiment," so the lives of our terrified little victims were wasted. I felt very sad and guilty about taking part in this cruelty, but there was no avoiding it if I wanted to get my MD.

I had had expectations of being prepared for humanitarian work, but this—memorizing masses of useless information and torturing little animals needlessly—was not what I had been expecting.

I didn't consider withdrawing from school or turning to some other career. I just put my head down, put one foot in front of the other, and kept going one day at a time. This had been my principle in past difficult situations: don't think of the future or of the goal, just think of doing the work required today and try to get through the day. The next day, do the same. Try not to make enemies and try not to burn your bridges in anger or out of spite. Know that one day, some day, the unpleasantness will be at an end.

XXXXXXXXXXXXXXXXXXXXXXXXXXXXXXXXXXXXXXXXXXX

As the year progressed, I heard from some of my friends in Houston about the gay bars in New York. There were several on Third Avenue in the fifties, about a twenty-minute walk from the school. The famous "bird circuit" of gay bars still existed, so-called because they had names like "The Blue Parrot," "Faison d'Or," and other bird names. I began to explore them, going in about 9 PM for a couple of beers, sometimes chatting a little with other customers.

One evening about three months into the first term, two men in the Lodge, one of my favorite bars, suddenly said to me, "Have we seen you at Cornell Medical School?" I was terrified, somehow thinking they were threatening me and that I might get expelled. I replied, "No. I don't think so," and immediately left the bar.

A week later, I encountered them again in the same bar, the Lodge, and they smiled and said, "No need to be afraid of us. We're connected with Cornell ourselves." I found out that Jack was a senior, and the other man, Pete, his lover, had graduated the year before and was now an intern at a hospital in New York. They lived together in a pleasant apartment not far from the medical school. They introduced me to the three other gay senior students, a serious bunch with twinkling eyes.

They told another of their gay friends, a sophomore at the medical school, to keep an eye out for me. He eventually introduced himself, and we soon became friends. His name was Emery Hetrick, and he, with his lover, Damian Martin, later founded the Hetrick-Martin Foundation and the Harvey Milk School for gay students, who for a variety of mostly homophobic reasons could not attend ordinary public schools. Emery was one of my closest friends in medical school. When he graduated, our lives went separate ways, and we didn't see much of one another, although whenever we were in contact it was as cordial as ever.

I asked Esther Lee Blakemore, my piano teacher in McAllen, whether she knew anyone in New York with whom I could study. She recommended her friend Bernice Frost, who was an eminent pedagogue, having written numerous books of instruction, mostly for children. I played for Miss Frost at her studio in Steinway Hall on Fifty-Seventh Street. She accepted me as a student, and I had weekly lessons until I graduated from medical school, except for times when I was on duty and could not leave the school or when she or I were out of town.

Olin Hall had a new Steinway grand piano in the student lounge, which was sometimes free for me to use, and also a new very good Steinway upright in a soundproof practice room in the basement. I could practice late at night or very early in the morning without disturbing anyone. My time at the piano helped sustain me psychologically and spiritually, and Miss Frost was a fine teacher and a gracious and positive influence.

Olin Hall was under the care of a group of housekeepers, all of whom were Russian émigrés. One of them was said to have been a countess; perhaps it was so. The housekeeper for my room, Madame Kudrina, was a middle-aged, dignified, strong, and distinguished-looking woman. Eventually we got acquainted. When she found out I was studying the piano, we had some interesting talks about music.

She told me she was a graduate in piano from the conservatory in Kiev, where she had studied with the eminent pianist and teacher Felix Blumenfeld and was a fellow student of Vladimir Horowitz. She never said what had happened to her between then and now, but I assume there were troubles arising from the post-revolutionary turmoil in Russia and also World War II.

I asked her to play for me, and she agreed. We went down to the music room in the basement. She said she did not have a piano currently and was very out of practice. We took some of my sheet music with us. She looked through the music and suddenly exclaimed, "Oh, I used to play this piece." She had chosen Scriabin's *Poeme Satanique*, an extremely difficult concert piece. *Uh-oh*, I thought.

Propping the score on the music rack, she played a few scales and arpeggios and then began playing the Scriabin. Her performance was very impressive, passionate, technically secure, and beautifully phrased. She was a true artist. I was stunned. She smiled and asked me to play something. I played a Schubert Impromptu, and she graciously praised my performance.

"How sad," I thought, "for an artist like Mme. Kudrina to have to make beds in a school dormitory." Perhaps I was wrong, considering all that she might have been through.

Later that year, Walter Gieseking, the great German pianist, was returning to America for his first performance after World War II. I invited Mme. Kudrina to go to his Carnegie Hall concert as my guest. She was an imposing figure when dressed for the concert: very erect, dressed all in black, her white hair pulled back severely, with a strand of pearls reaching below her waist, and a long black onyx cigarette holder. She remarked, "The last time I heard him was in Berlin before the war. He still grunts too much when he plays."

Twice she invited Emery Hetrick and me to Russian Easter parties at her family's apartment downtown. The guests were all Russian émigrés, including the countess of course, and it was a festive occasion. Mme. Kudrina had made a *paschka*, a traditional Russian Easter dessert. It was so delicious I asked for the recipe, which she gave me.

I did not notice the coincidence of becoming connected and attached to Russian émigrés both at Rice and at Cornell until later.

One of the pleasures of living in New York is to sample the enormous amount of music and theater available. I went about twice a month to a recital or concert, to the opera or the theater. I heard many of the great artists of the time.

With my parents I heard "Lucia de Lammermoor" at the Metropolitan Opera three times in one season: the first time with Lily Pons in her farewell season of singing—an exciting but seemingly precarious performance, as she was tiny, frail, and getting old. The next time was with Maria Callas, who was at the height of her career and could sing beautifully while lying head downward on a staircase in the "Mad Scene." The third Lucia was Joan Sutherland, her debut year at the Metropolitan Opera. Her performance was spectacular, and the audience went wild.

XXXXXXXXXXXXXXXXXXXXXXXXXXXXXXXXXXXXXXXXXXXXXXX

As for my studies, some subjects were more interesting than others. I found neuroanatomy a boring course, mostly memorizing tracts of nerves inside the central nervous system and spinal cord. These tracts were generally indistinguishable to the eye; that is, it was required to memorize the location of these numerous structures, all of which looked like strands of spaghetti to me. I had not been diligent in my homework, although I attended all the classes and paid attention. The final exam in the spring seemed a little difficult, but I assumed I had done okay.

Two days later the professor called me in. "This is the worst final exam I have ever seen. Obviously there must have been something wrong. If you would like, you can repeat the exam in the fall, before school starts, or you can repeat the course next year. Which do you prefer?" I nearly fainted and thought this might be the end of my medical school career. I opted for repeating the exam before the fall term started.

All summer I read the neuroanatomy text over and over, committing essentially the whole book to memory. I was super-prepared. Just before the start of the fall term, I went to the professor's office; he gave me a test form and sat me down in the corner to complete the test. I knew every question cold. The professor said later, "Well, I knew something was wrong and you needed another chance. This is one of the best exams I have ever seen." He gave me an A plus on the test and a passing grade on the course as a whole.

The professor was right: there was something wrong with me, but neither he nor I had spotted exactly what it was. The problem would remain undiagnosed for many years.

XX

Summer Job—Hermann Hospital Again

Hermann Hospital in Houston welcomed me back to a summer job in the record room transcribing dictated surgical reports. I was able to rent a room in the Rice dormitory again and looked forward to a repeat of the previous summer's pleasant experience. Although the form was similar, the content was not. Many of my classmates were gone. Fred was attending graduate school at the University of Oregon. Many of my gay Houston friends from last summer had drifted away. The summer was pleasant enough but somehow felt thin, like a pillow which had lost half its feathers. I paid many visits to my grandmother, who was always very glad to see me. I regret that I did not realize more clearly what a treasure she was to me.

At every age and stage of life, we should try to recognize and appreciate what is valuable to us and not take for granted and dismiss the value of our treasures, which do not always dazzle us with flashing tinsel. Sometimes we do not recognize what we have or that some treasures do not last forever. This was unfortunately my situation.

XXXXXXXXXXXXXXXXXXXXXXXXXXXXXXXXXXXXXXXXXX

Medical School: The Second Year, 1955–1956

The second year at medical school was of varying interest. Emery Hetrick and I had become close friends, and we decided to be suitemates. I felt the support of another gay classmate was important. I regretted telling Dick that I was not going to be his roommate this year, but I think he soon forgave me.

New York continued to be an exciting place for me, certainly more than McAllen or even Houston could ever hope to be. I had heard that the finest restaurant in New York was the Chambord, on Third Avenue at Forty-Ninth Street. Saving my pocket change for a year, I felt sure I now had enough money to dine there, even though it was very expensive. I asked Emery to go with me as my guest. At the restaurant, a moderate-sized room, the tables were beautifully set with linens, silver, and crystal, with large floral arrangements throughout, and there was a formal French menu. Emery and I were able to pick out some recognizable items. The food was delicious.

Looking to my right, I recognized a famous profile—it was Gloria Swanson, the silent movie star. This was before her comeback in *Sunset Boulevard*. Her dinner companion was a distinguished-looking gentleman, and they were having an intense, serious conversation. She noticed me looking at her, and she turned and gave me a charming smile. I was thrilled. A real movie star sitting next to me!!

Later in the year I invited Dick Roberts to be my guest at another Chambord dinner, which was equal to the first, except there was no Gloria Swanson the second time.

In September of 1955 one of the new freshmen, Alden, and I spotted each other with the instant mutual recognition that we were both gay, although we were both as far back in the closet as we could manage, as was prudent in those days and in that situation. I told Emery, and he confirmed that he had the same reaction to Alden.

Alden was handsome, six feet two, well-built, with good posture and dark hair and eyes, looking something like Sean Connery. He was intelligent and hardworking, eventually graduating first in his class. We became great friends and remained so for years, eventually sharing a professional office in New York and living as close neighbors in Connecticut.

Alden Whitney, 1956

There was never any sexual contact between us, which made the relationship easier and more pleasant. When he had problems, I was always attentive and solicitous and tried to be helpful. Eventually he developed a pattern of treating me respectfully when my finances were doing well and dismissively whenever I had financial stress.

XX

The classwork that year was as hard as ever, with much memorization. I continued going to the gay bars and had several small, short-lived, mild affairs which grew out of pleasant sexual contacts. Again I thoughtlessly dismissed relationships, and I was unaware of this at the time. Would I never learn?

As the school year drew to a close, one of my favorite classmates, Dick Evans, and I landed summer jobs working for Dr. Peter Regan in the psychiatry department, helping him with his research into serotonin metabolism. He was doing some of the first work in the field of serotonin reuptake in the brain and its relationship to mood disorders.

As part of the research, we had to obtain twenty-four-hour urine samples from some of the inpatients in the Payne Whitney Clinic, the psychiatric hospital attached to the medical center. This was my first contact with patients in a psychiatric hospital, and I was very interested to interview them for this project. They all seemed curious about the project and were willingly cooperative. The staff always smiled when they saw us carting the gallon jugs of urine down to the lab for our research.

Dr. Regan was an inspiring teacher, a brilliant researcher, insightful, articulate, and patient in making sure his students understood what he was teaching. He was very kind and encouraging, and Dick and I both subsequently became psychiatrists, partially due to his influence.

At the end of the second year at Cornell, we were all promoted to the third year, starting in the fall. I was delighted, as I never took any promotion for granted.

I was halfway through medical school!!!

But my chronic feeling of inadequacy and lack of self-esteem continued as strong as ever.

XXXXXXXXXXXXXXXXXXXXXXXXXXXXXXXXXXXXXXXXXX

The Lecture

Alden had philosophical and religious bents. He had considered entering the priesthood and yearned to live at the foot of the cross. Having developed a keen interest in wearing ecclesiastical drag, he once commented that he had heard the call of the costumes some years before he heard God's call to the priesthood, as he put it. Some years after finishing medical school, he enrolled in Yale Divinity School. Falsely pleading lack of funds, he persuaded me to foot the bill for this three-year course. He graduated and was ordained an Episcopal priest.

After finishing his theological training, he worked in a hospital as a priest as well as a psychiatrist and was active in one of the local churches. He told me an odd story about his first day as a physician pastor in the hospital:

An elderly woman wanted to have confession and communion, so Alden was called to her bedside.

"Who are you?" she asked.

"I'm Father Alden. I'm here to give you confession and communion."

"Thank you, Father. Bless you, Father."

After the rituals were finished, the woman lay back peacefully on her pillows with a benign smile. She appeared to be dozing. After a few minutes, she opened one eye and looked at Alden.

"Now get the hell out of here," she barked.

XXXXXXXXXXXXXXXXXXXXXXXXXXXXXXXXXXXXXXXXXX

Alden became interested in taking flying lessons. I joked that he knew how to manage on Earth, how to manage in heaven, and how to fly between the two. He didn't smile.

He looked wonderful in his ornate clerical outfits made of velvet, silk, lace, and other rich fabrics, which he cared for lovingly at home. He enjoyed ironing while listening to opera and then modeling the costumes inside the house, twirling about for guests, especially after some martinis. Sometimes this led to a dialogue of the sodomites. He bought a secondhand chasuble for a thousand dollars—heavy silk elaborately embroidered and set with stones—quite beautiful, a triumph of ecclesiastical sartorial artwork.

Eventually he grew a long grayish white beard, and when he wore his black velvet robes covered with a snowy white lace surplice (lovingly ironed) and a long golden chain with a cross, he looked like a medieval Russian saint—holy and very impressive. He approved of the impression he made.

I sometimes went with him on his shopping rounds of the ecclesiastical garment emporiums in Rome, which had fine selections of priestly outfits, including undergarments and socks, offered for sale to the public. I was shown a most attractive cardinal's outfit for myself. "Just right for you," the salesman said. Perhaps they had a sideline of furnishing ecclesiastical costumes to lay persons. But I was not much interested, and besides, it was quite expensive. Sometimes I have regretted not buying this interesting costume. Alden wanted very much to own a papal outfit, including the adorable embroidered silk slippers; however, this was not available to the general public.

In later years, after buying a farm in Connecticut, he was very proud of his donkey, King, which had been given to him by his friend Consuelo Vanderbilt Earl as a pass-along gift from the Holy Father himself, from the Papal Stable of Asses. He usually spoke of King as "the Pope's ass."

His spiritual inclinations were somewhat in conflict with his stinginess and avarice. He once served a single rock Cornish game hen at a dinner for four. I was a guest and left hungry. He succeeded in cheating his eighty-year-old father out of some money, a maneuver he was quite proud of. There was also perhaps a touch of conflict with his extremely enthusiastic admiration for the male physique, an inclination definitely in the fleshly realm. Some friends went so far as to say they feared this admiration was overly enthusiastic.

In fairness to his spiritual life, it must be said that in the last twenty years of his life, Alden on rare occasions manifested what might be described as brief episodes of angelic possession, in which he went out of his way to be freely kind and helpful.

XXXXXXXXXXXXXXXXXXXXXXXXXXXXXXXXXXXXXXXXXXX

In an attempt to keep our horizons from becoming too constricted, Alden and I both wanted to maintain our cultural and intellectual interests, in addition to our medical education. In January 1956, just after we had returned from the Christmas holidays, we saw a notice that the world-famous theologian and pioneer in the field of psycholinguistics, Paul Tillich, was going to deliver a lecture, "The Mystery of Our Destiny," the following Tuesday at the New York Academy of Sciences. This was just our cup of tea. We decided to attend and looked forward excitedly to this magnificent event.

On the night of the lecture, we both put on our best suits and ties and left two hours prior to the lecture so that we could stop at the bar of the Stanhope Hotel for a couple of pre-lecture martinis to limber up our minds.

We arrived at the Academy of Sciences twenty minutes early and found the auditorium already two thirds full with what appeared to be the usual high-toned crowd appropriate to such an occasion: people who might have been scholars, ecclesiastics, teachers, scientists, physicians, and intellectuals of all stripes and appearances. By eight o'clock, the hall was filled, and excitement hung over the audience.

The president of the academy led the great man to the podium, to prolonged applause, and made a brief introduction. Dr. Tillich was about five-ten, looked his seventy years, was quite thin, dressed in a drab suit, and wore coke-bottle glasses. He shuffled his papers on the podium and glared at the audience. Appearing to be hovering somewhere between befuddlement and volcanic rage, he cleared his throat a few times and finally began to speak.

"Essteemed correcks, honkered gwests, hradees und ghenturmuns, honohr and purivuridge." It is beyond my abilities of phonetic transcription to present his talk accurately, so please use your auditory imagination to add a strong, almost incomprehensible German accent to this account of the Reverend Tillich's remarks.

German was the language of Kant, Schopenhauer, Luther, Nietzsche, Wagner, Sacher-Masoch, and Freud: a language of profundity. Not many laughs with any of them, and not with P.T. either.

He commenced his lecture. "A burning question of utmost importance for all persons is their relativistic relations with former and current beings, historical and possibly otherwise, and with the one almighty God, but at the same time trying to avoid the excesses of pan-adaptationism." He glared at the audience.

In this way, he cleverly got rid of half the world's population, since, for the billion Hindus there are said to be three hundred million gods, and for the billion-plus Buddhists a single supreme being does not exist.

He went on. "Inversely relativistic though the exigencies of relationships might be ... as we look to the future or even to the past ...." My attention began to wander to thoughts of having some more mind-limbering fluid.

Scowling grimly through his thick glasses at the audience, he dropped his first bombshell: "And so you can see, ladies and gentlemen, that the mystery of our destiny is the history of our tragedy." This was the most profound statement I had ever heard. Alden and I looked at each other and nodded gravely—this is what we had come for. He spoke further about the matter and then said, "It is also true that the tragedy of our destiny is the mystery of our history." We nodded again. How thrilling that we were being initiated into these profound secrets.

A little later, we learned, "The destiny of our mystery is the history of our tragedy," and after a while, "The tragedy of our history is the mystery of our destiny" and "The mystery of our tragedy is the destiny of our history."

Gravely and slowly, with tremendous intensity, Father Tillich's lecture went on. Gradually I lost track of how many of the nineteen additional permutations he revealed to us.

The extreme weight and gravity of his profundity finally caused our underdeveloped intellects to collapse, and Alden and I began to giggle and to wink at one another. Our reaction was not what we had expected, and we were embarrassed at our frivolous superficiality, until we noticed that others were also snickering, although the more serene were quietly snoozing.

After about another hour, Saint Paul decided he had favored us with enough enlightenment for one evening, and so the lecture ended, to loud applause. The audience left quickly, trying to look serious and wide awake; many had the severe pursed-lip look of those who are trying hard not to laugh. Alden and I hurried to a gay bar for a beer and some craziness more cheerful than we had just experienced.

The next day one of my classmates asked, "How was the Tillich lecture?"

"Oh, it was fascinating, but shatteringly profound," I said. I then looked down and shook my head slowly as if in recollection of a celestial visitation.

Was this a case of snot-nosed arrogant know-nothing kids (pearls before swine), or was it the aftereffects of having our snoots in the gin bottle, or was it a case of the emperor's new clothes? Or all three?

This mysterious history may have a tragic destiny, or perhaps not only one or two, relativistically speaking.

XXXXXXXXXXXXXXXXXXXXXXXXXXXXXXXXXXXXXXXXXXXX

Medical School—
Conclusion, *1956–1958*

The Third Year, 1956–1957

The third year was spent in clinical studies. We actually began serving, or at least interacting, with patients on the wards.

It was our job to draw all the required blood samples each morning and to do the blood counts and urine exams on all newly admitted patients. Today these tests are done by machines.

The first day on the surgery service, we were attending an introductory lecture from one of the chief surgeons. The lecture was on triage, separating those who could be helped from those who couldn't. The teacher asked us what we would do if we came across someone who had an abdominal wound and whose intestines were lying on the ground. One of the more unorthodox students said he would urinate on the intestines, which cracked up the class and the teacher too. The answer is not so wrong, as urine is sterile and might be the best thing available at the scene.

The professor, Dr. M., one of the chief surgeons, was not so benign in his treatment of Beverly, one of my favorite classmates. She had married an air force officer the previous spring and had taken a two-year leave of absence from school so she could go with her husband to Japan, where he was stationed. The Korean War had recently started. They had not been in Japan long when her husband did not return from a mission over Korea.

After staying in Japan for a month waiting for news, Beverly chose to return to medical school. We all gathered around her when we saw her on the first day of classes. She was in torment wondering about the fate of her husband. Was he alive, dead, or captured by the enemy?

On the second or third day of surgery class, Dr. M. was lecturing further on trauma. He well knew Beverly's situation but started in on her anyway. "Tell me, Doctor, how can you tell whether anyone is living or not?" There

171

was a hush in the class as Beverly gave a reasonable answer. Not enough for Dr. M.—he continued his pressure. He put question after question of living versus dead to Beverly until finally she broke down, started crying, and left the room. He gave the class a broad smile. I am ashamed that the rest of the class, including myself, didn't have the integrity to stand up and walk out of this sadist's lecture.

One of my classmates, who had had a radical neck dissection years earlier for thyroid cancer, applied for a surgical residency at New York Hospital. His operation had been a success, and he was most probably cured. The same Dr. M. interviewed my classmate and rejected him, with the comment that New York Hospital didn't accept candidates for residency who did not seem likely to live through the training. My classmate was shocked and distressed at this cruel response. He was a fine student and doctor, full of kindness and integrity, and lived for at least another twenty-five years. Most of us saw this as yet another example of the beast's usual mode of behavior.

Fortunately there were only a few of these sadist doctors on the teaching staff, although they were not unknown. We should all hope we never fall into the hands of one of these monsters. I have encountered a few, both as a colleague, a teacher, and as my physician. Some were peacocks; some were scorpions; some managed to be both. There should be a term for these hybrid psychopaths: perhaps "scorpicocks?"

We had to practice operating on dogs. These were strays who had been supplied by local dog pounds. We would perform an operation, say open and close the abdomen, or remove a kidney. The dogs would be returned to their kennels. We would visit them twice a day, take their temperatures, and inspect their wounds. A week later, we would do a second operation on the dogs, and after another week, we would perform a third operation on the dogs, again checking their postoperative progress, which was usually good.

The dogs looked at us trustingly, wagged their tails, and tried to lick our hands. I always spoke to our dog, patted and stroked it for a while, and tried to give it a little comfort in its tragic situation. Sometimes I brought it a little piece of meat from the cafeteria, which was against the rules. After the third operation the dogs would be euthanized, and new dogs would take their place for further operations. This procedure made me very sad, and I felt guilty to be a party to such useless and hideous cruelty. The dogs seemed to be offering love to their murderers. It was a nightmare for me.

Later on I met many people who had grown to love their tormentors, and many tormentors who expected and insisted that their victims love them, or at least convincingly pretend to do so. This can be a repetition of what unfortunately transpires in some families.

I continued my nighttime life in the bars, looking for sex, looking for love. One night I stayed out until closing hour, 4 AM. The next morning, at 8 AM, I was on the medical ward, with my partner that day, examining a new patient, an old man who was practically comatose. My partner said after we had finished, "Did you smell the alcohol on his breath? I wonder where he got it, and so early in the morning, too?" "Yes," I said, "I wonder too." I made haste to leave the floor to brush my teeth again. I knew I had gone too far and resolved to be more moderate in the future. This was one of many such resolutions I was not able to keep.

XXXXXXXXXXXXXXXXXXXXXXXXXXXXXXXXXXXXXXXXXXXX

Next we rotated to the delivery service. Divided into groups of four or five students, we had to spend the days and nights on the delivery floor for the six weeks of our rotation. We were each required to deliver twelve babies and to assist and observe the delivery of all the rest of the babies born while we were on the service. I was in a group of four students. Each of us in my group got every fourth night off; otherwise we were on call day and night and took turns in the delivery room.

For my first delivery, I had done an examination and thought the baby was in the usual position, as did the intern and the resident. When the big head finally emerged, the baby was looking toward the ceiling. Uh-oh. This is not the usual position and often means a difficult delivery. I was shoved out of the way like a bowling pin, and the resident took over. The baby, weighing twelve pounds, was safely delivered, and happily all was well. But all of us were embarrassed by the misdiagnosis of the baby's position. My next five deliveries were more usual, thank goodness.

My first night off I went to the bars, picked up someone, and we had pleasant sex. Four days later, I noticed some urethral discharge and burning on urination, symptoms of gonorrhea, a condition which I had had before, always promptly relieved by a penicillin injection when I had gone to visit the discreet specialist in venereal diseases in gay men.

I did not want to explain why I needed time off from the delivery floor (to see the VD specialist), so I began treating myself with heavy doses of Achromycin, an oral antibiotic, which was an acceptable, but not preferred, treatment, and which probably rendered me noninfectious after the first dose.

I was very careful on the delivery floor, observing strict sterile precautions, washing my hands very frequently, and wrapping myself in Kleenex held in place by rubber bands. This would all have been sufficient to keep the situation under control and out of sight if a serious complication had not arisen.

The same day I began treating myself for gonorrhea, I began to feel slight malaise. My jaw hurt, and I had a slight pain in one testicle. I went to the school physician, a kindly and competent man, who misjudged that I was malingering and trying to be excused from the notoriously stressful delivery service. I did not tell him about the gonorrhea.

"Take an aspirin and come back tomorrow if you are not better," he said—the age-old and usually good advice for many situations. The next day I was worse and told him so. "Take another aspirin," he said. The following day I had severe malaise and headache, my face was swollen on both sides, both testicles were painful and quite enlarged, and I had a fever of 104. The doctor thought therapy other than aspirin was indicated.

I had the *mumps*! Complications had set in.

There had been a gypsy "queen" with mumps in the hospital a few days before. I had passed by her room but had not entered it. This was my closest known contact with someone with mumps. Mine was the first and only case of mumps I have ever seen.

Naturally, I had to be removed from the dormitory and so was admitted to a private room on New York Hospital's infectious disease floor, with sterile precautions for all visitors, including the hospital staff. Gowns, masks, and gloves were required for everyone who entered my room.

The treatment for mumps, a viral disease, with testicular involvement was steroid injections for their anti-inflammatory effects. But this would hamper the body's natural immune resistance to bacteria, so the gonorrhea bacteria could then produce a massive invasion, perhaps affecting the eyes, joints, and kidneys. The steroid treatment for mumps was like pouring gasoline on a fire so far as the gonorrhea was concerned. Penicillin, the treatment for gonorrhea, had no effect either way on the mumps.

At present, gonorrhea is usually considered a mild disease. Before antibiotics, this was definitely not the case. Urethral complications included stricture, which required periodic painful mechanical dilatation. Sometimes scabs formed in the urethra. This required the insertion of an umbrella-like device with sharp edges. The umbrella was partially opened and then slowly withdrawn, cutting the scabs loose as it went. Another complication was painful joint infections. The writer Katherine Mansfield suffered from this chronic affliction from the time she acquired gonorrhea at age eighteen until her death years later. The organism sometimes attacked the eyes, and blindness could occur.

I realized with a sinking heart that I had both gonorrhea and mumps, felt like a walking cesspool, and was in danger of getting much more seriously ill. I sent word to the resident that I needed to talk to him, and he came in promptly. With great embarrassment I told him the story, omitting what I might have done to contract the gonorrhea, which was irrelevant at that point anyway, and he did not question me about it. Within a few minutes a nurse came in and gave me a penicillin injection, and my recovery was underway.

New York State and New York City had rigid reporting requirements for infectious diseases, including contact information, but if anything was done in this line, I knew nothing about it.

The next day the professor of obstetrics, a kindly and distinguished man, came to visit me, along with his two assistants. I thought he was going to scold me or perhaps even expel me from school for my misdeeds, which I assumed he knew all about. Perhaps he only knew about my mumps situation. To my relief, he said that because I had only delivered six babies before I had to leave the delivery floor, I was still lacking six deliveries to make my required quota.

He gave me a choice of when to make up the deficiency: I could work during the Christmas holidays until I had delivered the required number of babies, or I could wait until the summer break to do the makeup work. I knew the break between the third and fourth years was only three weeks; the rest of the summer was mostly scheduled for regular classwork. I chose the summer break, expecting the six-baby makeup would only take two or three days.

Mumps was well-known for making men sterile if there had been testicular involvement, and in my case, it had been severe. The sterility was not related to male hormone levels, which remained normal, but was an aftereffect of swelling and pressure on the sperm-producing cells during the acute phase of the illness. As I was being discharged from the infectious disease floor, I asked the resident if he thought I might now be sterile. I tried to feign a worried look. He was uncomfortable with this question and mumbled something about doing some tests later to see what the situation was.

The common view was that for a man to be sterile was a big shadow on his masculinity: embarrassing and damaging to his self-image because he could not father any babies. No tests were ever done. I assumed that I was sterile, and that was okay with me, as I neither intended to marry nor had any desire to have children. This was an odd fringe benefit of being gay.

I spent a few days of the summer break working on the delivery floor. As there were no other students present and competing for deliveries, I didn't have to take turns. I was called for all suitable deliveries and completed my six-baby makeup in two days.

This mumps-gonorrhea episode was my most serious mess-up during medical school. I am most grateful that I was able to continue my education. No faculty member ever mentioned the incident to me, and I believe that none of my fellow students knew about it, thanks to the discretion of the resident. Otherwise I would have received at least a few very pointed remarks from my colleagues.

XXXXXXXXXXXXXXXXXXXXXXXXXXXXXXXXXXXXXXXXXXXXX

The first day I returned to class after the mumps, an obstetrics seminar was on the schedule. The teacher, Dr. G., asked me a difficult question about the use of a certain hormone in a problem delivery. I gave a poor answer. He glared at me and said, "That's the kind of answer that makes me feel sick that I ever went into teaching." The other students looked wide-eyed. Reminiscences of Dr. RATsanoff at Rice. His reaction was quite overdone. I had not yet learned that this was another of the scorpicock variety of professors. After class, several of my classmates said, "Whew!! I'm glad he wasn't after me. Why does he have it in for you?"

We learned that Dr. G. enjoyed insulting and terrifying the students. He was rude and surly to me for the remainder of the semester, during which time I saw him also exercising his sadism on a number of my fellow students, taking obvious pleasure in insulting and embarrassing them.

Two years later I insulted him back, I am ashamed to say. I was with my parents for a short Christmas visit to Caracas. We were staying at the Tamanaco Hotel, which at that time had the reputation of being the most expensive hotel in the world. Perhaps it was.

One day I approached the elevator on my floor, intending to go downstairs to meet my parents for dinner. I saw a familiar figure already waiting for the elevator. It was Dr. G. When he saw me approaching, he gave me a big smile, stuck out his hand, and said, "Oh, hello. How are you? What are you doing here?" I looked him right in his eyes, turned my mouth down in a scowl, made no reply, and did not shake his hand. Going down in the elevator, I stared at him without speaking. He looked uncomfortable. Later I thought this was a poor way to handle the situation, although he certainly didn't deserve a cordial greeting from me. Preferably, I should have been masklike and coldly polite.

XXXXXXXXXXXXXXXXXXXXXXXXXXXXXXXXXXXXXXXXXXXXX

That year, 1956, I wanted to go home to Houston for Christmas. My grandmother had been in the hospital for a month with inoperable lung cancer, even though she had never smoked a cigarette.

My grandmother, Houston, 1954

The doctors told Granny she had swallowed a watermelon seed which had gone down the wrong way and had become stuck in her lungs. She barely lived through a bronchoscopy. At age eighty, her doctors thought she was too old to survive a major lung operation, so there was nothing much to be done except try to keep her as pain-free as possible. When I went to visit her during the Christmas vacation, she was lying comfortably in bed in an attractive private room in Hermann Hospital, where I had worked in the record room during two recent summers.

When I said goodbye before returning to New York, I knew I would never see Granny again. My eyes filled with tears, but I had to keep a straight face so as not to alarm her and ruin the fiction that she was going to get well soon. Perhaps she believed this; perhaps not. She was a wise old lady and was not afraid of death. Like others in the family, she occasionally saw deceased loved ones and had a pleasant visit with them. She smiled at me, gave me a kiss, stroked my head and hands, and said good-bye. I had a hard time walking down the hall and out of the hospital without sobbing.

After I returned to New York, I kept in touch with frequent phone calls to my mother and to Granny. She was slowly declining. My mother or my Aunt Nellie were with her all day every day. I was aware that there was some kind of tension between my mother, my father, and my aunt Nellie on one side, and my uncle Van and his wife, Sadie, on the other, but I assumed it was merely the usual intrafamily hatred.

One evening in February 1957, I had just gone to bed in Olin Hall. As I turned out the light, and definitely before I had fallen asleep, I saw a glow in the corner of my room. Granny was there, hovering perhaps two feet above the floor, wearing a pink silk gown and surrounded by a rosy light. She was looking at me with a loving and kindly expression, holding out her right hand as if in farewell. I knew immediately that she had come to say good-bye and that she had either just passed away or was in the process of leaving her body. Mentally, I received her blessing, and I gave her mine. After about sixty seconds, the vision slowly faded.

Although her death was not a surprise, neither was it expected at just that time, as she might have lived another month. I found out later that just at the time I saw her in my room in New York, she had asked her nurse to play the little butterfly music box I had given her. She said, "I hope John will be all right." And then she died.

The morning after my vision, Sunday, I was scheduled to attend an autopsy in the hospital as a required part of my training. I had been there only about thirty minutes when an intern came in and handed me a telegram. The pathologist stopped his work and told me to open the telegram. It was the message that my grandmother had died. The doctor asked if I needed to be excused or preferred to continue. I said I could continue, but there were so many tears in my eyes that I couldn't really see much of what was being done.

I did not feel I should leave school to attend Granny's funeral in Houston. My parents agreed.

I report this visitation event as it occurred. I believe that my grandmother actually visited my room, or alternatively, projected a thought form telepathically into my mind. Maybe there is not much difference between these two explanations. Her purpose was to say good-bye for her benefit as well as mine. I am grateful to my grandmother for this parting gift.

If someone wanted to maintain that this was only a fantasy, or that I had fallen asleep and dreamed the event, I would answer, "Perhaps."

About six months before Granny entered the hospital, she had had pneumonia and had been admitted to a small private hospital, where she slowly recovered over about two weeks, with some residual cough remaining. She was under the care of her very long-term physician, Dr. Wright, who was quite elderly and in whom she had total confidence.

We asked to see her chest X-rays from that time and were disturbed to find that a tiny lung cancer was visible then. Perhaps if she had been operated on at that time, she might have survived.

I was angry about this and advised bringing a malpractice action against Dr. Wright, who in my view had killed my grandmother through his negligence. The family didn't want any part of such a thing, and so the idea was abandoned. Perhaps that was best; perhaps not.

XXXXXXXXXXXXXXXXXXXXXXXXXXXXXXXXXXXXXXXXXXXXX

I later found out the nature of the trouble which had been brewing in the family. My grandmother owned a large two-story house in a good section of Houston. It was divided into two apartments; the upper one was rented out, and the lower one was for her, but she also rented out two bedrooms in her own. There was a garage apartment in the rear, also rented out. These were her assets. Other than the rents, her only income was her widow's pension from the Southern Pacific Railroad and a tiny bit of savings.

This was before the days of widespread medical insurance, which she didn't have. Her medical care was obviously going to be expensive and would need to be continued until she passed away.

My father proposed to my mother and her three siblings and spouses that he would pay all her medical bills and when the house was sold and the estate was settled, he could be reimbursed. Her remaining estate would then be divided equally among her four surviving children. The children and their spouses thought this was a good and fair plan, with the exception of Sadie Mae, Granny's new daughter-in-law.

Sadie said, "That would be a big waste of money. Since she is going to die no matter what care she gets, there's no sense in paying for expensive care. She should be transferred to the Harris County charity hospital and left there until she dies. If it isn't so luxurious as a private hospital, then so what? No use to waste money on her." Sadie was one of the first to advocate what came to be known as "Granny dumping."

My mother, Aunt Nellie, Uncle Edmund (Mother's oldest brother), and all their spouses disagreed with Sadie. Even Uncle Van, Sadie's husband, disagreed, but very mildly, as he had to live with the battle-ax. Later, Sadie argued strongly for a funeral as cheap as possible, but the others wouldn't listen to her. I knew nothing of Sadie's cruelly stingy attitude until just before my mother died nine years later, when my mother told me the story.

My mother and Nellie doubled their hatred of Sadie. Two years later, when my mother and Uncle Van were both in New York, they had cocktails in the Palm Court at the Plaza Hotel. I was to join them for dinner that evening. When I arrived, Van, red-faced and angry, was just leaving. He said, "Your mother is just impossible. She demands that I divorce Sadie."

My mother was drunk, also red-faced, furious, and babbling about how her brother, Van, whom she had mistakenly thought was a nice person, preferred that bitch he was married to over his own mother; how evil Sadie had kicked out nice Matt, Van's former wife, and she had also tried to kick Van's mother into the poor house; he was going to help her do this, and on and on. I didn't understand what she was talking about, as at that time I didn't know of Sadie's attitude about my grandmother's medical expenses.

After that, my mother was no longer on speaking terms with her brother Van and the now unmentionable Sadie. Van was my closest relative, and we had always been on very good terms. I didn't much like Sadie myself, but that was Van's business, and I tried to remain cordial. Sadie, ever free with nasty remarks, was not so obliging, although she did me some tremendous favors at the cost of a good deal of effort. Sadie talked ugly but acted nice, quite the reverse of more usual troublesome behavior.

Years later, after both my parents had died, Sadie moved all the things in my parents' house to an apartment I had chosen in central Houston and arranged it all for me. About ten years later, when I gave up that apartment, Sadie arranged and supervised the packing and moving of all the apartment contents, including a concert grand piano, to my new house in Ridgefield, Connecticut. Both moves entailed lots of work, and Sadie was quite free, gracious, and charming about both these transfers. Sadie was the first person I had to deal with regularly who was truly unpredicctable. It was an education in taking one day, or one action, at a time.

Whenever I went to Houston on a holiday, I would quietly, surreptitiously, go for a short visit to see Van and Sadie. My mother, somehow, always checking my whereabouts, would find out, and I would not lie to her. She would become enraged, and then I had to barricade my bedroom door at night, putting large pieces of furniture against it, as she would scream, curse loudly, and throw dishes, lamps, and glasses against it. I never got used to that.

I was always glad to return to New York after a holiday visit to Houston.

XXXXXXXXXXXXXXXXXXXXXXXXXXXXXXXXXXXXXXXXXXXX

In May 1957, on one of my numerous excursions to the gay bars, I went into the Sans Souci, a piano bar on the corner of Sixtieth Street and Third Avenue. As the evening wore on, and the clientele became more intoxicated, the quality of the performances declined—or perhaps collapsed would be more accurate.

I noticed a young man standing alone, smiling at me. He had a handsome face, a good build, and strikingly beautiful blue eyes. We gradually shuffled closer together and began to talk. "I'm John Puckett," he said.

He was obviously well educated, friendly, and was fun and interesting to talk with. From Iowa, he had been in New York for less than a year. He had worked the previous two summers at beach resorts in the Hamptons and Amagansett, but he knew these were not career jobs. He then found a job in the copy room of J. Walter Thompson, one of the leading advertising agencies.

John Puckett, Brooklyn Heights, 1957

His lover, Roger, was still in Iowa but was planning to move to New York in the fall so they could live together. John also had a girlfriend back in Iowa, who was hoping to marry him, a very unlikely prospect, which she did not want to acknowledge. He was living at the moment with a friendly admirer who had an apartment at Lexington Avenue and Seventy-Fourth Street.

He came home with me that night to my room in Olin Hall. I had brought many previous sex partners home from the bars to Olin Hall in the past three years, and luckily there had never been any trouble. The first year, when Dick Roberts, who was not gay, had been my suitemate, I rarely brought pickups home, and then only when he was away. The next two years, when Emery Hetrick, who was gay, was my suitemate, I was more relaxed about it and would sometimes even introduce Emery to my visitor.

Emery and I were not attracted to the same physical type, except for the evening when we were both talking to and trying to seduce Gore Vidal, whom we had just met in a gay bar, the East Five-Five, an elegant, gussied-up place.

That evening, we were absolutely united in wanting to be with this beautiful and brilliant man, preferably one at a time. Gore Vidal seemed interested in Emery but then decided not to follow through. He showed no interest in me. I struck out. *Too bad for him*, I sighed to myself.

John and I had an exciting and delighting night in my Olin Hall room. We knew we had clicked. This time I asked for his phone number. Three days later I called him, and we arranged another date, to meet at the Sans Souci again. Again we had a very hot evening. We continued to meet two or three times a week. John introduced me to some of his friends, and I reciprocated.

The school year came to an end, and I started my two-day, six-baby delivery makeup. After that, I was free to enjoy the official school summer holiday and had planned to go to Houston to visit my parents for the three weeks. I knew there would be a lot of trouble from my mother if I cancelled my vacation and stayed in New York, which was what I really preferred to do.

John and I said good-bye and planned to get together when I got back. We exchanged letters several times during our separation. The summer holiday in Houston was less stressful than usual, as Mother was controlling her drinking. I was in a better mood than usual and was excited about my new relationship.

Miss Frost had arranged for me to play a recital at her Steinway Hall studio in the fall, and I should have used the holiday to practice hard and perfect my pieces, which were already in fair shape. I preferred to go out drinking with my friends, read, and otherwise relax. I practiced some, perhaps forty-five minutes a day, which was not enough to prepare for a solo recital.

XXXXXXXXXXXXXXXXXXXXXXXXXXXXXXXXXXXXXXXXXXXX

By the time I got back to New York, John had decided to share an apartment with his old college friend Jim, who was also from Iowa. They found a place on Sixty-First Street, a fourth-floor rear walk-up apartment with one bedroom and bath. Jim and I liked each other, and he didn't object to John's and my using the apartment as much as we wanted for our intimate activities. Jim was a social butterfly and was out most evenings. I visited John almost every night, at least for a few hours, somewhat neglecting my final year of schoolwork—even more than usual, that is.

Eleanor Roosevelt was a resident in the building and had the duplex apartment on the first and second floors, along with the large back garden. She entertained frequently, and when I entered the building in the evening around 6 or 7 PM, she was often standing at her front door waiting to welcome guests. Eventually we began speaking and having tiny conversations. She was most charming and usually looked quite lovely; her radiant spirit illuminated her somewhat plain physical appearance. I would have liked to have known her, but there didn't seem to be an appropriate way to do this. She might have been more welcoming than I thought; it was another case of my being too timid to reach out to someone.

Within a month, John's friend Roger came to New York for a visit. By then John and I were romantically involved, and John told him that he had met someone here in New York and their plans to live together as lovers had to be cancelled. Roger was crushed, according to John. I was ecstatic but at the same time felt guilty for being complicit in the misery of someone else.

The rest of the year was a happy dream. Sex was red-hot; we were highly attracted and compatible. We drank some but not as much as we had been doing separately. We spent some time in gay bars visiting our "friends" there but not as much as when we were single. We talked and laughed and had a very fun time together. This was love at its best, I thought, even though I was inexperienced. Was this what I had been looking for all along? I hoped so. We made plans to live together after I graduated.

Two months after school had resumed, my piano recital took place on a Saturday afternoon at Miss Frost's studio. I played the first Bach Partita; "Petizada," a set of charming small pieces by Villa-Lobos; a concert etude, "By the Sea," of Smetana; the B-minor Scherzo and the D-flat Nocturne of Chopin; and I concluded with "The Banjo" of Gottschalk—a respectably difficult program. My playing was only fair, and I had a couple of embarrassing memory lapses due to my lack of practice, but Miss Frost seemed pleased and invited me to play at Marymount College in Westchester, where she was on the faculty, which I had to decline because of too much schoolwork. Perhaps a concert career had temporarily opened.

Not long after my recital, Miss Frost and her husband sailed on the North German Lloyd ocean liner Bremen, bound for Hamburg and a vacation in Europe. I went to the sailing, which included a champagne party in their stateroom and an oompah band on deck, along with streamers, confetti, and horns when the boat sailed away. I cried; everyone cried at sailings. They were somehow very impressive and emotional events. These sailing parties no longer exist because of terrorist concerns.

XXXXXXXXXXXXXXXXXXXXXXXXXXXXXXXXXXXXXXXXXXXX

Medical School: The Fourth Year, 1957–1958

I was moving into the home stretch in medical school.

My instructor in internal medicine, Dr. S., was a senior internist, perhaps sixty years old, presumably skillful and experienced. He had piercing blue eyes, a bright red face, perhaps caused by high blood pressure and/or alcoholism, and a striking smile. When he pulled his thin lips back in a smile, his huge teeth made him look as if he were a predatory animal about to attack. The whole effect was ghastly. If I were sick and he were my physician, I would fear for my safety.

Even as his student, I feared for my safety. Sometimes he taught by inviting the students to hear each other present patients. In previous weeks I had done reasonably good work in the clinics, being well prepared and careful in examining the patients. As we were presenting a patient, Dr. S. was usually sarcastic, confrontational, undermining, insulting, and generally unhelpful. Every week was very unpleasant.

In my presentation to the other students, I mentioned that today's patient had a problem with her "submandibular glands." This really set him off. Appearing enraged, he said, "I don't know what you are talking about, and obviously you don't know either. What kind of glands are those? Where did you dream up that crazy terminology? How do you expect to become a doctor when obviously you don't know anything? What excuse do you have for this terrible performance?" And on and on he went. I felt like falling through the floor, briefly considered leaving school that minute, but mumbled something like, "I'm very sorry, Dr. S. I'll try harder in the future."

The other students looked embarrassed. I was so rattled I couldn't defend myself. The glands in question are sometimes referred to as "submaxillary glands" and sometimes as "submandibular glands." The terms are interchangeable—something like calling a finger a digit or calling an arm a limb. Presumably Dr. S. understood this fact, perhaps his vocabulary was limited to only "submaxillary glands," or perhaps he was drunk and in a bad mood.

He glared at me and at the other students and then marched out of the room. Class over, dismissed. I asked the other students if they had had trouble with Dr. S. Those who had had contact with him said he was terrible—rude, insulting, inappropriate, destructive, demoralizing. Another scorpicock on the loose.

The next week when it was time for medical clinic, I told the head of the clinic that I was requesting a reassignment to a supervisor other than Dr. S.

"Oh, but that's who you are assigned to for this term." Then he asked, "What is the problem?"

I told him, and he said, "Well, you just have to learn to get along with people."

"I'm sorry. I couldn't ever learn to get along with a sadist like Dr. S. I can't take up for myself against him. It's not possible for me to survive another session with him."

"I'm sorry. You can't be reassigned."

"Well, I'm very sorry too. I guess this is the end of my medical education. I very much wanted to be a doctor. I've spent nearly four years in school and am almost finished. Just for my own information, has Dr. S. wrecked many of the other students?"

"I don't know."

"Thank you. I'm leaving now. Good-bye. Good luck to you."

As I left the floor, Dr. S. glared at me, ready to begin our regular session. I went right on by but told two of my classmates that I couldn't take Dr. S. anymore and that I had to withdraw from school.

Later that day I got a call from the dean of students requesting me to come in for a talk immediately. I told him what had happened. He said he had heard previous stories like this about Dr. S. and would speak to him about behaving better with the students.

"That's good. I hope it works. But I'm afraid then he would be nastier than ever to me. I can't defend myself against him now, much less if he gets even more abusive. I just can't work with him again. You know that nothing like this has occurred with me in the four years I have been at Cornell."

"I know that. I'm sorry you have had to put up with behavior like this. I will send word to the clinic chief that an exception is to be made, and you'll be assigned to another supervisor in medicine clinic."

"Thanks very much. In that case, I would prefer to stay in school and complete my coursework. When should I go back to medicine clinic?"

"Next week will be fine. Good luck."

"Thanks very much for helping me out."

This was a very close call. I knew there wasn't much to lose by taking the position I did, as Dr. S. would have eventually succeeded in breaking me down so that I would have had to run away or even perhaps attack him physically, losing my MD degree either way.

XXXXXXXXXXXXXXXXXXXXXXXXXXXXXXXXXXXXXXXXXXXX

Other than dealing with lurking prima donnas and scorpicocks, clinic sessions were usually informative and pleasant. In our senior year, we had the option of taking a couple of elective courses. I chose dermatology and venereal disease clinic. Since antibiotics had been discovered, venereal disease treatment as a specialty was fading away.

But there were still some interesting older patients in this clinic, former prostitutes who had worked in San Juan, Veracruz, and Havana, who had unusual venereal diseases like yaws, granuloma inguinale, and *mal de pinta*, as well as tertiary syphilis. They came in once a month for routine checkups. All were jolly, high-spirited ladies who favored bright red hair and exhibitionistic clothing. I imagined they had been stars in their profession before they became incapacitated. They seemed happy to have a nice young medical student to talk to, and I enjoyed hearing about their lives and experiences.

XXXXXXXXXXXXXXXXXXXXXXXXXXXXXXXXXXXXXXXXXXX

The psychiatry lectures were sometimes enlightening, sometimes dead wrong. The professor of psychiatry and head of the department, Dr. Oskar Diethelm, about fifty years old, had trained under leading psychiatrists in Europe and the United States. He was especially skilled at detecting brain tumors and other brain lesions. Dressed in an immaculate, snowy white, rigidly starched lab coat, he made rounds frequently at Payne Whitney, the psychiatric hospital, and he saw every newly admitted patient within twenty-four hours after admission. Once, when M.M., probably the most famous actress in the world at that time, had been admitted the previous evening and had been making an uproar, his opening remark to her was, "I am told, Miss M., that you are an actress. Is that correct?" That was rather like asking Joe DiMaggio if it were true that he was a baseball player—ridiculous. Miss M. was highly offended, screamed for a while, and shortly checked herself out of the hospital.

One afternoon he was lecturing at a seminar on homosexuality and the other perversions. He said, "Homosexuals are all psychopaths. They are impulse-ridden. They cannot control their impulses, so any desire which enters their consciousness must be satisfied immediately; sometimes very inconvenient for them. They can rarely graduate from college, and almost never from medical school. I do not know of any practicing physicians who are homosexual, and there are most certainly no homosexual psychiatrists." He was quite definite, perhaps a little too definite. It was not necessary for him to add that gay people were immoral, disgusting, and evil; that was common knowledge.

This was the official psychiatric party line as recently as 1958 and was being taught by an eminent doctor who was head of the department at one of the country's leading medical schools. Perhaps he believed what he was saying. Fortunately, in the fifty years since then, more accurate information has been slowly and often unwillingly accepted by the psychiatric profession.

At the time, The New York Psychoanalytic Institute would never certify the training or award a certificate to practice psychoanalysis to an analyst who was gay, because he was too "sick." The head of training there was the bigoted and eminent Dr. Sandor Rado, who will appear later in this volume in the chapter entitled "The Queen of Neptune."

The seven other gay students in the audience glanced at each other, careful to keep any smiles suppressed.

There had been many years of police and judicial bigotry, persecution, and extortion of gays. The police had developed clever and elaborate methods of entrapment. A gay man could be arrested for propositioning an undercover decoy, who usually had been acting in a provocative or obscene way.

In 1964 John and I rented a house at Fire Island Pines, the mostly gay resort off Long Island, sharing the place with Alden and his lover, Rolf. On Saturday night of the Fourth of July weekend, John had been out drinking at the Boatel and was coming home late. He saw two good-looking men standing together about ten feet from the boardwalk. They appeared to be mutually masturbating. John left the boardwalk and went toward them. When he touched one of the men, he was immediately arrested. They were both police decoys. He was taken to Sayville, on Long Island, and jailed. Bail was five hundred dollars, which was not easy to obtain on a weekend—ATMs had not been invented yet. I managed to borrow the money and pay the bail, and we went back to New York.

There were two female lawyers in New York City who specialized in homosexual entrapment cases. All gay people knew who they were. The fee was five thousand dollars, part of which was for bribes for the police and the judges. The clients all got off if they could pay. It was an extortion racket, no doubt quite profitable. Safe for the police thugs too, as gays did not usually fight back or even resist, unlike real criminals, who tended to be more forceful. This persecution of gays was a continuation and intensification of the notorious homophobic Mayor Abraham Beame's attempt to "clean up" the city in preparation for the World's Fair of 1964–1965.

As part of the "cleanup," over two hundred gay bars, all but the one rumored to be owned by the police Athletic League, were raided and closed. All baths were closed, except the Everard, said to be owned by the Patrolmen's Benevolent Association.

The Plaza Hotel installed high stools at the Oak Bar and forbid the customers to change seats or to walk around, to discourage cruising. The St. Regis Hotel's King Cole Bar was even more direct. They were said to put ipecac in the drinks of men who looked gay, so they would soon be throwing up and leaving the bar. A bar could lose its liquor license and be closed for serving homosexuals, and many were closed, perhaps victims of police shakedowns.

The police entrapment agents were even walking the streets, trying to catch gay men who might proposition them after they had made provocative gestures. Of course, these same agents also used an old favorite: loitering in public restrooms, playing with themselves and making sexual gestures to the other customers.

John refused to go again to Fire Island, although I continued to go each weekend. There was definitely a tense atmosphere there, and we all thought we could spot the decoys loitering around. There was even an amphibious assault, closer to Cherry Grove, which netted dozens of gay men loitering in the meat rack, as the cruising place in the bushes was known. The persecution on Fire Island was so intense that for the first time property values began falling, and the next summer many properties did not rent. The property owners objected strongly.

At the same time, all kinds of illicit heterosexual activities in New York City were subject to similar extortion. The atmosphere in New York became like a Sunday school. Many national organizations stopped having their conventions here, as there was not enough entertainment for the delegates.

Many gay men moved to San Francisco, which had a more benign attitude toward gays. So many gay men left that businesses dependent on gay men started closing. Florists, beauty salons, art galleries, clothing stores, restaurants, and theaters all were decimated, or worse.

The Stonewall riots of 1969 were the first time gays resisted the police brutality, and they marked the turning point in persecution and bigotry in New York City.

Eventually the bigot mayor Beame was voted out of office, and the new mayor, John Lindsay, had a definitely more liberal attitude toward gays. Lindsay told the police to stop the entrapment and to concentrate their efforts on real criminals. But by that time much damage had been done, and thirty years later the city has not completely recovered.

The civil rights movement also helped us. The idea of not hating and persecuting others because their skin or religious beliefs or sexual lives were different than yours began to spread. We knew that we were not sick, or wicked, or evil threats to children and society.

But this widely despised condition of homosexuality, the "love that dared not speak its name," hung like a dark cloud over my life and many others and was present at all times. This made the educational process more strained for me. In 1973, after much discussion and controversy, the American Psychiatric Association removed homosexuality from its list of illnesses. This angered some "therapists" who made their living from their purported "curing" of homosexuals.

Now, in 2010, to be gay is definitely not a plus in medical circles, but it is not so dangerous as it was fifty years ago. Perhaps now even Dr. Diethelm, if he were still alive, might be acquainted with a few homosexual physicians, even psychiatrists!

This is not to say that homophobia, even in virulent and/or lethal forms, has disappeared. As recently as 2007 a United States senator was entrapped and arrested by an undercover agent making homosexual overtures in an airport restroom.

XXXXXXXXXXXXXXXXXXXXXXXXXXXXXXXXXXXXXXXXXXXX

Christmas of my senior year, 1957, my parents came to New York for a ten-day visit. Being caught in my parents' crossfire was stressful and exhausting for me. I thought my mother was too emphatic, too vitriolic, and too prolonged and repetitive in her criticisms of my father. Generally I secretly agreed with her that my father was an uncouth and sullen slob, unable to take up for himself against her, apparently cowardly and generally unattractive. There really was no "crossfire"; the firing all went one way. My mother fired at my father, but he never talked back or took up for himself. I often wished he would tell her to shut up.

My father and I continued to mutually dislike each other. I had no use for him, never consulted him about anything, and preferred not to talk with him at all. But because of the always hovering presence of the virago, he and I were fellow sufferers and managed to treat each other with a detached and flabby politeness.

Christmas was tense and dismal. I was relieved when my parents departed for home.

XXXXXXXXXXXXXXXXXXXXXXXXXXXXXXXXXXXXXXXXXXXX

The major concern of the senior year was getting a good internship. I had considered going back to Texas or perhaps out to California, but once John and I met and became serious, the only choice was an internship in New York City. I applied to several hospitals and had a number of interviews.

The interview with a board of doctors at Lenox Hill Hospital, a good institution on Manhattan's Upper East Side, was amusing. One of the doctors, beautifully dressed and with an English accent, perhaps a real one, looked at me, tipped his head back, and drawled, "And tell me, young doctor, where did you go to prep school?"

"I didn't go to prep school, sir. I went to the local high school in McAllen, Texas. That was the usual practice there, and it was a very good school."

"Oh .... thank youuuu sooooo much. We'll let you knooow. That's aaahhll for today."

189

I knew I had flunked the interview due to lack of educational social credentials acceptable to Dr. Fancy Clothes. Likewise, he flunked my interview.

I was accepted for a rotating internship at Brooklyn Methodist Hospital, in the Park Slope area of Brooklyn, to begin July 1, 1958. I was disappointed to not have been accepted at a Manhattan hospital, but I was happy about staying in New York and continuing my relationship with John.

Around June 1 commencement took place. My parents came up from Texas. My father seemed surprised that his sissy fag son was graduating from a prestigious medical school. I invited John to the ceremony. My parents liked him, as he was polite and easy to be with.

I had never "come out" to my parents and didn't do so in the future. My mother would not have objected much. I think she would have been relieved to know that in the future I would not be owned by another female in competition with her. My father would probably just have considered he had some further reason to despise and have contempt for me. I think they both knew at some level of awareness, but so long as I didn't declare myself, the subject could be kept out of sight and discussion. I certainly didn't feel any urge to tell them, to discuss the matter with them, just as I had never felt there was any reason to ask their help in understanding my gayness. To keep part of myself invisible to my parents had always been the safest course.

I sighed with relief that I had completed medical school. I was sorry to leave school and some of my classmates, whom I had grown to like, but I was relieved that my MD degree was finally in my hand, so I no longer had to worry about thugs like Dr. S., Dr. G., the sadistic obstetrician, Dr. Moore, the cruel surgeon, or some of the unpleasant homophobic students.

I am happy not to have to associate with these difficult beings anymore.

Most of the medical school professors were dedicated doctors who did a fine job teaching. The chairmen of the departments were leaders in their fields and were enormously skilled and knowledgeable practitioners in their various fields, generous with their knowledge, and kindly and helpful in their work with the students. It was both intellectually stimulating and inspiring to study with them. Frank Glenn in surgery, R. Gordon Douglas in obstetrics, the truly magnificent David Barr in Medicine, and Samuel Levine in pediatrics were among many who worked miracles in turning us all into doctors. My thanks and gratitude to them all.

XXXXXXXXXXXXXXXXXXXXXXXXXXXXXXXXXXXXXXXXXXX

For many years the students kept track of each other, at least casually. A student one year ahead of me, a classmate of Emery Hetrick's, had a particularly tragic fate. Abbe Ghasghai was Iranian royalty. His grandfather and the Shah's grandfather had been rivals for the throne of Iran. The Shah's grandfather won out, but the situation between the two men was peaceable.

Abbe had the best of equipment at school, a purple Cadillac convertible, and attractive girlfriends. He occasionally had visitors dressed in elaborate robes with golden headbands. He was always polite and very gracious, charming, and friendly to all of us. He was an excellent student. His father built him a modern hospital in their home district in Iran, and after he finished his training Abbe went there to practice and run the health program. He was not interested in or active in politics.

When the Shah was overthrown in the Islamic Revolution, Abbe felt in danger and went into exile in the United States, as did his other family members and many other Iranians. As a prince, and as a doctor, his presence in Iran would be desirable publicity for the new regime. It was said that the Grand Ayatollah Khomeini sent word to Abbe to ask him to return to Iran, that he was greatly needed there, that he and his family would be perfectly safe. At first he was hesitant but finally gave in to the repeated entreaties. When his plane landed at the Tehran airport, he was taken directly to jail and beheaded. I feel sure that the government had some reasonable-sounding reason why Abbe was viewed as a dangerous criminal. What a wicked, tragic waste.

XXXXXXXXXXXXXXXXXXXXXXXXXXXXXXXXXXXXXXXXXXXXXXX

I had said good-bye the previous year to Emery Hetrick, who had graduated a year ahead of me, and now I said good-bye to the other students in my class and other classes. Good-bye to Olin Hall, good-bye to Dick, good-bye to Alden, good-bye to Miss Frost, hello to the rest of life.

It is better if a physician has both good technical ability and is reasonably mature psychologically. I tried to keep a balance but sometimes failed. I am grateful to have been able to attend Cornell Medical College and feel I got a very good education there.

I was able to survive by working as hard as I could, trying to conform as well as I could, concealing my homosexuality to the best of my ability, not being pugnacious, and really wanting to be of service to my fellow humans.

In retrospect, my performance at Cornell was somewhat hampered by early alcoholism, time spent in a search for love without any guidance or help, increasing feelings of inferiority, and an increasing social phobia. On the other hand, if I had been more diligent in my studies, my emotional and social development, already severely stunted, would have been even further retarded.

I was not afraid of the approaching internship, although it had the reputation of being very difficult. I was looking forward to the next stage of my medical education and of my life education too. The future was welcoming, and perhaps I had already found a permanent love in John.

Remsen Street, Brooklyn

July 1958 to July 1959

I graduated from medical school on June 1, 1958, and was scheduled to start a one-year internship on July 1 at the Methodist Hospital in the Park Slope section of Brooklyn. John, my partner of one year, and I were looking for a rental apartment, our first shared place. We wanted a furnished apartment but couldn't find one. We saw an advertisement for an unfurnished one-bedroom place in Brooklyn Heights, on Remsen Street, one-year lease, $150 per month. Not too close to the hospital, not too far.

We called, and a cultivated, husky female voice said, "Well, yes. I'm Gladys Green. I'm the owner of the building and I'm currently occupying the apartment, but my new husband wants me to move to his place." We made an appointment to see the apartment the next day at 2 PM.

The apartments at the front of the building had a panoramic view of New York Harbor and the lower Manhattan skyline, but this was a rear apartment—not much of a view, we thought.

When we rang the intercom, Gladys told us to come up to Apartment 2B. The door was already open, and she said, "Come in, come in. Don't be afraid of Harry." She motioned to her brownish miniature poodle, who looked at us with bleary eyes and growled listlessly.

"Would you care for a drink?" Gladys asked. She was a startling vision, about sixty years old, garishly made-up. Her makeup and lipstick were heavily smudged. Dirty dyed red hair, showing white roots, was piled messily on her head, some strands drooping carelessly over her face. She was dressed in a sheer peach-colored floor-length peignoir trimmed with white marabou feathers, à la Marlene Dietrich, 1930. The garment flared open frequently and widely to reveal that Gladys was wearing nothing underneath. A silk leopard-patterned scarf tied around her neck and high-heeled bright red patent leather shoes completed her costume.

She held a pitcher of brownish liquid in her right hand and a pitcher of clear fluid in her left. Perhaps tea and water, I thought. "Stingers," she said, waving the brown pitcher, and "martinis," waving the clear fluid. "I always keep something in the fridge for gala occasions, like now. I think I'll have a stinger," she said, putting some ice cubes in a tumbler and filling it to the top. John and I asked for martinis, which she served in large matching tumblers.

We all lit cigarettes, hers in a medium-length black onyx holder, and began the tour of the small apartment, which didn't take long. A pleasant terrace with a wrought-iron fence ran the length of the back of the building, overlooking the small well-tended rear garden. Gladys dropped some remarks about singing at La Scala and at the Metropolitan, which we let pass on by. After a few drinks, the negotiations were concluded, not a moment too soon, as Gladys was on the verge of total nudity and total drunkenness by the time we left, and John and I were both getting increasingly nervous.

We were scheduled to move in on June 25. As the day approached, phone calls back and forth kept everything progressing pleasantly and on schedule. On the 25th, we arrived at the apartment in a rented car, carrying our clothes and essentials for setting up housekeeping. Our two new mattresses were tied to the top of the car.

Gladys was in high spirits. This time she had pitchers of manhattans and Bloody Marys, and we hesitantly shared a bit with her. Perfectly attired for moving day, she was again dressed with great flair—in a foxhunting outfit, red coat, gray riding trousers, and high shiny brown boots. She had on a black flamenco dancer's hat, flat-topped and wide-brimmed, with a fringe of sequins and small cloth balls. A sheer, wide-meshed black veil completed the ensemble. She proudly told us that she had sewn the fringe and the veil onto her hat just that morning. When she moved her head, the little balls danced and jerked around, giving her an air of surreal gaiety. Dog Harry was hiding behind the sofa, snarling occasionally.

Gladys introduced us to George, her burly husband, who told us he was in the garbage hauling business. He ogled his foxhunting-costumed, flamenco-hatted sweetie with obvious protectiveness, admiration, and lust.

Then Gladys and Harry and George and John and I all went down the stairs carrying Gladys's final boxes and her suitcase. George's huge garbage truck was parked in front of the house, waiting to carry Gladys and Harry to their new home half a mile away. George climbed up into the high driver's seat, and John and I helped Gladys and Harry climb into the passenger seat and get settled. Gladys was sad and cried a little. Her mascara and eye shadow ran down the right side of her face in a short, slender line. As the huge rig slowly moved off down the street, like a Spanish galleon bearing a queen into exile, Gladys stuck her small hand out the window, waving her lace handkerchief in farewell.

"Good-bye, good-bye, good luck," we said. Then we turned with a happy smile and went up into our first connubial dwelling. What bliss, we thought.

Two days later, as we entered the building, we met the tenant in the garden apartment, which occupied the whole ground floor under us. Mrs. Terwilliger was a middle-aged widow, trim, fashionably dressed, well-groomed. Two large diamond rings flashed on her fluttering hands.

Without a pause, she began to give us an account of a recent event in the building. "Oh, that hideous Harry. How I despise the disgusting fleabag. What trouble he's caused me!! Just last week, I had been to the beauty salon and was all dressed for my monthly bridge luncheon at the Brooklyn Club. When I stepped into the garden for a moment to get some flowers, suddenly my head was all wet."

Her voice rose in pitch and volume. "That awful dog had peed through the fence right onto my head. I know he did it on purpose, just to be mean and filthy." As she continued her tale, she became more agitated. "I screamed, and Harry ran back inside to hide with his mistress, that foul pretentious bitch Gladys Green, witch, tart, trollop, and that stinking George piece of garbage."

She stopped abruptly and collected herself. Then in the most dulcet and refined tones, "Oh, pardon me, I never talk like this. It's only that I was so upset. Well, I'm so glad that you boyeez have moved in. Have you lived in Brooklyn Heights before?"

We were appropriately sympathetic about Harry's sneak attack on Mrs. Terwilliger's coiffure. After that we always spoke politely and smiled faintly whenever we saw her. For a while she fluttered her eyelids at us as if we might be two stud princes who had moved in above her, intending to sweep her away to a tent in the desert, the same way Rudolph Valentino treated poor, lovely, helpless sex toy Vilma Bankey in *The Sheikh*, one of her favorite movies. But thanks to her good sense and worldly experience, she eventually realized that the territory in Apartment 2B was already occupied and was not waiting to be conquered by a social Circe like herself, and so the fire slowly died out of Mrs. Terwilliger's lovely eyes.

The other neighbors of note were the tenants in Apartment 2B in the building behind ours, just across the rear garden courtyard. We thought the place was vacant, until one night about 9 PM the lights went on, and we saw a young couple, a man and a woman, both tall and slender and with masses of long black hair. They immediately took off all their clothes and set to. Their vigor, stamina, and imaginative positions were wonderful to behold. They might have been professional contortionists, perhaps practicing for sexual exhibitions or rehearsing scenes from the *Kama Sutra*. They threw their heads and masses of hair around so vigorously that they suggested two medusas having a violent wrestling match.

Three or four times a week, at random hours, the couple repeated this skillful performance. The curtains were never closed, the shades never pulled. I imagine that most of the other neighbors enjoyed the truly virtuoso performances. (Many years later, three weeks after having an operation for a detached retina, I asked the doctor if I could have sex yet. "Yes," he said, "but don't move your head." I thought of the skillful Medusas and their muscle control.)

Two other men living on our block had names identical to mine. We got each others' telephone calls by error, but I soon learned which of the other two should get the referral. Some of the calls were very interesting, lubricious, and demanding. One of the men had a lurid social life of intense activity and variety; the other was a social slug, and of course I was out of circulation because of my schedule and my conjugal duties.

And so the year passed haltingly. I rented a small piano, which I loved to play, although I had almost no free time.

Until we moved in together, I had not realized how indiscriminately and compulsively promiscuous John was. It was a nasty shock to me. He was attracted to anything that wore pants, and with his good looks and charm he had no trouble picking up new sex partners. At the time, many stable gay relationships, perhaps most, were "open." The partners had occasional sex outside the relationship, and this was usually acceptable if it was not flaunted.

John said, "As long as you are number one, why do you care if there's a number two and a number three?" I knew that I did care, but I couldn't explain why—maybe because I had hoped for a more monogamous love relationship. He was always irritated when I refused to cook dinner for his new boyfriends and didn't care how offended I felt. This promiscuous pattern eventually became very destructive to our relationship.

As the year of internship was finishing, I committed to a three-year residency in psychiatry at a hospital in White Plains, New York. So John and I looked for a conveniently located apartment in Manhattan. We did not even think of splitting up; we thought we had a good relationship.

We found an attractive apartment close to the East River Drive, handy for commuting to White Plains by car. It even had a partial view of the East River. The renting agent in the new place was very grandiose but decided to accept us as tenants even though we were not rich or famous, and we signed a three-year lease.

And so in late June 1959 we said goodbye to Mrs. Terwilliger, had a final look at the Medusas, and moved out of Gladys's little Remsen Street love nest and into our new and somewhat grander residence on East End Avenue.

My partially satisfying love relationship was as good as I had ever known or expected. The possibility of a better relationship was not in my mind, and I was too busy to think much about it.

Internship, Brooklyn

July 1958 to July 1959

At the same time as the year at the Remsen Street apartment was occurring, I had another, separate life going on across town. They were so separated it was as if I had a double life, innocent, but difficult.

The internship started July 1, 1958, at Methodist Hospital, in the Park Slope section of Brooklyn. The twelve new interns, three women and nine men, gathered in the cafeteria. We introduced ourselves as we waited for the directors of the program to arrive. This was to be a "rotating" internship, the usual variety, during which we would work for a total of two or three months in each of the various services of the hospital: internal medicine, surgery, pediatrics, obstetrics, and the emergency room.

My colleagues were mostly graduates of East Coast medical schools. The new interns were all white, all twenty-five to thirty-five years old, but otherwise a group with a wide range of interests and backgrounds. Mostly pleasant, polite, and cordial, they were a conscientious, intelligent, and well-trained group. However, none of us had any practical experience, such as what kind of a needle to use for suturing a laceration.

The chief doctor greeted us and started our orientation. He looked at me and said, "Your first assignment is one month in the Emergency Room, starting *right now. Go!!*" He said the same to another new intern. This gave me a big scare, as I thought I didn't know enough to do emergency medicine. I was both wrong and right. The other doctor and I went to the ER and reported to the head nurse, who immediately put us to work interviewing the patients, examining, treating, suturing, and prescribing. Whenever we didn't know some point of procedure, the nurses would steer us. They kept the ER and the interns functioning smoothly.

A steady stream of new patients came in. The ER was busiest on Saturday nights and icy mornings, because of fractures, and slowest on (non-icy) weekday mornings.

If we needed help, we could call one of the specializing residents, who always promptly came. Every specialty service had several residents, and they also helped us when we rotated through their specialty departments. In case of more severe problems, the attendings, or senior doctors, were on call and were usually willing to come in to help if the resident called.

We were on call every other night and had to sleep in the hospital on those nights. Our sleeping rooms had no window screens, so mosquitoes were a problem. The worst ones were the vicious New Jersey salt marsh mosquitoes, which were blown across New York Harbor and over to Brooklyn when the wind was wrong.

One night at 2 AM I was awakened by a call from the head nurse, who said a woman had just come in complaining she couldn't breathe. This seemed to be a true emergency, perhaps life-threatening. I dressed and was in the ER in two minutes. The nurse had an unreadable expression, perhaps a faint smile, as she pointed out the emergency patient's cubicle. On entering, I saw a thirty-something woman, heavily made-up, sitting on the examining table, wearing fancy high-heeled shoes and swinging her legs, smoking a cigarette, smiling, and reeking of alcohol.

"The nurse called me and told me you were having trouble breathing?"

"Oh, yes, Doctor, but not right now. It was on the subway. I often have trouble breathing on the subway. I had some spare time, so I thought I would come in to be examined."

I began to understand. She was drunk and was just killing time by flirting with the young doctors in the ER. After a short examination which revealed nothing, except the patient's inclination to lean heavily against me, and after some flirtatious talk from her, I said, "Your examination is normal."

"Well, Doctor, I have been told that this is a psychological problem. Do you think that's possible?"

"Yes, indeed. Go home and go to bed. Bye-bye." As I left the ER, I said mildly to the head nurse, "Thanks. You know where you can find me." I gave her a big wink to signal her that we were both on to the fact that this "emergency" she had called me for was not a true emergency.

At the end of the month, I rotated to the pediatrics service for a two-month tour. The work there was a big surprise, as many of the patients tried to kick and bite me and otherwise screamed a lot. I had not encountered uncooperative patients before but soon got used to it. I learned to draw blood from the top of the heads of infants and to do other specialized procedures. Some of the patients had very sad situations, and there were a number of deaths. Again, the nurses came to our rescue and gave moral support.

The work at the hospital was hard, with very long hours. The interns generally worked thirty-six hours or more at a stretch and had every other night and every other Sunday off. I usually spent the time trying to catch up on rest, uncontrollably falling asleep at parties, at dinners, at movies, and the theater.

The hospital was in a heavily Italian section of Brooklyn, and many of the patients were Italian. Some of the older female patients, who had been in New York for forty or fifty years, couldn't speak English. They had spent their entire lives in a completely sheltered, Italian-speaking home environment. The hospital had a number of interns, residents, nurses, and other employees who were fluent in Italian, so this was not a problem.

The hospital served delicious Italian food. There was no lounge for the doctors when they had free time, so we all gathered in the cafeteria, where food was offered twenty-four hours a day, free for staff members. We used the cafeteria to discuss our current cases, our difficult situations, and to give each other moral support, encouragement, and friendship.

The next service was obstetrics. On Christmas Day, I worked on the delivery floor. There was a special, serene, benign atmosphere. The senior doctors were not inducing any deliveries for their own convenience that day. All the deliveries were easy; all the Christmas babies and mothers were well. Everyone seemed happy. It was a sweet event for me and for the mothers and babies too.

After two months on OB, it was on to the surgical service. The time on this service was busy, with many new patients, including trauma victims, to evaluate daily. I enjoyed scrubbing and assisting in the operating room but was confirmed in my decision that surgery was not really my first choice among the specialties. Two months was enough.

The medical service was even busier. For the first time, I encountered attending doctors who admitted their patients on Friday afternoons so as not to have to bother with them over the weekend. A number of these patients were real complainers, but on examination sometimes I couldn't find anything wrong with them. I entered the diagnosis of "well adult male" or "well adult female" in their charts and shortly found myself receiving an angry telephone call from the attending and was forced to write something more insurable. "Possible upper respiratory infection" or "rule out colitis" were bland and serviceable, even if untrue. There was no choice.

I felt an outrage at the behavior of these unethical, lazy, greedy doctors. One physician was well-known for sending in many patients on Friday afternoons. His patients were usually quite well, except they hadn't yet received the doctor's sizeable bill. We all had to become hardened to occasional unethical practices by some of the greedy senior doctors. Perhaps they were overworked or were saddled with extravagant wives.

However, most of the attending doctors were ethical, pleasant, skilled, and genuinely interested in the welfare of their patients and in teaching the junior doctors.

Of the other eleven interns, my special friends were Carl and Carmella, a married couple. Both were diligent, intelligent, agreeable, and generally a pleasure to work with. I invited them to dinner several times, and they invited me back just as often. They had a beautiful and charming two-year-old daughter, whom I met, but she generally did not come out to dinner with us. When the internship ended, we all went our diverse ways. Carl started an anesthesiology residency, Carmella an internal medicine residency, and I started a psychiatric residency.

About eight months later I saw in the *Times* that Carmella had died of a heart attack, the youngest woman on record to die of coronary artery disease. I thought it seemed odd and had a hard time believing it. Something didn't seem right.

A year later a friend on the staff called to tell me that Carl had been arrested and charged with murdering Carmella. The sad and sordid story involved the wealthy couple who lived next to them in suburban New Jersey. It was alleged that Carl and the neighbor's wife were having an affair and that they had conspired to murder her husband. Carl and Carmella then moved to Florida, soon followed by the widow. The next step in the plan was for Carl to murder Carmella, which he accomplished using anesthetic drugs.

But when it came time for Carl to marry the widow, he declined, having become involved with a younger woman. The jilted and enraged widow went to the police. She said she thought it odd that his wife and also a close friend of Carl's had suddenly died without apparent convincing causes of death. The bodies were exhumed, and tiny amounts of a rare and fatal drug were found in both. There was a highly publicized murder trial. Carl was found guilty and sent to prison for many years. I didn't know the widow's fate.

I was distressed by this situation and thought about how guilty, sad, and confused Carl must feel. I wavered about getting in touch with him but finally decided it was not a prudent idea. I never talked to him again. I was afraid I might make a great deal of trouble for myself. I have never been sure I made the right decision.

Twelve years later Carl was released from prison and married the younger woman. I don't know any further details.

Generally the work at the hospital was straightforward, but sometimes very odd and troubling situations arose.

One Saturday afternoon when I was working in the emergency room, a middle-aged man was brought in by his family, who were rude, hostile, and abrupt with him and with the hospital staff. He seemed terrified, had severe abdominal pain, and his blood pressure was falling. Physical examination, cardiogram, and X-rays were normal. Blood count was normal. He had not had a heart attack or a stroke. Residents and an attending came in consultation, but a diagnosis could not be made. Blood pressure continued to fall, and he died about two hours after arriving at the ER.

I asked the family for autopsy permission, and they indignantly refused. It was my duty to sign the death certificate. Although I suspected that the man had been poisoned, perhaps by his nasty family, I listed the cause of death as unknown. This was unacceptable and caused an uproar and made everyone angry with me, including the chief medical examiner of New York City, and the hospital internists, whom I hoped would insist on an autopsy. Nobody wanted the extra work this would make, as it was 4 PM on a Saturday afternoon, an inconvenient time for everyone. A proper investigation was out of the question.

I then learned an important lesson about my own weakness. Surrendering to the pressure from all sides, I changed cause of death to "possible bleeding ulcer," which was not impossible, although I didn't believe it. Nothing further was done. I have always been ashamed of my cowardice that afternoon.

Over the year of internship, I was called a number of times to attend patients who were dying. One was a fifteen-year-old boy who had leukemia and had been in the hospital for four days. His parents had been with him constantly but were exhausted and had gone home for a short rest. In spite of multiple transfusions, he was bleeding heavily and uncontrollably from his disease. He understood something very serious was happening and was terrified, whimpering, crying for his mother, and asking if he was going to die. Shaking my head, I said, "It will all be okay. Try not to be afraid; it makes the bleeding worse." My comments did not seem to help him, and I stayed by the bedside for a few hours, holding his hand, trying to soothe him. Suddenly, at 3 AM, he gave a muffled groan and died.

Another patient, a strong and healthy-looking middle-aged man, had come into the hospital the previous evening, complaining of severe chest pain. Physical examination, X-ray, cardiogram, and blood tests were all normal. All night he would shout loudly, "I'm dying. I can't stand the pain. Give me morphine. Morphine!!!" Not wanting to cover up whatever was wrong with him, we did not give him morphine or any other painkiller. Although he showed no signs of withdrawal, we all wondered if he were an addict trying to force us to give him narcotics. He repeatedly tried to climb out of bed and took swings at the two attendants who were with him all night. Physical exam, including blood pressure and repeat cardiograms, showed nothing. At 10 AM the next morning, he was again shouting loudly and jumping vigorously around in the bed, when he suddenly died. An autopsy didn't reveal the cause of death, which remained a mystery. Perhaps an arrhythmia killed him.

These two patients knew they were dying and were terrified and agitated. I was not able to quiet or console them. Of course I did not agree with them that they were dying, nor did I deny it. This is a situation most young doctors, including me, are not equipped or trained to confront, and it is always difficult for anyone with compassion, even when death might seem a relief.

I sat with perhaps twenty other patients who were dying from various ailments, usually cancer. If they wanted to talk, I listened and responded. Otherwise, I sat quietly and watched. I stepped out of the room if a clergyman arrived to administer last rites or if a relative wanted to be alone with the patient. A few hours before death, the patients began to sleep more frequently. About two hours before death, they began to look around occasionally. They usually had a tranquil expression and perhaps said a few words. About thirty minutes before death, they appeared to be asleep but still might open their eyes and say something. Breathing became slower and deeper. The breaths became further apart and finally stopped. Death had come quietly.

In none of these patients, except the two described above, did I see agitation, fear, pain, or physical distress. All the other deaths were truly peaceful. I always watched to see if the person seemed to be looking at any spirits or deceased relatives, and I never saw anything to suggest that. Neither did I see anything startling or unexplained at the moment of death, other than the tremendous central fact of death itself.

These deaths were powerful lessons of reassurance for me. After that, I could say with certainty to people who were concerned about their own death that I had seen many deaths, and they were almost always peaceful and comfortable, nothing to be afraid of. This was an invaluable lesson in my training.

I finished the year with another month's assignment in the emergency room. I was surprised how much more I knew this time, how much more competent and assured I was than a year before. The doctors still knew more about scientific matters, and the nurses still knew more about procedures. Everyone got along.

We had all looked forward to the finish of the internship year, but when it came, we were surprised how moved we were to be completing this stage of our educations and to be separating to go our own ways. I had never before bonded with a group, and this was another benefit from my year at Methodist Hospital. Since we were so busy, there was little time for socializing; the bonding was an increasing feeling of mutual respect, openness, trust, and support. We discussed our patients freely and advised one another. I liked the feeling, but it was years later before I bonded with another group.

The medical education I received was quite helpful later on in my psychiatric practice. When patients complained about physical ailments, I had a good idea of whether they were physically or emotionally caused and if the symptoms pointed to any particular diagnosis.

When the year of internship was finishing, I committed to a three-year residency in psychiatry at a hospital in White Plains, New York.

Years later, I look back with some sentimental fondness on the internship year. The work was too hard, and the hours were too long, but it was a period of considerable personal growth. I was surprised that I had been able to tolerate this difficult experience without collapsing and without permanent damage. Perhaps I was stronger than I realized.

Psychiatric Residency

East End Avenue, Residency—June 1959 to June 1962

June 30, 1959, the first day in our new apartment on East End Avenue, we rode up in the elevator with Don Ameche, the penthouse tenant. A movie star of past years, his career was just about to take on renewed life. We were surprised that the renting agent had permitted such a "show business person" to live in the building, as she had made a point of telling us that only last month she had not permitted Marilyn Monroe and her husband Joe DiMaggio to move into the building because they were show business people. Hearing her pretentious lie, John and I looked at each other and suppressed a giggle.

Don Ameche was always a pleasure to encounter, and there was a rumor in the building that Carmen Miranda, the Brazilian sparkler, and one of my favorite actresses, was a frequent visitor to his apartment. We were disappointed never to encounter her, but the anticipation of elevator glamour was always exciting.

On July 1, I began a three-year residency in psychiatry at the New York Hospital, Westchester Division, in White Plains. Most mornings I drove the forty-mile journey to work in my new two-door black Buick, the latest model, with fins that stuck out on each side at a jaunty forty-five-degree angle. Because I usually drove over the speed limit, I soon learned the locations along the road where the traffic police hid, and so I avoided ever getting a well-deserved ticket.

The work at the hospital was much less strenuous than the internship had been, and it was often very interesting, although definitely not without occasional problems.

I was on duty one night each week and one weekend each month. One evening I admitted a leading businessman, who had driven himself alone to the hospital for admission for the treatment of alcoholism. He looked very sad, but I was later told he had a good result from his treatment.

Most of the physicians and their families lived on the grounds. Only a few nonconformists (like me) commuted from New York City or elsewhere. The married senior medical staff and residents were assigned individual houses; the most junior ones were assigned an apartment in the staff house. Each of the unmarried residents, including me, was assigned a room with private bath in the staff house, very comfortable and spacious.

Meals were served in a formal, white tablecloth dining room. One of the mentally challenged waitresses liked me and knew I enjoyed bacon, so at breakfast she would serve me thirty to forty strips of bacon from the adjacent kitchen, with fully predictable effects on my waistline.

There was a Steinway grand piano in the parlor of the staff house, and I enjoyed playing after lunch and sometimes in the evenings. This was stress relieving. Occasionally some of the staff would sit and listen.

Generally, the staff got along cordially, although the most senior members could be aloof or even frosty. The head psychiatrist was a tall, portly southern gentleman with piercing blue eyes and a booming voice, a pupil of the famous Adolf Meyer, founder of the psychobiological school of psychiatry. Dr. Wall was brilliant, had an imposingly benign personality, and had a very positive effect on the patients: one patient told me that to talk with the chief was like being hypnotized by Santa Claus.

My boss was a grandmotherly-looking woman, short and overweight, also a pupil of Adolf Meyer. She waddled along like a living dumpling, wearing orthopedic space shoes and cheap dresses that looked like bathrobes. She had gray braids in a severe knotted hairdo, a sweet smile, twinkling blue eyes, and was meaner than cat shit. She seemed to enjoy denying patients' requests and was referred to (behind her back of course) as "Bad Mother," or more affectionately as "The BM." She was rumored to have a long-term relationship with the thoroughly disagreeable Miss Bundle, martinet head nurse of the electric shock treatment department.

The hospital was the second-oldest psychiatric hospital in the country and was one of the last of the old-fashioned asylum-type places. It had formerly been known as the Bloomingdale Asylum when it was located in Manhattan for about a century, where Presbyterian Hospital now stands. It moved to White Plains about one hundred years ago. There were extensive grounds and gardens for the patients to stroll about in, and it had a nine-hole golf course. The riding stables and the private dairy had been closed some years earlier.

Of the 350 patients, many were famous, rich, talented, and successful. The average stay for the active patients was eighteen months, but many of the chronic patients had been there for years or even decades.

The first two tranquillizers and the first two antidepressants had just become available and were used with a few patients, although the senior staff was suspicious of such "crutches." I enjoyed working with my patients, usually found them interesting and likeable, and did good work in helping them with their problems.

One of the members of the occupational therapy staff, Margaret Stewart, who lived in New York City, met me at my apartment most mornings for the drive up to the hospital, and she would sometimes drive back to the city with me in the evening. Her company was very pleasant, and we discussed some patients we were both working with and laughed about the foibles of the staff and other trivial matters in the Hospital. This contact was very helpful to me.

On visiting days the mother of one of my teenage female patients would also ride back to the city with me, which was frowned upon by the senior staff, as it smacked too much of some kind of personal erotic involvement or sexiness—a bunch of nonsense, if the fossilized old bigots had only opened their eyes. The mother had limited funds, and the free ride was helpful to her. Her daughter, my patient, didn't seem to care.

I settled into the routine of commuting to and from White Plains and enjoyed the drive. It was a good way to start the day gradually and a good way to finish the day by decompressing on the way home. I liked the monthly weekends on duty—making hospital rounds morning and evening, seeing my patients in an unhurried way, taking care of the occasional emergency or admission, reading, playing the piano, and having some quiet time.

Gotham Merriment

In New York, John continued to cruise the bars and the streets, picking up men frequently. He was handsome, had light brown hair, bright blue eyes, a charming smile, and was friendly and sociable. He behaved seductively, and many men responded to his obvious and enthusiastic admiration. He drank heavily, and this led to numerous all-night absences from home. I was always distressed by these, but I managed to say nothing to him about my feelings, as in the past that had always precipitated severe arguments but no change in his behavior. Sometimes he had to go to his advertising job straight from his extramarital bed of passion.

I eventually took my cue from John and began to cruise the gay bars myself, an activity which was not very fruitful, so to speak, but expensive and conducive to hangovers. I soon decided it was more practical to go to the baths when I wanted to meet someone or many ones for physical intimacy.

John usually spent Saturday nights out drinking and whoring about, while I was at home innocently sleeping. Sundays John would sleep off the excesses of the previous night, and often I would go early to the baths, arriving fresh and rested at 8 AM. There were fewer drunks among the early morning clientele, but many of the customers had the hangover hots.

There were a number of gay bath establishments in New York, the largest and most popular of which, the Everard Baths, was on West Twenty-Eighth Street and was rumored to be owned by the Policemen's Benevolent Association, which we all thought protected us from police raids there.

The Everard had formerly been a synagogue, and the very pretty stained glass dome was still in place, serving as the ceiling for the top floor. There was a small swimming pool in the basement, previously used for ritual bathing, and a steam room about fifteen feet square. Both watering spots were used for pickups and for sex play.

The first floor had lockers, showers, and a small café. The second floor had a dormitory arrangement with perhaps thirty cots in rows in the center, with private rooms lining the four sides of the rectangular space. The third floor featured an H-shaped corridor layout, with many private, double, or multiple-occupancy rooms opening off the corridors.

The whole place had a disagreeable smell of unwashed, overheated bodies, cheap bathroom deodorizer, stale cigarette smoke, vomit, beer, and other spilled fluids. There was very little conversation or laughter to be heard, but there were other sounds, ranging from delicate, mouselike sighs to stentorian grunts, curses, and cries of passion as someone passed the point of orgasmic inevitability. There were occasional loud slapping and spanking noises followed by moans of pleasurable pain.

Some of the room doors were open in invitation; some were closed, the occupants presumably busy or resting. Holes of varying sizes had been cut in the walls between the rooms for peeping and to be used as glory holes.

The male clientele was of all ages, sizes, shapes, and degrees of intoxication, ranging from completely sober to passed out. One or two angels of death, carriers of disease or other disasters, were usually present in the crowd. No one knew who they were, and no one cared. There were even occasional prostitutes trolling for drunk victims who would prefer to pay. Everyone was dressed in long, thin, ghostly white cotton robes and wore flimsy paper slippers, necessary because the floors were so filthy and sticky.

The seekers shuffled around and around the corridors and up and down the stairways on either side of the building, inspecting the offerings, hoping to meet Mr. Dreamsex. Sometimes they retired to a dark spot or to a private room (or not), or to an orgy room, for attempted consummation of whatever private or group fantasy was being played out.

As I shuffled along in lockstep with the other ghostly members of the chain gang, in my head I could hear a cruel Cupid singing Bessie Smith's song "Baby Doll." ("I want to be somebody's baby doll.") By 4 PM, there had been enough time for a satisfying variety of Baby Doll events with five to twenty of my cohorts.

Then home again, where John and I would have dinner together, perhaps a pot roast and apple pie, or other wholesome Midwestern dishes which Iowa-born John cooked very well.

We sometimes had guests for drinks or dinner and usually played bridge afterward. One of the frequent guests was John's friend and college classmate, Steve Paine, usually called Crystal Pane. Crystal was a redheaded charmer and sociopath, constantly moving on the continuum between elegant courtesan and manipulative whore, whatever was appropriate for the situation. A friend who knew from experience told me that Crystal was magnificent in bed—very helpful in his chosen line of work.

Sometimes he would tell us with a laugh that he had a new "victim" and that he was holding out for some expensive present for his birthday the following week. Crystal had many birthdays each year for his various victims to celebrate—I don't know how he kept it all straight (so to speak).

At our little parties, John drank heavily. When drunk, he would repeatedly play the same musical. One of his special favorites was Irving Berlin's "Call Me Madam." I would eventually ask him to stop playing the same thing over and over. He would refuse. I would get enraged, tear the phonograph from its connections, and, after looking down to the street to see that nobody was walking below, hurl it out the window, putting a sudden stop to the music. This became expensive, so later I just tore off the tone arm and threw it out the window; eventually I just tore off the cartridge and threw that out the window, which was equally effective and not so costly to repair.

John Puckett, New York, Christmas 1962

Crystal roared with laughter. John became sullen and said to Crystal, "Let's get out of here and go somewhere where we can have some fun." He turned to me and said, "You're a piece of shit." Inwardly, I sorrowfully agreed with him, as I remembered my father's similar opinion of me. Then John and Crystal would both leave for a night on the town. *Good riddance*, I thought. We all had been sticking our snoots in the gin bottle of course.

Sparky

However, it was through Crystal that Sparky, our adored wirehaired dachshund, came into our lives. Sparky was born in November 1958 of championship canine lineage, in the upstate kennels of Averell Harriman, New York financier and former governor.

At two months of age, he was given to one of Governor Harriman's friends. Sparky was such a handful that three months later he was given away to Philip van Rensselaer, two months after that to his brother Charlie van Rensselaer, and two months later to Crystal. He was also too much for Crystal, who one month later offered him to John.

After consulting with each other, we decided to accept. I immediately fell in love with Sparky. He was one of the dearest beings in my life: intelligent, loyal, stubborn, mischievous, and refusing to be house-trained. He was full of abandonment anxiety and would sit outside the bathroom screaming if John or I went inside and closed the door. He definitely objected to being left alone.

Sparky working as a model, 1962

I liked Sparky better than I liked John. Sparky liked John better than he liked me. And John liked me better than he liked Sparky. This was a miniature cross-species version of Arthur Schnitzler's "Reigen."

Evening Exercise in the Fresh Air

One evening after our usual dinner and drinks and argument, John went off cruising to the bars.

At Seventieth Street there was a pedestrian overpass across the East River Drive and down into the park running along the river. Adjacent to the overpass was the Cornell University Medical College, where I had gone to school, and the New York Hospital, where I was still in training at its Westchester Division.

The overpass was designed so as to include a secluded recess about three feet deep and twenty feet long, facing away from the Drive and toward the East River. Men standing in the recess could not be seen from cars on the Drive, from the buildings along the Drive, or by strollers on the overpass. This was a popular gathering place for open-air gay sex.

That night, it seemed to me that this was exactly where I should go, and I was glad to see that there were about ten men already there. Most had taken off all their clothes except for their shoes and socks, and I rapidly joined the fun. This broke one of my cardinal rules for good interpersonal relations: when having sex, a bed should always be nearby.

After about an hour of this frolicking, with some men leaving and some new ones arriving, someone hissed in a low voice, "Here come the police!!" Suddenly, a searchlight mounted on a police boat in the river came on, and it shone brilliantly on us, exposing all. The clothes went back on with frantic speed.

I started walking north in the park along the drive, but the police were coming toward us from that direction. I then went south, but the police were coming from that direction too. I tried to escape across the overpass, but the police were already standing on top. I considered diving into the East River, but the police boat still had its searchlight on, so even that was blocked.

We were all caught in a raid: very lurid and right next to New York Hospital. I could see my career evaporating in disgrace, and I was really afraid. After what seemed like an hour, the police merely said, "Go home, and don't come back here again!!" and we all scattered like frightened birds.

A demon had led me to the recess, and an angel must have helped me escape. I ran the eleven blocks up the street to the apartment. John was still out, so at least I didn't have to cope with him. Sparky seemed worried, and we kissed each other. I gave him a hug, and we went to bed. I was so scared that I didn't go back to the overpass and its recess for almost three weeks.

Eight years later, John suddenly moved away with a new boyfriend, and Sparky began to mourn. For the next five years he sat by the front door for several hours every evening, waiting for John to come home. Sometimes tears would come when I saw him waiting so faithfully. Sparky was a truly pathetic little dog who never recovered from his last and worst abandonment. He died suddenly of a heart attack in 1972, age thirteen years, eight months, and thirteen days. Then it was my turn to mourn.

We were all in danger, as a friend said, of becoming roadkill on the highway of love.

Soon afterwards, my mother decided to take us on a winter holiday in Barbados, and I was glad for the change of scene.

Author and his mother, Barbados, 1962

Lilac Time in Vienna

Two months before the end of my residency training and four months before my twenty-ninth birthday in 1962, my mother decided to honor the occasion by taking me on our first trip to Europe. My father, predictably, decided to stay home, which was better for us all.

The first stop was Switzerland: the Beau Rivage Palace Hotel in Lausanne, deluxe and very formal. When we checked into the hotel, the desk clerk, unsmiling, snooty, and supercilious, asked my mother how she intended to pay the bill: an unfortunate choice of words, implying his doubt that she could afford to stay in the hotel. Mother immediately entered her paranoid world and went on the attack—a snarling Doberman could not have been more startling. Pounding the desk with the side of her left hand, she demanded in a loud and stuttering voice to see the manager. While waiting two minutes for him to appear, she skillfully and viciously berated the desk clerk for his insolence and stupidity. I found Mother's low-jinks tedious and slightly embarrassing but knew she had great staying power when angered and could get even nastier.

The manager, looking rather alarmed, was able to sooth Mother's injured feelings—so sorry, a misunderstanding, please forgive, never happen again, honored guests. He handled this very smoothly and appropriately and soon showed us upstairs to our beautiful rooms. I'm sure he was expert at dealing with disgruntled and disagreeable guests. Large rooms with murals on their high domed ceilings, marble pillars, oriental carpets, French doors opening onto views of Lake Geneva, the Alps rising up behind Evian on the opposite side, hushed voices: all gave an air of luxury, refinement, and expense.

At lunch the first day, I ordered Swiss cheese. The waiter gave me the fish-eye and said, "But sir, all our cheeses are Swiss. What do you wish?" Five days of looking at Lake Geneva and the Alps and eating Swiss cheeses were enough for us both.

After a short flight from Geneva, the plane made the descent to Vienna, the second stop on our itinerary. As we lost altitude, we could see houses, roads, extensive farmlands, and the Danube.

It was late April, lilac time, and on the drive into town, the air was filled with the sweet fragrance from thousands of large lilac bushes blooming everywhere.

On arrival at the Imperial Hotel, reputedly the best in the city, my mother wasted no time in throwing a tantrum because she didn't like her room. The hotel manager knew he was dealing with a loose cannon, so he immediately moved her into a large suite, which was more in keeping with her fantasies of grandeur. The beautiful two-bedroom suite with a terrace cost twelve dollars a day (memories of the distant past). I had a perfectly nice small room located in the back part of the hotel, one floor above my mother's suite, a desirable geographic separation.

After a fine dinner at the hotel and a wonderful performance of Strauss's "Ariadne auf Naxos" at the Opera, we walked back past more lilacs to the hotel, had a nightcap in the bar, made plans to meet the next morning at ten for sightseeing, then said goodnight and retired to our rooms.

Once in my room, I took off my necktie and considered going to bed, but I began to think of poor beautiful Archduke Rudolph, who had died for love along with his Marie, and poor beautiful Archduke Maximilian, who became emperor of Mexico and died there tragically. It was only a short jump to think of the jolly beautiful acrobats in their harlequin-patterned tights who had appeared in this evening's opera, displaying their fine legs as they tumbled about the stage. Feeling restless and feeling a pleasant stirring below, I went out on the Ringstrasse, the large street in front of the hotel, walked a block away, and hailed a taxi.

The driver did not speak English, and my German was not only rudimentary but had a strong Texas accent. I asked the driver to take me to "ein Bar für Menschen" (a bar for men).

"Jawohl," he said, and we began to drive around. He soon pointed to a woman leaning against a streetlamp and said to me, "Mädchen, Ja?" (A girl, okay?)

I said, "Danke, kein Mädchen, aber Menschen." (Thank you, not girls, men instead.) I could see he was puzzled but agreeable, so we drove around for a while. He had mistaken my word "Menschen" for the word "Mädchen," meaning maiden or young girl, but also hooker, tart, lady of the evening.

"Mädchen," he said again.

"Nein. Menschen," I said.

We continued speaking ping-pong and driving in fruitless loops for about ten minutes. What to do now? I suddenly remembered another plural for men, "Männer," which has overtones of little, unimportant, effeminate. So, "Männer," I said to the driver.

"Ach! Ja! Versteh!" he said. (Okay! I understand!)

He drove at high speed around the Ringstrasse, turned onto a main road, and drove out of the city. Before long we were in the countryside, which soon turned into deserted farmland. What now? Was I being set up for robbery or worse? I was ready to jump and run and fight to escape.

He stopped in front of a completely dark and isolated farmhouse. "Da," he said, pointing to the house. I couldn't tell whether it was more dangerous to stay with the driver or to separate from him. Flipping a mental coin, I paid, got out, and the car sped away and left me standing in an empty field before the dark house. I was frightened and disoriented, and the situation seemed completely out of control.

I tried to relate my location to the memory of what I had seen from the plane the day before, but I hadn't recognized any landmarks as we drove out of the city. It was 1 AM; I was turned around and was out in a cow pasture miles from town. There was nothing for it but to ask for help. I assumed if there were any people inside the house, they surely were all asleep. At the front door, I knocked softly, and then again a little louder.

A peephole opened in the door, an eye inspected me for a few moments, and then the door opened and the smiling doorkeeper motioned me in. What was I getting into? Perhaps something seriously sinister? Inside, in the very dim light, were about twenty men, nicely but casually dressed, ages about eighteen to eighty. Three couples were dancing; the rest of the men were sitting at tables or standing at the bar. I heard laughter and the familiar clinking of ice cubes. Apparently most people knew one another.

Three men sitting at a table near the door saw I was a stranger and invited me to join them, much to my relief, as I had not yet recovered my composure from the unnerving taxi ride. We drank beer and conversed in mixed English and German: Where are you from? Have you been in Vienna before? Do you like to dance? After about thirty minutes of primitive inconsequentialities, my new friends said they had to leave: good-bye, auf Wiedersehen. Now what?

My eyes had been caressing a good looker, a studly guy standing at one end of the bar, and he had been looking right back. Not wanting to sit alone at the table, I went over to the end of the bar and stood next to Mr. Studly. He was about six-two, two hundred pounds, maybe thirty years old, looked very solid and well-built, had a handsome face, blond hair, blue eyes, and a ready and charming smile. We smiled and began to talk as best we could.

"John," I said.

"Franzi," he said.

After an hour and a couple of beers, I asked him if he would like to come back to my hotel with me so he could see my room. Apparently interested in hotel furnishings, Franzi said yes, of course, but he was hungry and wanted something to eat beforehand. His favorite restaurant, named Hölle (Hell), was in the central city, but it did not open until 4 AM, and it was only 2:30. Thirty minutes later, after another beer, we called a taxi, which came surprisingly soon, and we arrived at Hölle right at 4 AM.

The restaurant turned out to be in a cellar, gloomy and smelling of stale cigarettes and beer. Customers soon started arriving and looked to be night people, to put it politely, with faces showing obvious signs of having lived strenuously dissipated lives, or worse. Equal numbers of men and women, ages thirty-five to fifty, they mostly looked as if they needed an emergency trip to the shower. In spite of juicy coughs, most of them had cigarettes hanging from their mouths. Several of them seemed to need a wrinkle lift. As at the gay bar, the customers seemed to know one another and to know my companion.

Franzi and I sat at a table; he ordered pea soup and beer; I just had a beer. Some of the others denizens joined us. I seemed to be getting further from my goal by the minute. Franzi and I played a stimulating game of knees under the table for about forty-five minutes, and I enjoyed massaging his excellent thigh. At the same time he slurped his pea soup, smacked his lips, and talked with his friends. I was getting discouraged and so said I was tired and was going home. Franzi gave me a dazzling smile and whispered something in my ear, "Ich bin wie ein Gott im Bett." Eager to understand, I tried to remember German vocabulary, and when I finally understood ("I am like a God in bed"), my fatigue vanished. It seemed like a good idea to stay a while longer, to eventually experience this divinity in action.

Franzi ordered more pea soup. If my handsome Franzi liked pea soup, so would I! Pea soup had always been one of my least favorite foods, bilious green, tasting of dirt, and with a revolting lumpy texture, as if it were made from mashed worms. To my surprise, it had now become surprisingly delicious, perhaps due to the power of suggestion, combined with erotic excitement and the beers which had gone before. Franzi's head began to droop occasionally, and his shining blond hair was close to falling into his soup. Using two fingers, I brushed his hair out of soup's way several times.

By 5:15 I began to wonder if there would be enough time for the hoped-for divine bedroom frolic before meeting Mother at ten. This was the moment of decision.

I whispered to Franzi, "We really need to go to my room now. I hope you'll come with me."

He said, "Oh, yes, of course," but first he wanted to have a ham sandwich and another beer.

"Okay," I said. I ordered the sandwich and beer for him. After five minutes, the sandwich arrived. At the same time, I gave up and decided to leave. I paid the bill, noticing that a number of Franzi-friends had piggybacked onto my check. I said good-bye to Franzi, who didn't seem to notice. He had gone to sleep and was snoring loudly, his sandwich and beer sitting untouched before him, his pretty blond hair floating on the surface of his soup. I was getting hungry and was tempted to eat the sandwich but restrained myself. Mr. Studly's friends smiled, and we all waved good-bye—bye-bye—auf Wiedersehen.

I walked back to the hotel past more lilacs, fantasizing luridly about what sex with Franzi might have been like. I arrived at 7:30 and slept for two hours before getting up (with a pounding headache and a fierce hangover) to get ready for a big day of sightseeing. At ten Mother and I met in the lobby.

Smiling, she asked, "How did you sleep?"

"Very well, fine, thank you, and you?"

Later in the day we were down in the Hapsburg crypt, looking at the coffins of various imperials, including beautiful Rudolph and tragic Maximilian. I thought, *Probably lucky to have escaped Mr. Studly Franzi without any trouble. He said he was like a god in the bed, but I suspect a pig-in-a-blanket would be more like it.* Curiously, I have been fond of pea soup ever since.

Author and his mother, Vienna, 1962

XXXXXXXXXXXXXXXXXXXXXXXXXXXXXXXXXXXXXXXXXXXX

Opening an Office

At the end of June 1962, my three-year residency finished, and I was ready to start a private practice in New York City. I was fortunate to find my way to Frances Arkin, MD, an elderly psychoanalyst who wanted to retire. She had a combined office and residence at 750 Park Avenue, at Seventy-Second Street, a prime location. The building management was willing to disconnect the two parts of her apartment by building a wall between them. My part would consist of a consulting room, small waiting room, bathroom, kitchen, and a small terrace.

Dr. Arkin and I had very friendly negotiations, and I bought her office furniture. I signed a two-year lease with the building and moved in on July 1. This was a momentous day for me, as it is for any young doctor when he starts practice and opens his own office for the first time. Within a few days I was seeing patients in my new quarters.

Dr. and Mrs. Nandor Fodor soon moved in to Dr. Arkin's former apartment, now across the hall from my new office. Dr. Fodor was a well-known old psychoanalyst from Budapest, whose special interest was poltergeists and hauntings. He was a friendly man, and we soon became acquainted. I had many cordial talks with him and also with Mrs. Fodor, who had the Hungarian charm and good looks of her countrywomen, Mama Jolie Gabor and her three glamorous daughters.

The Fodors soon invited me to the premiere of a movie, *The Haunting of Hill House*, for which he had been a consultant. On the screen were dark shadows, sinister-looking stairways, and supposedly real ghosts. In the audience were the stars of the movie and other celebrities. The movie was something of a dud. The audience was more interesting than the events portrayed on the screen. There was a gala party afterward, with Dr. Fodor the center of much interest.

He offered to take me to his next poltergeist case, and I looked forward to at last seeing this phenomenon. Unfortunately, Dr. Fodor suddenly died of a heart attack the following month, and so there was no poltergeist visit for me. His funeral was the first I had ever attended.

I didn't do much work to build a busy practice, so I had considerable free time in my office, which I used to catch up on long-neglected reading. Soon the practice was supporting about 50 percent of my living expenses. The other 50 percent was given to me by my mother on a month-to-month basis. She was very generous and would sometimes fund extra purchases, such as a particularly beautiful jade piece from an auction at Sotheby's. Her financial help continued until her death three and a half years later.

One afternoon about two months later, I heard piccolo music coming up from the street. Going out on my terrace to investigate, I looked down at the smallest parade I had ever seen. There were just nine men, dressed in red and black uniforms, trimmed with gold braid. They wore polished gold helmets with spikes on the top. As they marched jauntily along in a single file, one played a piccolo and another played a drum.

Only one lane of Park Avenue had been blocked off for this parade, and there was a police guard to see that the marchers were not bothered by the traffic. It was a parade of the veterans of the Spanish-American war, which had taken place in 1898, some sixty-five years before. In following years, I watched for the tiny parade again but never saw another, so I assumed that I had seen the final proud parade of this vanishing group.

Later there was a gathering of many major world leaders at the United Nations. Again looking down from my terrace, I saw several of them. The most impressive was Sarvepalli Radhakrishnan, president of India, who was also a world-famous philosopher. He went by in a large open car, sitting majestically in the middle of the backseat. He looked like a cross between God, as shown on the ceiling of the Sistine Chapel, and Santa Claus. Beaming benignly at the crowds along the street, he graciously acknowledged their applause as he passed by. Part of the fun of living in New York is to notice the many interesting, sometimes unexpected, sights.

I found my new office comfortable and convenient, and the first two years of my practice passed by pleasantly. After a year and a half, Dr. Arkin called. She told me she had retired to a beautiful house in Nantucket but had been bored there after a lifetime of practicing psychoanalysis.

She said she had become depressed and so had decided to return to New York to live and to resume her psychoanalytic practice. I was anticipating that she was going to ask me to give her office back, but instead she said that she was moving into a new building on East 68th Street, where she was going to live and also practice. By coincidence, John and I had been living in that same building for the past fifteen months.

In July of 1962, John and I had decided to move from East End Avenue to a more central location in Manhattan. At that time, there were plenty of apartments available in New York. Some buildings even offered two or three months free rent as an inducement for new tenants to move in. We had been watching a tall building going up on East Sixty-Eighth Street and signed a three-year lease there. On August 1, 1962, we moved into our new apartment.

We were the first tenants in the apartment, which was on the thirty-third floor and had a panoramic view of Manhattan. On clear days, the Atlantic Ocean shimmered in the distance. The apartment was unusual in that it had one bedroom but two full bathrooms, very convenient for our living arrangement. I bought a cheerful, fuzzy bright red rug for the front bathroom, which we called the guest bathroom. Dog Sparky adjusted well to the move.

The building was attractive, but the walls seemed very thin. However, as Louis Rudin, one of the Rudin brothers, our landlords, lived there with his family, the service was excellent.

One morning the kitchen window suddenly and spontaneously fell out of its frame and crashed down onto the street thirty-three floors below, fortunately not hurting anyone. We called the service department, and workers arrived within an hour to replace the window, this time more securely.

The walls were so thin that you could almost hear the neighbors eating toast in the mornings. When I was in the bedroom and the service phone rang, I could not tell whether I was hearing it ringing in my kitchen, through the wall from the next apartment, or through the floor from the apartment below. There were many useless and hurried trips to answer the call, only to find it was not for my apartment.

The neighbors, Donitra and Jan Lahki, and their beagle dog, Katy, were cordial when we first moved in. They had been living there about two weeks and were the first tenants in their apartment. Our font doors opened opposite one another across a hallway. Sparky and Katy sniffed each other cheerfully and wagged their tails.

John and I were both glad to move away from the scene of our increasing dissipation and depravity on East End Avenue. I hoped our lives would become more orderly and wholesome in a new location. Naturally, this was not to be. As Seneca said, "Change of sky, same self." He knew.

I rented a small piano and put it in the living room, against the wall shared with the neighboring apartment. As my psychiatric practice grew quite slowly, I had some free time and enjoyed playing the piano two hours on most days, usually in the early afternoon.

For a while there was no problem with the music. Then one afternoon, while I was playing, the doorbell rang. It was Donitra from next door. She shyly requested that the music stop for a while, as she was trying to take a nap.

"Oh, I'm so sorry. Sure—no more music for the rest of the day," I said. A few days later there was another ring at the door: again it was Donitra complaining about the "noise," as she called the music. Shortly there was a complaint every time I played, no matter what time of day it was. Then she no longer rang the bell but just pounded on the wall.

She must have liked Chopin, because there was no pounding during his music, but anything by Mozart would bring on a regular thunderstorm of pounding. Maybe my Mozart playing was not up to her standards. The neighborly relationship was getting quite sour by this time.

Neighbors from Hell

One Saturday night, John and I had been out at one of our favorite gay bars, where we knew a number of the regulars. When the bar closed at 3 AM, we invited several of our fellow barflies to come back to our apartment to continue drinking and having a good time. One of the group had a birthday that day, and another was a professional cabaret pianist. A loud and very extended version of "Happy Birthday" was begun. All joined in adding a vigorous and tuneless vocal part.

After about ten minutes, close to 5 AM by then, loud wall pounding began from the Lahkis' apartment. Several of the guests said, "Fuck you!!" in loud voices, yelling at the wall. The pounding got louder. "Fuck you," we all shouted with great energy and conviction. After a while, the pounding stopped. We were satisfied that we had vanquished the pesky Lahkis. We all enjoyed more drinks and more piano playing.

Soon the intercom rang from downstairs. It was the doorman, requesting that we lower the noise level, as he had complaints from our neighbors.

"Who?" I asked.

"Oh, you know," he said, "but still, they're within their rights, so please quiet down."

"Okay," I said. I told the guests that there were complaints about our music and singing, and that it was getting late, time to break up the party, bye-bye. Everyone yelled, "Fuck you," at the wall a few more times and then left. John and I staggered into the bedroom and passed out.

We were behaving like neighbors from hell. Demon rum was on a rampage and was causing a rumpus.

At 6 AM the phone rang. "How do you like being waked up?" asked Donitra, who then hung up. Every twenty minutes for the next five hours she called again. After that, three or four nights a week, without any further provocation, she would call multiple times at late (or early AM) hours. When we saw each other in the corridor or the elevator, there was a glacial silence. Even the dogs quit wagging their tails at one another.

If she heard our doorbell ring when we were having guests, Donitra would throw open her door and glare at our guests, startling them. She would continue glaring until they were safely inside our apartment. Eventually she progressed to asking our guests, "Oh, are you here to visit those fags?"

One day, a friend in the building told us that an agitated woman, probably our neighbor, was sitting in the lobby, telling other tenants and visitors about the two drunken degenerates who lived next to her, how dissipated we were, how much noise we made, how rude we were, disgusting queers, et cetera. I was a little surprised to hear Donitra was so upset that she had started a vendetta. The next day, another friend said he had been riding up in the elevator with an unknown woman, who suddenly began to tell him about the vile fags who lived next door to her and were persecuting her day and night with noise and evil looks.

We occasionally saw Frances Arkin in the elevator and always had a short, pleasant conversation with her. One day she told us that Donitra had approached her and started telling her nasty things about us. Dr. Arkin smiled and winked as she recounted this. Borderline psychotics were neither new nor socially interesting to her.

Donitra's increasing agitation began to worry me, and so I talked with the building management, who had an office on the first floor. They tried to be polite but obviously thought I was a paranoid complaining about a neighbor who was slandering me—a common delusion. They obviously didn't want to get involved in this sticky situation. I didn't blame them.

Ten days later, the management office called me and asked me to come down. I went immediately and was worried as I walked in. They told me that the owner and his wife, along with his attorney and his wife, had been in the elevator when an agitated woman unknown to them got in and immediately started telling them scurrilous stories about John and me. The owner and his lawyer were both displeased.

The building management subsequently spoke with Donitra and warned her to stop telling people nasty gossip about her neighbors, or she would be evicted. I was very surprised and pleased that the management was siding with me. After that, whenever Donitra saw me, she glared. If anyone could shoot feces through her eyes, Donitra had mastered the trick. But I heard of no more malicious gossip from her.

My peace gesture, which perhaps she never knew of, was to move the piano away from the common wall between the two apartments and into the bedroom. There were then two additional walls and about twenty feet more distance from the common wall. I bought a mute for the piano, a rather unusual and hard to find item. Relations did not improve, then or later.

I arrived home about 8 PM one evening to find two fire trucks just pulling away from the building. The lobby had a smoky smell. After checking with the doorman that it was safe to use the elevator, I went up to the apartment. John was home, looking somewhat agitated, and Sparky was also there, looking solemn. There was a smoky smell in the apartment. John told me there had been a fire somewhere in the building, and that the stairwells and elevators and lobbies had been full of smoke. Smoke was dense in our apartment, and John had worried that Sparky would be asphyxiated, so he had held him out the window for some time in an attempt to help him breathe. Neither John nor Sparky was harmed. The firemen had taken care of the trouble.

Later, my father thought this was an interesting (and perhaps lucrative) problem and said he would make a hydraulic escape device which would lower a seat at a constant rate the thirty-three floors down to the ground. Unfortunately, he died before he could construct this apparatus.

We hired a cleaning lady, Sarah Nell, who claimed she was eighty-five years old. I believed she was at least that age. She was cheerful and did a fair job of cleaning the apartment, was reliable, didn't break things, and didn't steal, with the major exception that she drank the liquor from the back of the liquor cabinet. She probably thought we wouldn't notice that she drank the Punt e Mes or the Calvados or the blue Curacao and had emptied the bottles.

I found this out one day when I was making one of my favorite dishes, sautéed veal with apples, Calvados, and cream. It was then I discovered there was no Calvados in the bottle. I found the other empty bottles and deduced what had been happening. There was a little Grand Marnier left, so I used that instead, which gave a peculiar, although tasty enough, result. I put a lock on the liquor cabinet.

Sarah Nell was also given to using our food in an inappropriate way. I had bought a large cucumber to put into a salad and had stored it in the fridge. When it came time to make the salad, I took out the cucumber and started to wash it. I noticed that several small clumps of bright red fuzz were sticking to its skin. What could this odd material be? And then I remembered the bright red fuzzy shaggy bathroom rug. The fuzz on the cucumber matched the fuzz on the rug exactly. The cucumber had become a monument to the longevity and strength of the human sex drive. I sighed, scratched my head, and threw the monument into the garbage. No cucumber was in that night's salad.

One afternoon when she finished work, Mrs. Nell put on her hat and coat, said good-bye, then went into the hall closet and closed the door behind her. In a few moments she emerged looking confused and said good-bye again.

This time she wobbled toward the front door and successfully made her exit, probably with some of my liquor inside.

Moving Again

And so the months staggered by as we continued to work, drink, carouse, quarrel, and generally act in a disreputable way. We were living out *A Rake's Progress*. By autumn of 1963 we had been at East Sixty-Eighth Street for fifteen months and had worn out our welcome there. We decided that the situation had become too uncomfortable and thought we should look for another place.

I consulted a highly recommended real estate agent and told her I was a serious musician and played the piano at least six hours daily, often in the middle of the night, and so we needed an apartment with very thick walls, thick enough to be soundproof. I thought this exaggeration was justified in order to get the point across that we really needed an apartment soundproof enough to protect both the neighbors and ourselves.

"I have just the thing," she said, "two penthouses in an old building." We went to look at them. They were both very comfortable, had high ceilings, fireplaces, walls covered in moiré silk, and large terraces. They were both rented by Olivier Coquelin, a handsome and elegant young Frenchman who had introduced discotheques into the United States. He owned Le Club, which was his second discotheque and very fashionable at the moment. Later, he opened another exclusive disco, the Cheetah. Coquelin had a small pink cheetah painted on the door of his black Rolls Royce convertible, and he certainly looked dashing in his sleek auto. His good looks and café society chic helped persuade us to rent from him, along with the real estate agent's recommendation of the building's soundproofing.

We decided on the penthouse on the Fifty-Fifth Street side of the building and signed a two-year lease as subtenants of Mr. Coquelin. We were able to get out of our lease On sixty-eighth Street, and we moved into our new soundproof palace on January 4, 1964. We were happy to move out of the Paperwall Tower and away from psychotic Donitra. We said good-bye to Sarah Nell with relief, lying to her that we were moving out of town.

As an inducement for Mr. Coquelin to rent to us, we had to buy all his furniture in the apartment. There were some good quality antiques, and some not so good, but the price was both mandatory and reasonable.

We already had an apartment full of furniture but thought we could manage the excess furniture problem after we moved in. There was so much furniture that many pieces were on top of each other (literally), and there was only a narrow aisle down the center of each room. We later called the Salvation

Army to donate some of the furniture. When they saw the expensive and hideous custom-made mustard velvet sofa, they said, "Oh, no! We don't want that." We begged them to take it. They agreed and removed the five-thousand-dollar monstrosity, along with some other less hideous pieces. The terrace had an inflatable pink plastic swimming pool, which we soon discarded.

We liked our new apartment and our new handsome landlord. Sparky seemed happy in the new location, and he marked the territory as his by gently lifting his leg in various places, both inside the apartment and also outside on the terrace.

We sat on one of the several sofas, smiled, smoked cigarettes, and had some celebratory martinis. We were both drunk by the time the sun went down.

We had no idea of the sadness that was coming.

XXXXXXXXXXXXXXXXXXXXXXXXXXXXXXXXXXXXXXXXXXXXX

We enjoyed making the terrace more usable. A red maple tree was already growing there, and it was joined by a flowering crabapple, a willow, a mulberry tree, and other planters full of annuals: morning glories, sunflowers, moonflowers, zinnias, marigolds, and various plants which changed with the seasons and the years. We arranged some chairs and a table on the terrace— just right for bridge games, usually drunken ones.

I again rented a small piano from Steinway and began taking piano lessons from a wonderful teacher, Willard Macgregor, who had studied with Artur Schnabel, Isidor Phillip, Ernest Hutcheson, and other eminent teachers.

Over the years of studying with Willard, he became a friend as well as a teacher. He knew many musicians, and he introduced me several times to Igor Stravinsky, a small man, formal, polite, and quite pleasant; Giovanni Martinelli, the operatic tenor star, charming and still full of energy at age eighty; Polly Kazlova, former child prodigy violinist; Samuel Dushkin, violinist and friend of Horowitz; and many others. He had known Madeline Mannheim as a child in St. Louis (she is the honoree of Busoni's Third Sonatina entitled *Par usum infantis MM*), had heard Busoni play in Saint Louis before the First World War and remembered the program, had played Ravel for Ravel, Roussel for Roussel, Emil Blanchet for Emil Blanchet. He had played first performances of a major piece of Hindemith (*Ludus Tonalis*), and also of a piece for two pianos of Stravinsky, with Stravinsky at the other piano.

He told me of an unprinted change in the manuscript of Liszt's *Sonnetto del Petrarca #104*, which Liszt wanted pianists to perform differently from its printed version. Liszt had told his pupil Isidor Phillip, and Isidor Phillip had passed the information on to his pupil, my teacher. I was thrilled to have a piece of interpretive information passing straight down from Liszt to me. Liszt had studied with Czerny, who had studied with Beethoven, and so the tradition goes on. Willard knew many of the major concert pianists of the twentieth century and told me dozens of amusing anecdotes concerning musical personalities.

Life was beginning to seem interesting, comfortable, rewarding, and even relaxed at times.

However, after our move to the new apartment, our pattern of drinking, quarreling, and dissolute promiscuity continued seamlessly. We thought we were leading an interesting, amusing, even glamorous life. The truth was that we were starting the slide downhill into dead-end alcoholism.

XXXXXXXXXXXXXXXXXXXXXXXXXXXXXXXXXXXXXXXXXXXX

Before we moved to Fifty-Fifth Street, our friend Steve (aka Crystal Pane) had told us he was acquainted with Clarence Sarlox, the man who lived in the apartment above us, and suggested we might like to meet for a drink to get acquainted. The apartment above ours, the so-called "Tower Penthouse," could only be reached by taking the elevator to our floor, going out onto a public terrace, and then climbing an external iron staircase to the floor above. The Tower Penthouse was unusual for New York. It had twenty-foot ceilings and a terrace so large that it was planted with grass; the lawn needed to be mowed on a regular basis.

I slipped a note under Sarlox's door, inviting him to call us to arrange a date to meet and have a drink together at our apartment. A few days later he called, and a date was set for 7 PM the next evening.

Clarence arrived punctually. He was about forty years old, heavyset, with dark hair and eyes. Well dressed in a suit and tie, he looked tired and remained unsmiling through the meeting. We chatted about the history of the building and about famous past and present tenants, a long list which included Maggie Teyte, Lotte Lenya, Noel Coward, Van Johnson, Lucille Ball, Paulette Goddard and Erich Maria Remarque, Joan Fontaine, Hermione Gingold, and many more. We found out nothing about him personally, and he asked no questions of us.

After one martini, he suddenly said, "Well, I accepted your invitation this time, but I'll never accept another invitation from you. It's best that we don't become personally involved, in case we need to bring legal proceedings against one another in the future."

We were taken aback by this abrupt comment, which didn't seem to follow from anything in our conversation, but answered, "Oh, yes, certainly.

We understand." The fact was that we did not understand what he was talking about. He then said good-bye and departed. The whole meeting had lasted less than thirty minutes. This struck us as very sophisticated and proper New York neighborly behavior. We never found out what he had in mind, if anything, about litigation. Perhaps he was just unhinged, a condition not unknown among middle-aged New York gay men with too much money and too much free time.

He was a quiet neighbor, and there were no problems of any kind between us, or so it seemed to John and me. When we met in the elevator, we exchanged greetings pleasantly but formally. We occasionally saw him with young men who were limply handsome. This was not enough to make us want to know him better or to know anything further about him. After six months he moved back to Oklahoma. We never heard anything from or of him again.

Meeting Clarence should have been a cautionary event for John and me, but we didn't envision that we could become so jaded, blasé, and enervated. He was not our future, we thought.

The first six months in our new apartment was a time of more than usual happiness and security. I began to hope that increasing peace and stability would continue to develop in our lives. My security was short-lived, and my hopes receded.

My Father's Death

Screams

On July 23, 1964, John and I had dinner with our friend Gerald Prince, who lived in Murray Hill. The movie critic Rex Reed, charming and intelligent, was also there. We were sitting outside, in the back garden, having cocktails before dinner.

Suddenly I heard a loud scream, or bellow, or wail, which seemed to be coming from the next building, several floors above where we were sitting. I looked around and up at the next building but saw nothing unusual. The horrifying scream was repeated six more times, at intervals of about ten seconds. Each scream lasted about four or five seconds. The sound was unusual, as if a giant dog or perhaps a bull were being severely tortured. There was a quality of desperation, despair, and pain which was quite unsettling. I had never before heard anything like it. My friends continued their conversation just as if nothing had happened. I spoke up, "Who or what do you think is making that terrible sound?"

"What are you talking about? We don't hear anything. When did it happen?" they all replied. I was puzzled that they did not hear such loud, strange screams but let the subject drop. Later I understood.

The Accident

Author's father, Houston, 1963

On the same day, July 23, 1964, my father drove to El Tovar, a hotel on the south rim of the Grand Canyon, a place my mother was considering visiting. He needed to see if it would be a suitable place for her to spend a couple of weeks. He knew from past experience that if she were in a place she found unpleasant, drunken tantrums and disorderly and violent public scenes would begin, and then he would have to make an emergency trip to wherever she was to extract her from the situation. Preview inspection trips were attempts to forestall trouble. He never received any thanks from her, neither for the prior inspection trips nor for the rescues.

On arriving at El Tovar, he looked over the premises and had lunch, including one cocktail.

Driving back to Flagstaff to catch a return flight to Houston, he suddenly put on the brakes and the car began to slide. It was sliding down the road when it was violently rammed, on the driver's side, by a car coming from the opposite direction. He would have been killed instantly if he were still alive at the time of impact.

The family in the other car, a young mother and father and two small children, were not so extensively damaged as my father. The man suffered amputation of one ear and some facial lacerations. The mother had a small facial laceration. The children were unharmed. After some searching in the vicinity of the wreck, the ear was found, and it was reattached at the Flagstaff hospital. The lacerations were repaired by a plastic surgeon, and I was told the results were quite good.

The other family only wanted its medical bills paid, with nothing extra for damages. My father's insurance company refused this modest request, claiming the cause of the collision was an act of God. A lawsuit eventually took place. I heard that the medical bills were eventually paid, plus a small additional settlement. I found the behavior of the insurance company shockingly callous and inappropriate.

My mother had been visiting in New York for the past two weeks. The next day, July 24, we got word of my father's death, and we flew to Houston that afternoon. Both of us went through the activities in a state of quiet shock. That evening, I went to the Houston airport to meet the small chartered plane which was bringing back my father's body from Arizona. I cried when I saw the heartbreaking sight of the black body bag, so limp and still, being removed from the plane and put into an ambulance for transportation to the funeral home.

Then I suddenly realized the wailing screams I had heard the day before were a message from the banshee, announcing a death in the family. The message was only for me, not for any of the others—which explained why they had heard nothing—the usual private style of banshee communication.

The next day Mother and I went to the funeral home to view the body and make the funeral arrangements. I was shocked when I saw the body. My father had a frozen grimace of extreme pain and fright. Dressed in a suit, it was obvious that his body had been crushed and flattened. He looked shrunken, distorted, and helpless, and I felt very sad that he had met such a violent and frightening end.

My mother was of course devastated, crying and sobbing from time to time, although she had always been very definite about her dislike and contempt for my father. I felt as if I had been knocked upside down and had spells of severe anxiety several times each day.

My father had never had a serious automobile accident before. We knew, because of the injuries suffered by the family in the other car, that a lawsuit was likely. We had an autopsy done for our own information and protection, although this was not legally required. The autopsy showed that my father had had one drink (presumably at El Tovar) approximately one hour before the accident. Blood alcohol level was well below the legal limit, and no other drugs were detected in his blood.

He had suffered multiple fractures of his spine and neck, both legs and both arms, pelvis, sternum, and most of his ribs. He had traumatic rupture of his heart and liver, as well as multiple skull fractures and lacerations of his brain. All this was from the tremendous force of the accident.

In addition, the autopsy revealed that he had had a severe heart attack about two hours before the accident. It could not be determined whether he was living or dead at the time of the impact. There was no significant bleeding, in spite of the multiple severe injuries. There was a small amount of oozing at the fracture sites, consistent with injuries in a person who had just died. (A dead person does not bleed when injured.)

The pathologist was of the opinion that my father possibly might have survived his heart attack had he been promptly treated but that he could not under any circumstances have survived the trauma of the accident. These facts were made known in the lawsuit which did indeed ensue due to our insurance company's refusal to pay the medical bills of the family in the other car.

It was my opinion that my father had not realized that he had had a heart attack, as he often had heartburn, and some heart attacks are minimally painful, mimic heartburn, or are even painless ("silent" heart attacks). When he was driving back to Flagstaff he either had a heart irregularity or perhaps his heart stopped. As his final dying act he had tried to stop the car.

The funeral was held in Houston three days later and was attended by many of my father's friends and business associates, including his disagreeable, hostile, conniving, and ungrateful partners.

My mother seemed lost without my father. I was surprised, since she had mercilessly and violently scolded him every evening for many years. If he came home for lunch, she would scold him then too. When we all went out to eat, she would also scold him there. I thought she hated him, and I wondered why they had stayed together for thirty-four years of a miserable marriage.

My mother said repeatedly after he died, "How could he do this to me?" Her life was off balance without my father. She had lost her whipping boy, the most stable relationship in her life.

XXXXXXXXXXXXXXXXXXXXXXXXXXXXXXXXXXXXXXXXXXXXX

Business Problems

When my father had wanted to start his own business, he didn't have the necessary funds. His partners-to-be, five businessmen living in McAllen, bought 50 percent of the new business for ten thousand dollars, which was of course a gamble for them. By the time of my father's death a few years later, the business had repaid them a hundred times over for this investment, while still leaving them with 50 percent ownership of a growing and profitable business. We had not yet learned that a 50 percent ownership division is an invitation for much bitterness.

This tremendous return on their money did not cause them ever to express any appreciation or even verbal recognition that they had made a very fortunate investment. Instead, at every opportunity they reminded my mother and me how generous they had been with my father (by investing in the business), how lucky he had been to know them, and how without them he would never have had any success. This perhaps had some slight truth, but the partners were only a minor part of the whole success story. The partners were ingrates of the most extreme sort and as avaricious and cruel as anyone I have ever met. The two younger partners, brothers, were a good deal better than the other three; unfortunately, they were the most junior, and their opinions didn't carry much weight with the others.

My father left behind a letter to be opened in the event of his death. There were two main points in his letter. First, he instructed us that in no event were either one of his sisters ever to be notified of his death. One of his sisters had already died. We were shocked when we read his letter but complied with his wishes, at least at first. Six months later, we told his remaining sister, who seemed to me to be a controlling, inappropriately invasive, and greedy person, of his death, explaining that we were complying exactly with what he had instructed us to do. This was not true; if we had complied exactly with his wishes, we would never have told her.

Second, and more importantly, he warned us in his letter that his partners would try in every way they could conceive to take our 50 percent of the business away from us. He said we should immediately contact his patent tax attorney in Washington, Harry St. John Butler, to ask him to help defend us against the partners and to act as general attorney for the estate.

Neither my mother nor I knew Mr. Butler, but we called him as soon as we read my father's letter. He agreed to help us and arrived in Houston the next day, in time to attend the funeral.

He was not only a brilliant and ingenious attorney, but he was also a highly ethical man. He had a good knowledge of the partners from working with my father during the last five years on patent and tax matters, and he already knew that they were not only insulting and arrogant, but also unethical and greedy. It was a help that we did not have to wait for him to find this out. Later on, when we had initial dealings with other attorneys and businessmen about various matters, such as tax and patent contracts, this getting acquainted process regarding the partners' characters became a considerable waste of time and money.

Harry St. John Butler, Houston, 1965

Outsiders usually thought the conflict was only a difference of opinion between the partners and ourselves, something that could easily be put to rights with a little goodwill on both sides. This was a cheerful and optimistic view of the situation, and it was also totally mistaken. Think of Al Capone and a bank he was robbing, or Jack the Ripper and his victims, or a cannibal and the missionary boiling in the pot; the trouble was more than a difference of opinion.

Two weeks after the funeral, Robert Elmore, the then-leading partner, called my mother to tell her that in auditing the books, they found my father had embezzled more than a million dollars from the company. He demanded immediate repayment and said they intended to ruin my father's reputation in court and that a lawsuit would be filed the following week. This call made my mother anxious, hurt, confused, and angry. She was very perceptive and could spot a rat from a long distance.

My father was not very organized about his papers, and although we did not believe that he would steal from his own company, we were afraid we would not be able to find proof against the partner's claims. We did not know of any previous instances of dishonesty on my father's part.

We immediately contacted Harry, who said he had expected something like this to occur. The next day he called Elmore and asked for a list of the claimed embezzlements, including dates, amounts, and supporting details. "We will be happy to give this to you," said the smug partner.

At the time my father started the foreign business, he had offered the partners a 50 percent interest in the new foreign enterprise, free of charge. They thought it was too risky and too far away from their control and had declined to participate, but they had assented to my father's developing the business at his own risk. Of course, they assumed that without their participation he was doomed to failure. The new business operated mainly in Mexico and Venezuela. It had been a struggle to set up and run and had been only modestly successful.

The week after Elmore's threatening call, we received a list of over three hundred items my father had purchased through his domestic company, of which he owned 50 percent, the other 50 percent being owned by the difficult partners. He had then sent these items on to his own similar 100 percent owned foreign business headquartered in the Bahamas.

The purchase and export procedure used in the "embezzlement" situation had extended back over three years, and the total amount purchased domestically and then exported to the foreign business was over one million dollars. We were shaken when we saw the list sent by Elmore.

We set to work immediately, combing through my father's records. He was in general careless about his papers. For instance, he made many of his original mechanical drawings on the walls of his office. A few years later, he decided to have his office painted and then was chagrined to find that all his mechanical drawings had been painted over. It took him several months to recreate the drawings, again on his office wall.

Fortunately, he had been orderly in his record keeping concerning items purchased through the domestic company, probably because he was always meticulous in record keeping for tax matters. We found records covering the three hundred items in question, and attached to the receipt for each one was a cancelled check showing that he had reimbursed the domestic company for each item.

The partners had possession and control of the books of the domestic company, and they therefore knew that all the items had been reimbursed. They probably counted on my father's well-known carelessness to make it impossible for my mother and me to find the proof that my father had not stolen or embezzled.

Harry presented the partners with copies of all the pertinent documents and cancelled checks. He pointed out to them that since they had a record of all the items in question, they must also have had a record of all the reimbursements; otherwise the company's books would be out of balance by about one million dollars.

They were furious that their sleazy scheme had not worked. Of course, they did not apologize.

This was the first of many such dishonest ploys, threats, and outright lies they used to try to beat my mother and me into submission or surrender so as to cheat us out of our interest in the company. They were unsuccessful, and their ongoing similar machinations eventually began to damage their reputations with their business acquaintances. They did not like to be seen by their community as the crooks and bullies that they were.

In fairness, in addition to the two better partners, the company auditor and attorney were fair and honest men, but they could not restrain their unethical employers, the partners. It was fascinating for me to watch these brazen machinations and manipulations play out.

At the next annual meeting of the board of directors, in front of all the partners and other officers of the company, the then current lead partner, John Stahl, who had been acting as temporary substitute president of the company, made a solemn promise to me. He promised that when we found a genuine permanent president for the company, he would promptly resign. It was on the basis of his promise that I agreed he could officially become temporary president of the company. It was a trap, and I fell for it.

At the next annual meeting one year later he announced that he was never going to resign as president, that he had no intention of ever stepping down.

Outraged, I said, "Your word means nothing. You have no integrity." There was a hush in the room.

Stahl stared at me with his icy watery blue eyes, smiled slightly, and then replied, "Now you know." There were gasps and throat clearings.

As an attempt to restrain Stahl's grab for total control of the company, I wrote to the company's banks informing them that he had not been authorized to sign checks on the company's accounts (which was true) and that they should not honor any company checks signed by him. They all demurred. I then threatened the banks that I would complain to the State of Texas Banking Commission that they were using "unsafe and unsound banking practices," a technical term implying illegal deliberate carelessness. The banks then all wrote to Stahl telling him they would no longer honor his signature on company checks. He was furious to be blocked in his illegal maneuver.

Further troubles arose from time to time with this reptilian man and continued until he mercifully passed away two years later. I did not choose to attend his funeral but heard that the atmosphere resembled a wedding: the attendees, including his widow, mostly looked very happy.

I continued to be as obstructive and unyielding as possible with the partners' machinations, and that eventually turned out to be the best course of action. They thought every business relation and negotiation had to have a winner and a loser, and they chose to win by causing the other party to fail or lose. They didn't believe that most negotiations could have two winners. They thought their self-interest lay in causing damage to others. Unfortunately, this idea has wide currency in the business world.

XXXXXXXXXXXXXXXXXXXXXXXXXXXXXXXXXXXXXXXXXXX

My Father's Legacy

It was unfortunate that we were never able to find my father's main bank accounts or other financial resources. We found one small bank account, containing around two thousand dollars, in San Antonio, and another, containing around three thousand dollars, in Maracaibo, Venezuela. Under Venezuelan inheritance law, it was required that I inherit at least two thirds, or two thousand dollars, of the Venezuelan bank account.

When my mother heard this, she was enraged, demanding that I renounce any rights to my father's Venezuelan estate. At first I thought she must be joking. But no, she was deadly serious. She did not want me to have any legal rights to any part of my father's estate, no matter how small it might be. Eventually, a formal document was drawn up for Venezuela, in which I renounced my rights to any part of my father's estate. And so I did not receive the two thousand dollars. It was probably appropriate that I did not receive any direct inheritance from his estate, as he would have been opposed to my receiving anything from him.

But luckily for me, my mother was willing to give me more than this amount each month, if I requested it of her. She was very generous with me, but she did not want me to have any rights separate from her inclinations.

The rest of my father's money was never found. We guessed that over a million dollars in cash was missing and could not be located. Eventually, when I knew more about my father's life and affairs, I suspected that his money had been diverted elsewhere. Perhaps Harry Butler knew where it was but didn't want to break my father's confidence.

About two months after my father's death, his assistant said to me, "I burned the letters."

"What letters?" I asked.

Looking embarrassed, he said, "Oh, the love letters."

Thinking quickly, I asked, "Were there many of them?"

"Oh, about fifty. And there was a picture," he said as he handed me a picture of a small boy.

As I carefully and gently quizzed his assistant, he told me that my father had another wife and another son in a foreign country. He had been bigamous for years. I never heard from the other family or made any effort to contact them. My father had probably given the missing funds to his other wife. I sometimes wondered if they knew what had happened to him, what accounted for my father's sudden disappearance.

When I heard about my father's bigamy, I felt shocked, betrayed, cheated. Even though I had never loved my father, it was very disorienting to realize that there was a large side of his life completely unknown to me.

I didn't mention the other family to my mother, and I never knew whether she knew. Later on, I had reason to think she may have found out some years earlier, but until the end of her life, we never mentioned the matter.

I had known for a long time that if my mother died before my father, he would have shown me the door in short order, as he had in general never liked me. I didn't much like him either, but as he was my only father, I sometimes had a faint hope, always disappointed, that he would show some warmth or approval. I could not have expected any help from him, probably no contact of any kind, and certainly would not have received any inheritance from him, as he disliked and had contempt for me for accepting any money from my mother after I reached the age of sixteen, as well as for other reasons.

But my father was a man of many faces.

Shortly after his death, about a dozen banks called in notes he had cosigned for amounts ranging from a hundred dollars to ten thousand dollars for some of his workers or other friends living in McAllen. There were about two dozen of these notes, totaling about twenty-five thousand dollars. We had known nothing of their existence before his death. We knew both the borrowers and the banks and were convinced that the notes were legitimate. We paid them immediately. A few of the beneficiaries thanked us.

At the time he died, I had not yet found out about his other family. He was a womanizer, and I am sure that within a few months after my mother's death, he would have been cheerfully cohabiting with another woman or would have married again, busying himself with his new wife and/or mistresses.

Some months after my father's death, my mother told me he had refused to participate in any way in paying for my college or medical school education. She had supported me for years from her own resources, without my father's participation but with his disapproval. After her death, I came across her bank statements, which showed this to be true. I had known nothing of this unhappy arrangement between my parents until she told me.

But, on the other hand, I also had known that if my father died first, the responsibility for looking after my mother, with her increasing alcoholism, periodic morphine addiction, uncontrolled rampages, and paranoid tantrums, would fall on me alone. There would be no relatives, siblings, or friends to help me with this. I saw this possibility as an almost unbearable burden, which it actually did become.

At any rate, my mother and I tried to educate ourselves as quickly as possible about the businesses, patents, tax matters, legal problems, and all that was necessary to try to keep our financial affairs in good order and the businesses alive and running and safe from the partners. We were both quick learners.

My mother never really recovered from the death of my father. She kept asking, "How could he do this to me?"

When I would go home to Houston for a visit, most evenings were very sad. My mother and I would sit in the sun room in two easy chairs with ottomans. We always had our favoritre drinks; for me a martini, for her a scotch and water. We were watching the TV with the sound turned off. Most of the lights were also turned off. As the light failed, the room became dark. There was almost no conversation between us, no lights, no sound on the TV, no music. Eventually, after several drinks, we might have a small dinner, or perhaps we might just retire intoxicated without eating anything. This was very dismal but was what my mother chose. She almost never wanted to go out.

For over forty years after my father's death in 1964, each year for a few days around the anniversary, July 23, I would be unusually anxious, irritable, and depressed, without any troubling events to account for these feelings. Eventually I realized this was an anniversary reaction, although usually I didn't realize the anniversary was at hand until two or three days afterward, when I would suddenly realize why I had been feeling so uncomfortable and so uneasy, and then any remaining feelings would immediately dissipate. In 2009, forty-five years after his death, for the first time there was no anniversary reaction. Perhaps I have at last been released.

For me too life was always different after my father died—sometimes better, sometimes not.

The Christmas Visit

The Christmas trees on Park Avenue were covered with sparkling white lights, and when the wind blew the lights danced around, making the whole avenue shimmer. The stores looked more festive than ever, and the big tree at Rockefeller Center was magnificent. The Salvation Army bell ringers were standing by their collection kettles hoping for generosity from passers by, and traffic was in its usual holiday jams. Blinking lights shone from apartment windows and from balcony railings.

Mother, Houston, November 1965

Christmas season of 1965 was at hand, and my mother was coming to New York for a month-long visit. She arrived from Houston in late afternoon on December 10, and I met her at the airport. She looked well, pleasant, and calm. Almost sixty years old, she was still had an attractive presence. About five feet six, slender, with good posture, graceful movements, and a lovely face, she was perfectly dressed and groomed, as usual. She was careful about her appearance; her seamstress came to the house weekly for minor adjustments to her clothes, and she went twice a week to the beauty salon to have her hair and nails done.

The limousine drove us to the Waldorf Towers. She had been staying there on her frequent trips to New York since my father had died nineteen months earlier. The manager greeted her and showed her to her usual two-bedroom apartment on the thirtieth floor. The hotel had several desirable features for my mother: the staff was very polite, and the maids were very agreeable, observing the "Do Not Disturb" sign no matter how late it hung on the doorknob and bringing as many extra towels as she wanted, whenever she wanted. When she checked out, there was never a bill presented. "Have a good trip, Mrs. Loomis. We hope you will visit us again soon." The bill would arrive in the mail several weeks later.

For me, the best feature of the hotel was the covered drive-in entrance to the small separate lobby of the Towers section of the hotel. From the car, there was only a four-foot secluded sidewalk to cross to the recessed side door, and then on about ten feet to the elevator used exclusively by the Tower guests. From the street, no one could see who was arriving or leaving the hotel by this entrance.

Mother was in good spirits but said she was tired, so we had dinner in her apartment.

The next day, she did some shopping, and then I met her for dinner. She again seemed in good spirits, only had two drinks at the hotel, and then we left in the limousine for the Four Seasons restaurant three blocks away, where we had an 8 o'clock reservation. The dinner started pleasantly but then began to deteriorate. In her sober state, she was shy, quiet, withdrawn, secretive, kind-hearted, a music lover. She was intelligent and inquisitive, read extensively in the Hindu scriptures and the classic and modern commentaries on the Upanishads and the *Bhagavad Gita*. This interest started years before when she heard lectures on Indian philosophy, and Eastern religions had become an important part of her life.

Alcohol opened the door for the emergence of another personality: half porcupine, half rattlesnake, bitter, argumentative, confrontational, and accusatory. This paranoid personality was formidable, repellant, and pitiful. All her selves wanted to be alone and to be left alone, an uncomfortable trait which she passed on to me. When she drank, she began to stutter, which would get steadily more severe through the evening until she could no longer speak. Her head, eyes, and mouth would jerk spasmodically as she tried to bring out a word, until finally in frustration she would pound the table with the side of her left hand. The stutter had started in childhood and had been an irritation to her all her life.

No matter how many drinks or how severe the stuttering, there was one phrase she could always say clearly: "By no manner of means." She would say this dozens of times in an evening; sometimes this was the only thing she could say: glaring, pounding the table, and obviously boiling with torment and rage: "By no manner of means. By no manner of means." I found the conversation almost impossibly awkward. She had the worst stuttering problem I had ever encountered.

If she let go and started to express her rage, the stuttering would decrease slightly, and she could speak more fluently as she berated whomever she was with, skillfully, cruelly, and at great length. The more vicious and lacerating her comments, the more fluent her speech became. The decrease of stuttering was usually a sign she was about to pass out.

That evening, while we were waiting for our dinner to arrive, she told me she had decided not to bring Ruth Lester, her nurse, with her, as Mrs. Lester wanted to stay in Houston for the Christmas visit of her two grown children. Mrs. Lester, a registered nurse, was a kindly middle-aged woman who acted as a helper, nurse, and companion to my mother. She was one of the few people who could get along with her and whom my mother could tolerate. Her most important duty was to administer once or twice a day the morphine injections to which my mother had been addicted on and off for the last twenty-eight years. The addiction had resurfaced again most recently eighteen months ago, because of pain resulting from a broken arm suffered in a drunken fall at a Houston club. Mother could manage the injections herself but preferred for someone else to give them.

I had declined to continue giving her the injections during a previous trip to New York, enraging her at the time. Because of her heavy drinking and profligate use of tranquilizers, sleeping pills and other drugs, I was afraid she might die after I injected her with morphine, and then I would be complicit in her death. As I was a physician, and her sole heir, this would be a very serious problem for me. It might even appear that I had deliberately murdered her. She said that lately she had weaned herself off the morphine but still occasionally needed some, which worried me greatly.

Her chronic emphysema and bronchiectasis had been slowly worsening, and sometimes she bled from her lungs, coughing up startling quantities of blood.

In recent years she had been drinking far too much, often appearing drunk, angry, unreasonable. The drinking was a daily routine. She would sometimes call me in the middle of the night, drunk, almost incoherent, angry, babbling, crying, sometimes screaming into the phone. These conversations would last between one and two hours and would eventually turn to the subject of what a bad son I had been, how I mistreated her, and how I was cold and uncaring. These were the same accusations she repeatedly made to my father.

She never asked me if I were dating or if I had a girlfriend, nor did she suggest she would like to see me married or that she wanted grandchildren. As I was a closet gay, I was grateful for this lack of maternal pressure to marry.

She spent much time alone, brooding and writing lengthy daily diary entries, which I have read, to my considerable distress. She had told my father several times that she was going to kill herself in such a way that it would look like he had murdered her, which greatly worried him. She never explained how she planned to accomplish this horrible plan. I was grateful that she had not started this threat with me but assumed it would be coming eventually.

Her insane nocturnal calls had been repeated many times over the last few years. There was never any proper resolution to these calls. She would gradually stop talking, and after a long silence she would suddenly hang up without saying good-bye. Usually my night's sleep was ruined by then, and I was exhausted the next day.

As she never commented on the calls the next day, I don't think she remembered them, or at least not clearly enough to mention. No matter how angry she had been the night before, the next morning she would be calm and pleasant, as if there had been no volcanic explosions just a few hours before. Most mornings she had the "flu," which was the code word for a hangover.

John and I continued our own pattern of heavy drinking and dissolute living. He went to work every day, and I went to my office. The business and estate responsibilities were heavy.

But life was not just a round of worry, sickness, drinking, stress, and legal problems. There were also placid and pleasant times, but they couldn't be considered innocent or carefree.

In 1964 and again in 1965, John and I gave large parties early in the Christmas season, before Mother arrived in New York. We would roll up the rugs, buy a case of liquor and plenty of party snacks, hire a bartender and a waiter, and look forward to the arrival of a hundred or so guests. The invitations were worded "Cocktails, 7–10 PM." The first guests, about equal numbers gay and straight, would arrive about that time, and the party would be at its height around 11 PM, with drinking, eating, dancing, and perhaps a little hugging, kissing, and groping in the darker parts of the terrace.

Clouds of cigarette smoke hung in the air, but none of the guests used marijuana or other street drugs, as these had not yet come into general recreational use, except in circles of jazz musicians and their followers. The last guests left about 4 AM. The parties were successes. I recently came across a list of supplies for a party—liquor and food—roast chicken, ham, cheeses, crudites, pates, cakes, the usual party foods, and felt a pang of nostalgia.

I told Mother that John and I had invited a few friends and co-workers in for drinks. She didn't show any interest, and it would have been big trouble for all to have included her in these parties.

As we were enjoying our dinner at the Four Seasons, she told me of the many medications she was taking for a variety of conditions. She pulled out a sizeable gold box and opened the lid. Inside was Ali Baba's treasure chest, with tablets and capsules of many sizes, shapes, and colors: various painkillers, sedatives, tranquilizers, stimulants, vitamins, and other medicines.

We had been exchanging a few pleasantries with the young couple at the next table, and after we had finished our dessert, Mother suddenly extended the treasure box to them and asked pleasantly, "Would you care for some pills?" They said no thanks but were obviously startled and uneasy.

Soon I asked for the check, and we started our exit. After the evening of drinking, Mother could no longer stand up and had to be helped by me and one of the waiters down the stairs and into the waiting limousine, which I used every time we went out, as I usually needed help from the driver to get Mother from the restaurant and into the car, and then from the car into the hotel. We drove home, using the hidden side entrance at the Towers. The driver and a bellboy helped get her into the lobby, and bellboys helped carry her upstairs to her apartment. I called for a maid to help me take off Mother's shoes and outer clothes, leaving her asleep (or passed out) in her bed. This was a common routine at the end of an evening and didn't warrant even a comment the next day.

XXXXXXXXXXXXXXXXXXXXXXXXXXXXXXXXXXXXXXXXXXXXX

The next few days were pleasant: one evening at the theater, another at the opera, dinner at a fine restaurant every night, sometimes a nightcap at El Morocco or the Stork Club, then home in the always-waiting limousine. About half the time, Mother was able to walk out of a restaurant with help, or on her own, and to manage the fourteen feet from the car to the hotel elevator.

One day we had lunch at the Palm Court at the Plaza Hotel, which Mother liked because of their string trio. She had been an accomplished violinist in her younger years. The violinist asked her if there were something she would like to hear, and she often requested the *Zigeunerweisen* of Sarasate. Violinists were usually pleased to be asked to play something brilliant of this sort and could more or less get through the difficult piece, although sometimes only in an abbreviated and simplified version. A large tip would follow. Fortunately, that day the violinist played the piece beautifully.

About twenty years earlier I had decided one Christmas to get Mother sheet music for some of the pieces she mentioned. When she opened the present, she looked surprised and sad but looked through the pages without comment.

I said, "Would you play some of these pieces?"

She answered, "I haven't played in over thirty years, and anyway the tuning post is down and needs to be repaired." Thoughtfully, she then said, "If you will play the accompaniment, I'll see what I can do."

I got her violin down from the back of the closet and handed the case to her. She opened it and sighed when she saw the violin. "This used to be my best friend," she said. She inspected and tightened the strings, tightened the bow, and then tuned the violin. Looking through the scores, she played a few bars from the Bruch Concerto, then moved on to play two pages of Sarasate's *Romanza Andaluza*. Putting Kreisler's *Schon Rosmarin* on the rack, she played the entire piece with considerable technique, brilliance, and good intonation. It was an impressive performance, considering that she had had no warm-up and hadn't touched a violin in over thirty years.

"That was one of my favorites," she said, with tears in her eyes. Tears were in my eyes too. She loosened the strings, put the instrument in its case, and asked me to put it back in the closet, resting on the new music scores. I asked her several more times to play for me, but she always declined. She never played again.

XXXXXXXXXXXXXXXXXXXXXXXXXXXXXXXXXXXXXXXXXXXX

December 18 was her birthday (officially her fifty-eighth, but actually her sixty-first). We again had a reservation at the Four Seasons. She said she had a new outfit for her birthday evening and a surprise she wanted to show me.

I arrived at the hotel about six for the pre-dinner cocktails. She looked lovely, as usual: perfectly groomed, poised, and pleasant. She had on a new long white silk dress, very feminine, soft and flowing, white silk shoes, a single-strand pearl necklace, pearl and diamond earrings, her favorite ruby and diamond bracelet, and a new white ermine jacket. These clothes set off her large hazel eyes and softly curled chestnut hair. I complimented her appearance, and she smiled and asked if I noticed anything else.

Well, *yes*: on her left hand she wore a new diamond ring. She was a favored customer of Kenneth van Atten at Cartier, and he sometimes urged her to take out jewelry on approval, hoping she would buy. This time he had outdone himself. The ring was an oval-cut D-color flawless diamond, twenty-six carats, a real fortune on a finger, constantly sparkling and refracting the light, spectacular but somewhat too demanding of attention, I thought.

When we arrived at the Four Seasons, many of the other diners watched our entrance. So far, the evening was off to a good start.

As drinks and dinner progressed, Mother became morose and started stuttering, "Nobody likes me, I'm so lonely, so afraid of people, there isn't any hope in life. I need help, and there's nobody to help me. I'm sick, I'm sick; I cough up blood at least twice a week. How could Glenn have done this terrible thing to me—dying and going off, leaving me alone." She began to cry, a very sad spectacle. Tears ran from her eyes; saliva and mucus bubbled from her mouth and nose.

After crying for a few minutes, she began to collect herself, and the anger began. "No matter how hard I try, it's never enough. People are mean and cold. I try to act and look nice and be a good person, but nothing is ever enough. Nobody likes me. I'm a complete failure. There's no use trying any more."

By now in a rage, she suddenly staggered to her feet, pulled the big ring from her finger, and hurled it across the room. It all seemed slow-motion: the ring floated slowly across the restaurant, arcing over the pool in the middle of the room, rising partway to the ceiling, turning slowly, sparkling and shooting out rays of light as it flew. Many of the other diners were watching this strange event, their heads following the trajectory of the ring. While the ring was still flying, Mother slowly slid to the floor, unconscious. Fortunately, her head did not hit anything on the way down. She landed crumpled on one side, her hair over her face, her dress partway up her legs, which were sprawled grotesquely, and one shoe had come off. Which had priority: Mother or the ring?

Quick practical analysis indicated that Mother was immobilized and could stay on the floor for a while, but the ring might grow legs and walk out the door. The choice was clear: I dashed across the room, weaving at high speed between the tables. The ring had landed on the floor between two tables of startled diners. Excited and breathless, I said, "There it is! It's mine!" and pointed to it. A waiter scooped up the ring for me, and I put it in my pocket.

Hurrying back to Mother, who was still lying quietly on the floor, I picked up her evening bag, her glasses, and the ermine jacket. Two waiters picked her up and carried her out; I cradled her head, which was flopping limply.

Down the stairs, into the limousine, over to the hotel, through the side entrance, and up to her room. The maid and I undressed her and put her into the bed. She was still unconscious but breathing normally. I wrote her a note saying I had the ring and sat with her for about an hour, until she roused slightly. I said goodnight, call you tomorrow, and left.

XXXXXXXXXXXXXXXXXXXXXXXXXXXXXXXXXXXXXXXXXXXXXXX

I stopped for a beer at a bar on the way home, hoping that some lively music and a cheerful atmosphere might break the gloomy spell of the birthday evening. It didn't. I was uneasy with the ring still in my pocket and so soon headed home, a ten-minute walk.

When I arrived home, Sparky was hiding under the bed, always a sign that he had been a bad dog. Angered that he had been left alone all evening, he had peed on my pillow.

I got a new pillow and case, undressed, and fell into the bed. Sparky jumped like a grasshopper into the bed and gave me a slobbery kiss. I said, "You've been a bad boy," and gave him a gentle thump on the end of his nose. Within five minutes I was asleep, holding Sparky in my arms.

XXXXXXXXXXXXXXXXXXXXXXXXXXXXXXXXXXXXXXXXXXXXXXX

When I saw Mother the next day, she was holding my note about the ring and pretending to fan herself with it. "I've been guarding this for you," I said. I handed her the ring. She didn't make any reply, just took it and put it into a drawer. There was no mention of the events of the previous evening—it was the customary veil of silence.

The routine of heavy drinking, heavy smoking, heavy eating, late hours, and the stress of trying to cope with my mother's violently unpredictable behavior, combined with working all day in a demanding profession, was exhausting. Every three or four days I had to take an evening off from the fiesta. This irritated Mother, who had all day every day to recover from the revels of the night before.

Not wanting to spend the evening alone, she would call cousin Georgie, her sister's son, and invite him to go out with her for the evening. I am sure he enjoyed the novelty of being taken around by his aunt Jean (my mother) in a limousine to his usual haunts. Mother said she enjoyed the evenings too. I was grateful to Georgie for helping to lighten the load on me, even though of course he had no such kindly intent.

Georgie had great charm and sex appeal, at least enough to live off both men and women for the past twenty years in Paris, London, and on the Riviera. He also played the piano beautifully. I didn't like him because of his manipulative lying. In return, he didn't like me because of what he said was my snobbish attitude. I believe he continues to live in New York, but we haven't spoken in over forty years, which suits me just fine.

And so the days and nights passed chaotically. On Christmas Eve, a Steinway Model L grand piano was delivered to my apartment as a Christmas gift from my mother, and I was overjoyed to get such a treasure. That evening five of us had dinner in her apartment at the hotel: my mother, John, and Harry St. John Butler. He had come up from Washington to spend the holiday with us, wisely leaving Jenny, his Inca princess girlfriend from Cuzco, at home (two queen bees are a bad combination), and also Dog Sparky and I. The evening passed precariously but without any blowouts; nobody fell off the high-wire.

We all looked forward to the next day, when we would be joined by our friends Claire and Gloria, who lived in the next building, for a gala Christmas dinner at our apartment.

XXXXXXXXXXXXXXXXXXXXXXXXXXXXXXXXXXXXXXXXXXXXX

Christmas Day, 1965, was warm. The doors to the terrace were open; the air-conditioning was on. John and I were making the Christmas dinner. The guests had been invited for 1:00 PM. Our kitchen was too small to prepare the entire dinner, so we had farmed out the turkey to our friend Claire, who lived in the next building. Claire was from a large, well-to-do Canadian Lebanese family. She was average height, somewhat overweight, had olive skin, large protruding dark eyes, wiry disobedient black hair, and was slightly bowlegged, very friendly, with a joyful personality and a radiant crooked-toothed smile.

She also liked to drink. At 11:30 I called her to see how the turkey was progressing. *Ring, ring.* "Uuhwuh wuh," Claire answered.

"Merry Christmas! Did we wake you? How's the turkey coming along?"

"Mezz Sismas to yoooo doo. Ono I've been wup for zowers. Turgey? Ohho: vine, vine."

"Good," I said. "We'll be over at twelve forty-five to pick up the turkey. You and Gloria be ready. Dinner's at one o'clock."

XXXXXXXXXXXXXXXXXXXXXXXXXXXXXXXXXXXXXXXXXXXXX

Mother arrived wearing a blue silk Chanel suit and her new diamond ring. She was the picture of charm, serenity, and self-assurance. She was accompanied by Harry Butler, who was in high spirits, roaring with exhibitionistic laughter and fingering his Van Dyke. Harry had had an eventful life, had known King Alfonso XIII and Queen Victoria of Spain and many other interesting people, but would only talk about such things as growing corn in the backyard of his house on Embassy Row in Washington, how fish liked to hide in holes—HAW, HAW, HAW. He could always be recognized by his loud gasping and booming laugh.

Also present were John, Claire, her roommate Gloria, Dog Sparky, and I. Sparky was excited and occasionally tried to climb up into the Christmas tree, a difficult maneuver for a dachshund. He enjoyed tearing the wrappings off his presents—dog biscuits and a squeak toy. He tried to hump my mother's leg, which made her laugh. She was very fond of Sparky.

The turkey looked beautiful, but it must have been cooked with a blowtorch, as it was done only to a depth of one inch. Carving the turkey was like peeling a basketball, but it was delicious. There was just enough of the cooked part of the turkey to go around.

I was pressed into playing the new piano and offered short pieces by Sibelius and Chopin, to friendly applause of course. The day was a success, and Mother and Harry left about 5:00. Claire, Gloria, John, and I finished up the remaining champagne. We gave the girls half of the raw turkey to take home for later, washed the dishes, and collapsed.

XXXXXXXXXXXXXXXXXXXXXXXXXXXXXXXXXXXXXXXXXXXX

The next week passed as usual. We went out for fine dinners every evening: Mother always ordered several courses but would only take a bite or two of each, preferring liquid refreshments. She had drunken temper tantrums and was carried out of most restaurants after she had passed out.

One evening we had a long discussion of one of her favorite topics: "What did I ever do to deserve a child like you?" This was not just an idle complaint or a rhetorical question; she wanted a reasonable answer as to what sins she might have committed to deserve her cruel, ungrateful child, as she sometimes saw me when she was drinking.

For some years I had dealt with the subject by saying that it must have been something really bad she had done in a previous life. Eventually, this evasion was not adequate, and she wanted to know exactly what she might have done. I tried desperately to deflect the conversation to some less painful subject but always failed. This led on to very unpleasant accusations about my cruelty and my rotten nature. Glaring at me, she would say, quoting from "King Lear," "Oh, sharper than a serpent's tooth." I hoped she would soon pass out, as the conversation never resolved or stopped before she became unconscious. These episodes always made me feel sad and hopeless.

Later a therapist suggested I might have told her, "Well, I don't know, but it must have been something very, very good to deserve me." I can't imagine what her response would have been. Explosive rage, I assume.

New Year's Eve was passed quietly in her hotel apartment, just Mother, John, Sparky, and I. 1966 started with a subway, bus, and taxi strike on January 1st.

On January 4th, a snowstorm began, twelve inches of snow forecast. Pleading fatigue, I took the evening off from the nightly carnival. Mother was not pleased.

At 11:30 PM, the phone rang: it was the night manager from the Towers. He said Mother had called down for room service and that her speech was so incoherent the operator was afraid she had had a stroke. The hotel doctor had seen her, and she had been taken, unconscious, by ambulance to St. Clare's Hospital. Her hotel apartment had been sealed.

I called the limousine company, explained that I had an emergency and needed a car, probably for all night or longer. The snowstorm was still going on, as well as the strike. As I was a regular customer of the limousine service, they were able to send a car for me, and I was at St. Clare's by 2:00 AM.

I could hardly register the news when the Sister in charge told me the prognosis was grave and that death would probably come shortly. The sister then led me into Mother's room. She was lying unconscious, with IVs and monitoring devices in place. Blood pressure was low, pulse was irregular, and she was having Cheyne-Stokes respiration: peaks and valleys of breathing, usually a sign of impending death.

Over the next two hours, each time she quit breathing I was afraid she had died. Then, with a loud gasp, she would start breathing again, and I was relieved. Gradually her breathing became more regular. The Sisters were surprised she had survived the night. By 5:00 AM she was breathing normally, and by 6:00 she had opened her eyes and looked around. At 7:00 she said, "Where the hell am I? How did I get into this goddamned place?" I told her what had happened. "Well, I want to go back to the hotel *Right now!!* Bring me my clothes," she commanded.

The waiting car took me to the hotel. The manager and the police unsealed her apartment, did an inventory, and I signed a release that all was in place. I packed a little suitcase with street clothes, some cosmetics, and her favorite wig and took her largest fur coat and an umbrella. It was still snowing. I left the new ring in a bedroom drawer.

Then back to St. Clare's. Mother was fuming, mean as a rattlesnake and demanding to be discharged. We both signed a release for the hospital, and she was discharged against medical advice. The whole episode appeared to be an overdose of alcohol/narcotics/sleeping pills, but more severe than usual, almost fatal.

Back to the hotel by 9:00 AM, where she had a large glass of scotch (I said nothing) and a cup of coffee. She said she was going to bed to rest up for our big evening ahead, when we were scheduled to have dinner with Harry Butler and his friend, Admiral Burke, who was on the executive committee of Texaco. This was an important meeting, which could result in a great deal of business for our little oil field service company.

Exhausted, I spent the day at my office, then rushed home to put on some fresh clothes and hurried back to the hotel by 6:00 PM. I found Mother staggering drunk. Horrified, I said, "How could you do this? You almost died last night in the hospital."

She looked at me for a while and then said calmly and without stuttering, "I know my drinking is hard on other people, but it makes *me* feel better. It would be even worse if I didn't try so hard. I'm not afraid of dying, but you know I'm afraid of people—afraid of living." I was left astonished and speechless by her admission. This was the only comment she had ever made about anyone's drinking, including her own.

Luckily, because of the snowstorm the admiral was not able to come up from Washington. The dinner with him was postponed, and a nasty business catastrophe was averted, as Mother became quite verbally abusive to Harry and me before the evening finished: demon rum at work again.

A week after New Year's, Mother decided her new Cartier ring was too ostentatious and exchanged it for a similar one half as large. Even so, the new thirteen-carat ring was like a headlight. Two days later, on January 9, she returned to Houston.

XXXXXXXXXXXXXXXXXXXXXXXXXXXXXXXXXXXXXXXXXXXXX

Since my father's death, Mother, Harry, and I had been working on a lengthy series of business documents. The complex agreements included my father's five disagreeable partners, our main oil field service business, several other related businesses, and the patents. My mother individually and my father's estate jointly owned about a hundred foreign and domestic patents necessary for the operation of all the businesses. The partners were hostile, suspicious, and uncooperative, and so were we.

From January 10th to February 10th, we did much negotiating and rewriting of agreements and patent assignments. During this month Mother was an astute and meticulous negotiator and businesswoman in the morning and afternoon and extremely drunk and almost raving in the evening. But she remembered nearly verbatim everything that anyone said, a startling ability she had always retained and one of the good and valuable things my mother passed on to me.

She decided against buying the ring, and so on February 8th, Mrs. Lester wrapped up the new "little" ring and mailed it back to Cartier.

Around noon on February 11th, Harry Butler called my mother from McAllen to tell her that the partners had agreed to and signed all the documents and that he was coming to Houston that afternoon and would bring the documents to her house the next morning for her to sign. She had finally won the biggest battle of her life, preserving her business interests against the fierce attacks by the partners.

Mother called me with this good news and said that she and I should go to the Bahamas two days later to register the documents and patent assignments in the Nassau office of the foreign corporation.

Because of her emergency hospitalization in New York just a month before, and her continued heavy drinking, I was afraid she might die in Nassau, a dreadful prospect. I told her I felt very uneasy about the trip. To me she seemed too ill to go to Nassau just now; it would be better to wait a little. This was only the second time that I had ever said no to my mother about anything (the other time was when I refused to continue giving her morphine injections). She was disappointed and then became furious. She said, "How could you do this to me? You're ditching me right at the end." She suddenly hung up without saying good-bye. I felt uneasy at this abrupt and unpleasant conclusion. I considered calling her back but knew there was no use just then.

Her big business battle was finished, her husband had abandoned her by dying, and now she felt her son had turned against her. She had had both a major business victory and bitter personal loss and disappointments.

XXXXXXXXXXXXXXXXXXXXXXXXXXXXXXXXXXXXXXXXXXXX

The next morning about 11:00, Harry called, saying he had serious bad news. He and Marian Regis, Mother's maid, hadn't been able to get into the house. They had to break through the back door and the metal door bars to get in and then had to break through the metal bar and the locked door to her bedroom. They had found my mother on the floor, lying on her stomach, her legs and lower body under the bed. She didn't seem to be breathing. Harry was trying to be gentle in delivering this message.

Marian took the phone and said, "Your mother's body is cold, congealed blood and vomit are coming out of her mouth, and one side of her face is blue. I'm so sorry to tell you that your mother is dead." She started to cry.

Harry called the police and her doctor, who signed the death certificate. Her body was taken to the city morgue, and a Pinkerton guard stayed in the house until I arrived from New York.

Crying, I packed a suitcase, called the airline, called the limousine company, and called John to tell him what had happened. I left for Houston that afternoon and arrived at 8:00 PM to find Harry, Marian, and the guard at Mother's house.

In her bedroom the large oxygen tanks with their arms, breathing masks, dials, and gauges, which Mother needed for her chronic lung disease, were still standing ready beside her bed, resembling giant grotesque insects ready to pounce. I looked at the spot on the rug where the blood and vomit had drained from her mouth.

I called her sister, Nellie, in Dallas, her brother Edmund in Arkansas, and her estranged brother Van in Houston. I cried some more and went to bed.

The next morning I went alone to the city morgue for the required identification of the body. An attendant wheeled out a gurney with a covered body and turned back the sheet. There she was, mottled blue and white, looking small and totally defeated, younger than her sixty-one years but very tired. I lifted up one cold eyelid, looked at her lifeless eye, and then let it close. Her tormented spirit had fled. I staggered slightly and said, "Yes, it's my mother." It was absolutely quiet in the room. I thanked the medical examiner and left.

The state required an autopsy because of the circumstances of her death: alone and not under a doctor's care within thirty days before. I had no objection to the autopsy. The report two weeks later showed that she had taken one drink and one sleeping pill a few hours before she died. There was no mention of other drugs or fatal physical conditions. The cause of death, confirming what her doctor had written on the death certificate, was listed as "acute and chronic alcoholism," and the terminal event was "inhalation of vomitus." But I knew the real cause was a broken heart. Life was too difficult and painful for her. She died because she no longer wanted to live. I felt I had killed her by refusing to accompany her to Nassau.

I cried in the car for a while and then went alone to the funeral home to make the funeral arrangements. As Mother had requested, her body was not embalmed, but was kept refrigerated until it was cremated. She had wanted cremation, with her ashes to be scattered in the same rose garden where my father's ashes had been scattered nineteen months earlier. Nine years before that, my dear Granny's ashes were placed in a grove of trees with singing birds, at the same cemetery, as Granny had requested.

When I returned home from the morgue and the funeral home, I found her three siblings and their spouses gathered at her house. I was glad they were there.

For the next four days, the house was full of Mother's friends, business associates, siblings, and in-laws. These visitations went on for twelve hours a day. There was much eating, drinking, smoking, talking, and laughing. It was exhausting for me, and I had to retreat into my room several times a day for an hour of privacy and quiet.

February 14, Valentine's Day, would have been my parents' thirty-sixth wedding anniversary, a wry choice of day as it turned out, considering the bitter and stormy course of their relationship.

The funeral on February 16 was a closed-coffin Episcopalian service at the funeral home, brief, calm, dignified, attended by two hundred people. "Beautiful Dreamer" and "Jeannie with the Light Brown Hair" were sung, as Mother had told me she wanted these to be part of her funeral service. I tried my best to remain stony-faced through the service, and perhaps I succeeded in revealing nothing.

Her five difficult business partners from McAllen attended the funeral. I nodded curtly to them as we were all leaving. This was probably not proper or wise behavior on my part, but I just did not have the energy to pretend they were anything other than gloating ghouls happy that their most recent victim was dead and out of the way and sizing me up as their next target.

Later that day, Mother's siblings asked if she had written a will. I didn't know how to deal comfortably with the real question, which was: had she left them bequests? The answer was: will, yes; bequests for them, no. I tried to give them this information in the foggiest and softest way possible. Even so, I could see they were all disappointed that my mother had not remembered them in her will.

In an attempt to compensate, I distributed fur coats, one each to her sister and two sisters-in-law, to her nurse Ruth Lester, and to her loyal maid, Marian, along with some pieces of jewelry and other personal mementos. This seemed to make the relatives brighten up somewhat. The visitors and guests departed, leaving Harry, Ruth Lester, Marian, and me to begin the sorting of her things.

The preparations for probate matters and for the ongoing business war with her partners were postponed for a few days. All the agreements and documents would have to be redrawn and signed again, with me as the principal and executor instead of my mother. This was not at all a sure thing because of the balky attitude of the partners, but all eventually proceeded smoothly. Just as the new set of documents was finished and partially signed, the oldest partner suddenly died, and the whole process had to be repeated once again.

A week after the funeral, I visited the cemetery where the cremation had been done. I told the owner I wanted to see the rose garden where my mother's ashes had been scattered just a few days before. He looked at me coldly, probably angry that no grave had been purchased, and said, "Oh, no, no—if we dumped all the ashes in the rose garden, they'd be knee-deep. We throw 'em in the woods over at the edge of the property." Shocked, I made no reply.

I went to look at the bedraggled, sad little rose garden and then walked over to the magnificent grove of trees at the edge of the property. As my eyes filled with tears, I could hear the grove was full of singing birds.

A Chapter Closes

I was devastated by the loss of my mother. Although she had become increasingly difficult, she was generally supportive of my efforts in life. She had a frighteningly good memory for conversations, being able to reconstruct them accurately months and years after they had taken place. I was lucky to have inherited this ability. She was spiritually curious and had read widely on various religions and philosophies.

It occurred to me that I was now an orphan. As in the bandstand at Ebano so many years ago, I cried and wondered who would take care of me, who would help me. I thought the answer was: No one.

I was habituated to both the good and the bad nocturnal telephone conversations, and I missed talking with Mother. For many years, when something interesting came my way, I would think, "Oh, wait until I tell Mother about this." Then the realization that she was gone would hit me again, always with a sickening jolt.

On the other hand, I was greatly relieved that I did not have to deal with the terrible drunkenness, the humiliating public tongue-lashings and scenes, and the dreadful middle-of-the-night telephone harangues.

Also, I had had considerable worry that she would, due to her drinking, either squander all her resources or otherwise ruin her financial condition and thereby destroy my chances of a sizeable inheritance.

Gradually a new life began to unfold for me. In the forty-three years which have passed since then, there has been no day that I have not thought of my mother with sorrow, regret, relief, and love.

HHHHHHHHHHHHHHHHHHHHHHHHHHHHHHHHHHHHH

Transitions, 1963

Ray

After my mother's death, I went to Houston on business for about a week or ten days each month. During a visit in July of 1966, I was car cruising in downtown Houston one evening and saw a very attractive man walking. I pulled up beside him, we had a brief conversation, and he came home to my apartment with me. The sex was very exciting. Before he left he told me he owned a bar downtown.

Ray was a retired naval officer, a former jet pilot. He had singlehandedly started to develop a historic, charming, but rundown suburban section of Houston. One of the buildings there was the location of his bar. This had become a mixing place for athletes, hookers, lawyers, intellectuals, barflies, and Houston society people, along with a few gay people, and it had the best jukebox in town.

Two nights later, I went into his bar, hoping to see Ray again. He was working behind the bar, served me a beer, and was pleasant but gave absolutely no sign of recognition. I assumed this was a message that he didn't want a repeat of our previous meeting or anything further of any other sort either. However, I enjoyed the bar itself, with its interesting crowd and good music.

A few nights later I went into his bar again, and this time Ray was effusive in his greeting. Later I learned that one of his business competitors had tried to burn Ray's face with a blowtorch, had damaged his eyes slightly, and so he had not recognized me on my prior visit.

Later that evening, he joined me at my apartment, spent the night, and a romance and highly charged sexual affair began.

Ray had chronic hepatitis, almost always a progressive and fatal condition. Before I knew him, and before his discharge from the service, he had spent two years in a naval hospital. He gradually improved, although he had occasional flare-ups of hepatitis which left him weak and discouraged.

James

Back in New York, John and I continued our usual disorderly lifestyle, but now my financial resources were much increased, due to my recent inheritance. My psychiatric practice was slowly growing and was a source of considerable satisfaction to me. However, now I was unable to do the extra work to develop the practice because of my heavy business responsibilities in Texas. My father's testing business was too small to run itself and too large just to close and abandon. My growing income from the business was an excuse for me to be too casual about developing my practice.

One of the most difficult aspects of my relationship with John had been his blatant sexual promiscuity. After our first two years together, perhaps partly out of self-defense, and fueled by heavy drinking, I also embraced promiscuity, which at that time had few serious physical consequences. These were the golden years of sexual abandon, as AIDS had not yet appeared. Other sexually transmitted diseases were for the most part easily cured with antibiotics, which had been discovered toward the end of World War II (about the mid-1940s).

The emotional stress produced in me by John's promiscuity was severe. It was common for him to meet someone new, to develop an enthusiasm for the person, and then to tell me at great length how superior this person was to me and in exactly what humiliating ways.

He often wanted me to cook dinner for his new boyfriend, and when I refused, an argument would start, often lasting several weeks. Once, using subterfuge and pre-arrangement, John introduced me to one of these men, a very sophisticated, forceful, and wealthy business executive. Much to my surprise, we later became friends, and Fred and I met for lunch two or three times a year until he died twenty years later.

In the spring of 1967, John met yet another new boyfriend, James Gregory, who claimed to be wealthy, to have a farm in France, and to be getting ready for his debut as a pianist with the Philadelphia Orchestra. He was planning to play Rachmaninoff's Third Piano Concerto. James had a letter confirming this from Eugene Ormandy, the longtime conductor of the Philadelphia.

In addition to being a much better pianist than I was, John told me James was also much wealthier, more sophisticated, was fluent in French, knew more people and more prominent people, and was much better in bed than I was. I was even privileged to be told the details of how much better his sexual equipment was than mine. All of this was painful for me to hear. James was also about one hundred pounds overweight.

My affair with Ray in Houston was still a secret from John, and I did not see it as a threat to my relationship with him.

I also did not tell John of my meeting with James about one year earlier.

I had been out cruising in the gay bars and encountered a casual acquaintance, Dick Sutton, whom I had always found attractive. After some conversation, we spoke of where we could go to have sex. I couldn't invite Dick home because John was there: we had not become hardened and blasé enough to have sex with outside parties in each other's presence, and we had never tried threesomes. So Dick, who was visiting New York, invited me to the apartment of a friend who lived across the street from the Frick Museum.

His friend, James Gregory, turned out to be a large man in his forties, about six feet four, overweight, with dark hair and piercing, frightening dark eyes. Later on, I heard several people comment on his strange, unsettling, and repellant eyes and his aggressive staring. There was a grand piano in his living room.

After a few minutes of polite conversation, Dick took me aside and asked if I were open to having a threesome with himself and James. When I declined, Dick seemed disappointed, and shortly James said goodnight with a surly stare and retired to his bedroom.

The sex with Dick seemed odd to me. He was the only person I had been with who needed to get up twice in the middle of the sex act to go to the kitchen for a glass of orange juice. Perhaps he was conferring with James as to whether the atmosphere in the bedroom had become more inviting. It had not. After three hours, I left and went home. I never saw Dick or James again, which was fine with me.

I did not hear anything further of James until a year later, when he was announced to me as John's new lover. I began to be treated to daily lengthy descriptions of all points of James's superiority to me.

I still had said nothing to John of my developing relationship with Ray in Houston.

XXXXXXXXXXXXXXXXXXXXXXXXXXXXXXXXXXXXXXXXXXXXXX

The Dinner Party

Saturday evening during Labor Day weekend of 1967, John and I were entertaining one of his old college friends, Don Riley. Don was a successful interior designer, intelligent, could be charming, was six feet six and a weight lifter, built like Hercules in his prime, and had blond hair and blue eyes. He was also the most serious, dedicated masochist I had ever met. That evening, we all three had too much to drink and were losing our self-control and perhaps talking too freely.

At our little dinner party that evening, Don spoke of the problem of finding suitable sadists. It was not safe to trust casual pickups to dispense the kind of bondage and extreme violence he craved. Most of his sadist contacts were referrals from European friends who were members of the loose group of international S&M devotees. The candidate had to be experienced and eager to dominate Don. Unfortunately, he said, most of the sadists who came to his apartment for the first time, on seeing his size and build, decided they wanted to have the masochist role, at least for that night.

One drunken night a few months earlier, I had gone to bed with Don myself. He wanted me to bite him.

"Bite me," he said. "You know where. Hard."

Inexperienced at this activity, I worried I might bite him hard enough to do real damage. On the other hand, I did not want to reveal myself as a sissy wimp by not chewing on him hard enough. To make matters more difficult, while we were trying to pursue this unusual masticatory version of the sex act, he made and received several lengthy telephone calls concerning his interior decorating projects.

"Harder. Harder!!" he grunted, putting his hand over the mouthpiece. I finally gave up chewing on him and went home. We were both unsatisfied, but as Don said, "Orgasm is only a detail." We did not repeat the attempt to get together sexually. We remained friends anyway, at least for a while.

At our Labor Day party, John had cooked a delicious dinner. The conversation continued on the subject of Don's problems meeting suitable sadists.

"I have a terrific new master," he said. "He gives me homework and punishes me if I don't do all my assignments."

"What kind of assignments?" I asked.

Don replied, "Well, for instance, when I get home this evening I have to eat a shit sandwich. My master has ordered me to eat six shit sandwiches a week. It's pretty difficult. It's hard to get them down. I just can't seem to get used to it. But I really get punished if I don't complete my assignments."

Trying to act as blasé as possible, I asked, "What kind of bread do you prefer for your sandwiches?"

Don shot me an irritated glance, but he didn't answer the question.

John Leaves

Later that evening John started telling me again about James Gregory and how wonderful he was in bed. I was fed up with this demeaning talk and so told John that I had also met someone in Houston and that we were having an affair. He became enraged, and we had a verbally violent and abusive argument. I stormed out of the apartment and went to my office, where I spent the night on the sofa.

When I came home the next day, Labor Day, 1967, John was gone. For years, I had been hearing of John's affairs, but within two hours of hearing that I had also been having an affair, he had left. There was no note. He never returned. He called a few days later to make arrangements to pick up his things. I was not at the apartment when he collected them.

In spite of knowing that our relationship had become very deteriorated, that we were constantly hurting each other, I had never thought we would break up, so it was an extremely painful surprise to me. Somehow, I thought we would be like my parents, scolding and hostile and sulking, never pleasant to one another but very stable, never breaking up.

Our lives had become very intertwined during the years we lived together, often unpleasantly so, and his departure left an enormous aching hole in my usual thinking and feeling. My drinking, which had been problematic for years, got worse. Every evening, in order to quiet the pain I felt from John's departure, I drank to the point of stupefaction. This marked the beginning of my daily drinking.

I was surprised and very moved to receive a letter from John's parents saying how sorry they were that we were no longer together and that they thought I was a very good influence on him. They invited me to keep in touch with them and wished me good luck.

John moved in with James and learned picture framing as a trade. They moved to New Hope, Pennsylvania. and opened a moderately successful business dealing in fine quality antiques. James turned out not to be wealthy, and the farm in France was under a legal cloud and did not become available to him. He was truly an accomplished pianist, but the debut with the Philadelphia Orchestra never took place, nor did he have any other public musical performances. Years later, John told me James was ragingly jealous and would not let him see any of his old friends. He was the only one of John's boyfriends ever able to control John's promiscuity.

Their framing and antique business flourished and became valuable. Eventually, James, a heavy smoker, developed lung cancer, and John attentively nursed him through his final illness, which lasted for two years. After James died, John was surprised by the contents of his will.

James left half his estate to a young man he had met during a trip to Houston nine months previously, and he had also named this young man to be executor of his estate. He left the other half of his estate to a local church, but he got the name of the church wrong, so the bequest did not go to the church he intended. John received nothing under the will, and there was considerable difficulty dividing the joint property of the antique business and the house in New Hope. John showed a surprising lack of anger or resentment about what James had done. By that time, John had stopped drinking, and his naturally kind and loving disposition again revealed itself.

After John left me, we did not talk again for many years. About 1995, twenty-eight years after we had separated, John called to tell me James had died. We started to talk by phone occasionally and began to have friendly lunches together about twice a year.

John told me he felt it had been a very bad mistake to have left me and gone off with James. I replied that considering our out-of-control drinking, I thought it was the best thing that could have happened for both of us. He was displeased at my unsentimental reply.

John's Death

John had been a heavy smoker all his life and was hostile to the idea of quitting. His emphysema was getting worse. He could not walk a complete block without getting short of breath and needing to stop for a rest, while he smoked a cigarette. After a bout of pneumonia which almost killed him, he was finally able to stop smoking. His breathing improved a little, but then the emphysema resumed its steady downhill course. He never complained, but when I asked him how he was, he would briefly mention his breathing status, which was usually bad.

He had affairs with two men who were very disturbed and caused him much trouble, embarrassment, and money. The first was a pedophile who preyed on the neighborhood boys, and the second was a thief who stole most of his money.

He eventually met a kind and helpful young man, who was with him to the end.

John Puckett and his friend Charlie, Rehoboth Beach,
Delaware, December 2004

His antique business in New Hope had declined greatly. He sold the house and the remaining antiques and bought a trailer house in Rehoboth Beach, Delaware, where he knew a few people. His devoted friend Charlie, much younger and of course stronger than John, moved in with him and helped to take care of him as his health failed. I visited him on a return trip from Washington at Christmas, 2005. His new place was attractive although very modest. He looked cheerful, but he had always been a good dissembler. He said he was lonely there and he missed the old place in New Hope with its streams of visitors.

His health declined further. He told me he was going into the hospital for an operation the following week and had a premonition that he would die right afterward. He was correct.

The ten years I spent with John, 1957 to 1967, were generally fairly happy, considering our life situations and our rapidly worsening alcoholism. We both had our faults, but were both basically good and kind people, and we both did the best we could with the relationship, even if it often did not look that way.

John Puckett and author, Rehoboth Beach, Delaware, December 2004

I felt sad when John died in February of 2006. He was seventy-five years old. His many friends at the funeral spoke lovingly of him, and several mentioned his beautiful bright blue eyes.

The New House

Following my parents' funerals, the mourning periods, sorting of their belongings, and legal and tax formalities, their assets were officially transferred to me, although many of my father's assets were never located. As a young doctor just starting out in a private psychiatric practice, I was used to just making ends meet, and this sudden change in my financial situation gave me the freedom to make some changes in my life.

In January of 1968, I started looking for a weekend place in the country and soon found an ideal house in Ridgefield, Connecticut. The house was a thirty-year-old one-story ranch with three bedrooms, three bathrooms, a large living room, dining room, kitchen, and attached garage, on five acres, high up on the side of a hill, with a spectacular fifty-mile view as far as Bear Mountain on the Hudson River in New York State.

Alden Whitney at his ordination, 1980

My friend Alden Whitney, and his partner, Rolf Vigmostad, had recently bought a house in Danbury, so we looked forward to seeing each other on the weekends.

Alden Whitney and his partner, Rolf Vigmostad, Phoenix, 1982

My small front yard had two huge maple trees and was surrounded by a white picket fence, perfect for Sparky. He could play in the yard without danger of falling over the cliff or wandering away into the woods. There was a small rental cottage at the beginning of the driveway, but no other houses could be seen from the property.

The elderly couple who had owned the house for twenty years had decided to move to a warmer climate in Arizona, or so they said. The price was negotiated, the survey was done, and the mortgage obtained. The papers were signed March 15, and the previous owners were due to move out on April 1. On their moving day, they left the house in very good condition, taking with them, as I had expected, all their furniture, but also the draperies and the roller shades, as well as the cleaning materials under the sink, all the light bulbs, and every roll of toilet paper. They were obviously thrifty and planning ahead.

The next day, the movers arrived from Houston with all the furniture from my parents' house, which had recently been sold. The largest, heaviest, and most valuable item was a forty-year-old nine-foot Steinway concert grand piano, which had been played in public by many of the leading pianists of the time. The piano and furniture were set up in the living room. The beds and bedroom furniture were installed in the bedrooms. Boxes were stacked up, and a few essentials were unpacked. An emergency trip before dark to the local grocery store was necessary to replace the unexpected removals by the departing owners.

I put out some towels, soap, and toothpaste, made up my bed, fed Sparky, and heated a can of soup for dinner. I sat in the living room eating the soup, drinking a martini, looking at the spectacular view, and feeling happy to be getting settled in such a beautiful place. Twilight came, and gradually the light completely disappeared. Feeling serene but a little tired, I decided to retire around 9 PM so I would be well rested for much unpacking the next day.

A straight hall, about thirty feet long, led from the living room to my bedroom at the far end of the house. The other two bedrooms also opened off this hall. Sparky and I got into the bed. I turned off the lamp on the bedside table and was just putting my head on the pillow when there was a distinct thump at the far end of the hall, the end closer to the living room and to the front door.

The sound was very definite, as though someone had jumped down from two or three feet onto the hall floor. THUMP!!! What could it be: A burglar? A crazed murderer? A ghost? A poltergeist? A ghoul? A demon? Some kind of large animal (perhaps a deer had somehow got into the house)? I called out, "Is anybody there?" but there was no answer.

Then, to my horror, loud, heavy hollow-sounding footsteps, about three seconds apart, started stomping down the hall toward my bedroom. They continued to the doorway, paused, and then came into the room and over to my bed, where they stopped. Sparky dog was very still but was making low growls. I thought I was most probably going to be attacked. I tried to arrange myself for a fight and then very slowly and silently put out my hand toward the chain on the table lamp. I found the chain, took a firm hold, and suddenly turned on the light.

There was no one to be seen. Sparky began to bark and jump around. This was the first visit from the invisible being I eventually named "Thumper."

Over the course of the next year, Thumper made many visits, always after dark and always walking in the hall. Sparky would growl or bark when the stomping was going on. Houseguests would sometimes ask me in the morning why I was walking up and down the hall last night, opening and closing the doors. When I explained the situation, some guests turned fidgety; others were irritated that I should be telling such lies. Others only laughed and thought it was a joke. Thumper walked the hall perhaps twice a week.

Regular houseguests eventually became convinced that there was an unusual presence in the house, and some friends declined to spend the weekend more than once. I almost became used to the visitations but was always a little on edge, although Thumper never did anything physical, until one day a year after his first manifestation.

It was about noon on a bright spring day. I was alone in the house and was washing dishes. There was the familiar loud thump, for the first time in broad daylight, and for the first time, the footsteps moved in a different direction, passing through the living room, into the front hall, into the kitchen, and then stopped right behind me. Sparky barked and then huddled by my feet.

Suddenly, there was a strong push on my back, not enough to make me fall down, but strong enough to make me stagger. Uh-oh. I turned around to face Thumper, if it were actually he, and said in the loudest and deepest voice I could manage (probably more like a squeak), "This is too much!! Stop it right now!!" For five seconds, there was a low crackling and rasping growl in the air about two feet in front of my head—then silence.

Thumper stayed out of sight for about two weeks before resuming his usual nocturnal visits, and there was never another daytime visit or any further shoving.

Aside from the pushing episode, I did not think Thumper had any connection with me. Like sitting in a restaurant and looking out through a plateglass window at people and cars passing on the street: I could see them, but their presence had nothing to do with me. Perhaps my house was somehow at a crossroad between this world and another.

A few months after Thumper's initial visit, a second and much more pleasant ghost began regular appearances. She was a very rare and exquisite perfume ghost, whom I named "Lovely Lady." She only visited at twilight, only when I was alone and playing the piano. I would become aware of a presence, a feeling that I was not alone. The presence would move behind me, coming from the long hallway and slowly moving to the center of the living room. There would be a strong floral perfume fragrance, which I recognized, but I couldn't identify. I felt she was watching me for a while and was very benign and wished me well. She charmed Sparky, who would look up into the air and smile and wag his tail when she was present. No one else ever experienced her.

Both ghosts stayed with me until I sold the house eight years later. I said, "Good-bye; good luck to you both." There was no more contact with Thumper, but for about ten years Lovely Lady would visit me two or three times a year, no matter where I was in the world.

Now, twenty-five years later, I sometimes wonder how they all are faring, including little Sparky.

Good-bye again, dears.

Author at the new house, Ridgefield, 1975.

The Queen of Neptune

Work was always interesting and was always a consolation.

A Miss Barber had called to make an appointment. When I returned her call, Miss Barber quietly told me she would like to make an appointment to discuss a problem. She seemed a little vague, and I pictured a Helen Hokinson lady, or a little grandmother with neat gray curls, perhaps bobby pins in her hair, maybe even wearing white socks and frumpy shoes, but a nice person, decent, shy, retiring. The appointment was set for Wednesday afternoon. Appearances can be deceiving, but in this case, her voice was deceiving.

When I met Bettina Barber in my waiting room, I was startled at the lovely vision. She was about thirty-five years old, medium height, had black hair in a fashionable coiffure, large dark eyes sparkling with amused friendliness, long dark eyelashes, even features, full red lips, perfect alabaster skin, and expert but understated makeup.

She had a voluptuous figure and was dressed in a mauve Chanel suit complementing her coloring. She had on pink coral and diamond earrings and bracelet, a delicate gold necklace, and on one of her perfectly manicured hands was an impressively brilliant marquise-cut diamond ring. Her full-length sable coat was draped casually over the back of her chair.

She gave an impression of extreme elegance, glamour, and wealth; she was poised, cool, perfect, and beautiful. So much for my judgment about her voice.

Entering my office, she tossed her coat on the sofa and sat down demurely, almost shyly. She crossed her shapely legs and looked at me with a slightly smiling, expectant expression.

I began with an opening statement which had often been helpful in getting things started with a new patient. "The purpose of our meeting today is for me to find out something about your situation and problems, and for us to decide, if we can, what, if anything, you might choose to do about them."

"Yes …. Well, you see …. my life isn't going anywhere, it seems pointless, and I feel there is something wrong with that."

Over the next few months, she told me about her life. She was an only child. She said her paternal grandfather had been a powerful and feared sorcerer, resident in Berlin early in the twentieth century. Her father, a doctor, with whom she had a very good relationship, had died about eight years earlier.

Miss Barber had never married and lived at home in Westchester with her mother, who was sixty years old and in good health. Miss Barber saw her mother as overly controlling, although with good intentions. Their relationship was generally cordial.

The family was wealthy, and Miss Barber had large trust funds of her own. She had a substantial annual income, so she was neither dependent on nor easily controlled by her mother. She had a good relationship with her uncle, one of the world's richest men. They were fond of each other, and she could turn to him for advice in practical matters. His son, her cousin, was also very fond of Bettina, perhaps a little too fond, but was helpful and protective toward her.

She had grown up in Westchester County, attended private schools, had extensive tutoring in languages and music, and in college had enjoyed courses in art, fashion design, and history. After three years she withdrew and did not graduate. She had dated without much interest and expressed a disinclination to marry. She had two childhood girlfriends whom she saw once or twice a month for lunch, and they talked by phone two or three times a week.

She did not have any interest in social life, hobbies, or volunteer work and seldom went out to any kind of entertainment. She had never had a job, other than a very short-lived part-time one some years earlier. She was comfortable with her own company, read several hours a day, and liked to listen to opera and other classical music. Intelligent, thoughtful, kindly, and cheerful, she was in good physical health and slept well. She did not use drugs and didn't smoke. Occasionally she would have a glass of champagne at some gala event.

Miss Barber was not troubled by any of the usual psychiatric problems, such as anxiety, depression, excessive anger, social phobia, or obsession. She had never consulted a psychiatrist or been in psychotherapy.

So far, this story sounds like that of many other well-to-do young women who cannot connect with life and while away their time in vague dissatisfaction and idleness, perhaps for years or even a lifetime.

After learning more about her, I agreed that her life seemed unnecessarily tedious and restricted and that nothing was apparent on the horizon which was going to change it, unless she took some action to make a change.

Her memory was excellent—perhaps too excellent; perhaps not.

But as the weeks passed by, she gradually revealed another side of her existence.

She enjoyed taking cruises on the Italian Line ships and was often seated at the captain's table. As she was fluent in Italian, French, Spanish, and German, she could talk easily with the other passengers and the crew. Sometimes she disembarked in Europe to visit friends in Paris, Rome, or on the Riviera; other times she stayed on board and sailed back to New York.

She often met interesting men on board and seemed especially drawn to Italian racecar drivers. She had a number of torrid affairs with various of these men and with a fierce Spanish matador.

If a man became serious, jealous, or spoke of marriage, she lost interest, as she definitely did not feel willing to be trapped, as she put it. Even if the man did not become serious, Bettina eventually became bored and discarded the relationship.

She sometimes enjoyed playing Circe, transforming men into swine, an almost automatic ability she had made good use of from time to time. She behaved rather like some of the grand horizontals at the end of the nineteenth century—La Belle Otero, for instance, although L.B.O. might have expired from jealousy if she had known who Bettina really was.

I noticed a surprising impulse in myself. Perhaps every other session, I would suddenly feel like suggesting to her that we should take our clothes off and make love, there and then. As a happily partnered gay man with little heterosexual inclination, I had never had this reaction before with any female patient, and not with a male patient either. I interpreted this impulse as my reaction to something that Bettina was unconsciously and automatically projecting, like a radio picking up signals from a nearby broadcasting station.

For various reasons, I never felt that it was the right time to introduce this countertransference matter into our therapy sessions. I feared it might harm her confidence in me. She knew she was extremely attractive to men, so I didn't have any news to give her in that regard, and we were meeting to discuss her life, not my reactions to her. As the psychoanalysts say, unconscious calls to unconscious, and here the call was loud but not so clear. Or perhaps this was witchcraft, or her Circe side manifesting.

As a result of her encounters with the racecar drivers, matadors, and other romantic partners, she had been pregnant thirteen times, each time by a different man. Each pregnancy had ended with an abortion, as she did not wish to have a child, not yet. She was obediently and happily saving her maternal ability for a greater plan, which had been outlined for her by some of the elders of the planet Neptune when she had lived there, first as a princess and later as queen of Neptune.

"At the time of one of my abortions, I met a former husband, Henry the Eighth of England, who was at that time reincarnated as a gynecologist in Puerto Rico. I was of course Anne Boleyn in a previous life." As she shared this information, she was watching me carefully to see how her unusual pronouncement would sit with me.

"Oh, that's very interesting," I said. "How do you know?"

"Well, how do you know anything about your own past? I remember." She seemed slightly irritated by my question.

"I see. What does Henry say about how he treated you in your past lives? Is he apologetic, or what?"

"Oh, no, Doctor. He doesn't remember. He doesn't know who I am. But he has a slight uneasiness with me—he feels some guilt but doesn't know why. He's just as fat this time as he was last time. He's like a pig, and I don't forgive him for that."

She lowered her eyes shyly and seemed about to enter a reverie but after a short pause continued: "But somehow I still find him cute and cuddly, in a disgusting way. I guess I still love him, at least a little bit. And he still has those revolting whiskers. Sometimes I know I just can't make my attitudes realistic and practical," she concluded with a faint smile.

In my practice I did not have any inclination to argue, much less to spring to the attack. In talking with patients, this was a definite asset; privately it was not necessarily so.

In the medical world, reincarnation was a taboo subject, especially among psychiatrists. To have an open mind about reincarnation, or to be interested in the subject, was even more unacceptable than having an open mind about telepathy, clairvoyance, spirit possession, or witchcraft.

The other psychiatrist who shared my office was of the opinion that Miss Barber was floridly psychotic and that there was no reason to pay attention to any of her conversation. "Meaningless drivel," the omniscient doctor said.

One of the common failings in psychotherapy was for the doctor to assume that what he saw as psychopathology was central to the patient's life and problems. For instance, when I was undergoing my first therapy, a psychoanalysis, the analyst kept referring to the fact that I was gay as central, embedded, and causing any and every difficulty I had. This of course was garbage but reflected the analyst's orthodox and old-fashioned Freudian bias.

Most of my personal problems had little or no connection with my sexual preference or behavior, and my gay life itself was not a problem for me, except logistically at times, but of course my analyst saw my failure to agree with her as a pathological resistance.

Later I had an ambivalent laugh when I found out that the analyst was a lesbian and had had a long-term affair with her female assistant. I was glad for her but disappointed that she could not have been less rigidly dishonest with me.

Likewise, in Bettina's situation, her beliefs and experiences concerning reincarnation, visitation by saints, astral travel, visions of the devil, and the like did not cause her any trouble and were not central to the problems she wanted to discuss with me. I accepted her occult experiences as existential facts, in the same way she saw them, and kept an open mind as to whether they represented psychopathology or some type of reality. For instance, she told me one day, "When I was out for a walk today, I saw the devil on the street. He was disguised as a large black cat. When he walked away, he turned and gave me an evil look. I see him now and then and am not afraid of him."

"I see," I said.

Bettina told me of some of her other past lives. "I loved my red-hot sexual affair with Alexander the Great when I was a Persian princess. I still haven't forgiven my mother, the Queen of Persia, for jealously interfering with my romance by spiriting me away from Alexander. My mother neither approved of nor liked Alexander, although she would have been open for a sexual affair with him, if he had asked her, which he didn't, as he didn't like her. Neither did I."

She described her life as a princess and then queen on the planet Neptune just prior to beginning her present incarnation on earth. She said she had been sent here as a goodwill gesture from the people of Neptune. It was to be her task to bear the new messiah for the world, and this was the reason she had all the abortions: none of the fetuses were destined to be the messiah. They would somehow interfere with her mission and so had to be aborted. This seemed illogical but was not a current concern for her.

As time went on, Bettina began to report trips out of her body at night, usually accompanied by a saint or an angel. They would travel somewhere to a person in trouble and would telepathically suggest helpful ideas to the person or to those around him. Eventually, St. Anthony came to call on Bettina early each night, and they would travel around the world performing benevolent and healing acts. She had considerable pleasure and benefit from her kind deeds.

Her nighttime adventures and her past lives were extremely colorful, interesting, and unusual. But her daytime life was a ho-hum matter; her life was still not going anywhere. Even the affairs, pregnancies, and abortions became a bore to her.

I suggested she might benefit from moving out of her mother's house, and so she took a beautiful apartment with a magnificent view on Central Park South in New York. She and her cat, Sheba, moved in.

Next-door to her apartment building was Rumpelmayer's, a branch of the famous old Viennese coffeehouse, known for its delicious chocolate-covered cherries and afternoon tea. She began to drop in every afternoon around 4 PM for tea.

One of the other regular customers was Dr. Sandor Rado, a world-famous pioneer Hungarian psychoanalyst, extremely powerful in the psychiatric profession and a dean of the New York psychiatric establishment. It was said he had been an analysand of Freud himself. He was also a leader of the homophobe contingent of analysts, advocating aversion "therapy" (giving a gay man painful electric shocks while he looked at a photo of a handsome man) to "cure" homosexuals. Some of us even thought the great man was a bigot. Unfortunately, he was head of training at the New York Psychoanalytic Institute. At that time it was said no gay doctor could ever graduate there. Dr. Rado would not approve a "sick" doctor to practice psychoanalysis.

He knew everyone who counted in the profession. I had heard him lecture several times. We had not been introduced, but he soon knew about me.

He developed an acquaintance with Miss Barber, got closer over time, and began to offer her presents, including chocolate-covered cherries, which she mostly declined. He finally began to invite her, then press her, to visit him in his apartment. Bettina amused herself by telling Dr. Rado that her psychiatrist had forbidden her to go to his apartment. He wanted to know who this might be, this unknown impertinent impediment to his pleasure.

At first he sent me imperious and/or threatening messages through her, commanding me to withdraw my opposition to her visiting his apartment. "Tell your young doctor that he is being countertherapeutic, a common failing among the inexperienced therapists."

I countered, "Tell him to try to restrain himself."

Then his messages became more polite, even wheedling, but to no avail. Quite unseemly, I thought. Bettina was using me as an excuse not to be cornered by Dr. Rado, and we were both amused by the situation. I felt like the mouse when he realized he had terrified the elephant.

Eventually, Bettina and Dr. R. became genuinely cordial, although never close, and his crude sexual overtures stopped, much to the relief of all three of us. Years later I learned from someone closely associated with New York Psychoanalytic during Dr. Rado's reign there that he was a notorious lecher and was known to grab at women who came within an arm's length, sometimes even trying to kiss them against their will. He was described as brazen and unembarrassed by his sexually inappropriate behavior. Perhaps he should have tried some of his favorite aversion therapy on himself to "cure" his lecherous tendencies.

I encouraged Bettina to look for a job, a formidable task for someone like her, who had never worked. Some years before she had joined the ranks of Mickey Jelke's "girls" for a short time and had occupied herself, if that is the right term, as a very high-priced call girl. She had hoped she might find this activity amusing and interesting but soon found it boring, so she resigned. And she didn't need the money.

One day she was almost crying in my office: "The only job I could find was as a model for a bubble bath company. They want me to pose for pictures sitting in a tub of bubbles."

"And how did you feel about that?"

"The problem is that they want me to be naked in the tub. I offered to wear a bikini, but they said no, and we couldn't reach a compromise, so I walked out."

"Too bad—perhaps this is not the right time to look for a job."

So she took another cruise to Italy instead.

Therapeutically, our work together had helped her to reach a plateau of more satisfying adjustment to the world. She was somewhat more comfortable with herself and her situation. She knew I was her ally, the only one she had except for her uncle and her cousin. She had stopped getting pregnant and had finally introduced herself to Henry VIII, who said he had known all along who she was and who he was. They became friends again, but she commented she could never really trust him after the way he had behaved last time. She felt proud of her nocturnal therapeutic work with St. Anthony and had a sense of accomplishment. She no longer had the feeling that her life was pointless and going nowhere.

About a year later, in 1977, I closed my office and said good-bye to all my patients, mostly with considerable sadness. I offered each patient a referral to the psychiatrist whom I thought was ideal for him or her. Bettina decided not to continue treatment with anyone else.

We had met for psychotherapy twice a week for a year, then once a week for two years, and we were both sad to say good-bye. I told her we could continue to be in touch by mail.

After that, we exchanged Christmas cards for over twenty years. She wrote me of events in her life: her mother's death, which she survived well, the death of her beloved cat Sheba, the death of her uncle, her discovery that she had a beautiful singing voice, and her delight in taking voice lessons. She developed a breast cancer, which was caught early and presumably cured. She told of her ongoing relationship with St. Anthony and her nightly trips with him to do good works. She continued to feel happy about her work with him and saw this as her purpose in life.

Each year at Christmas she invited me to visit her, to hear her sing, and to have a cup of tea with her. I am sorry that I did not accept any of her invitations, mistakenly feeling bound by psychiatric propriety.

One year recently I did not receive a Christmas card from her. I thought she might have been away or might have forgotten, or perhaps the card was lost in the mail. The following year, my card was returned marked, "Addressee Unknown."

I stopped by her apartment building on Central Park South and asked about her, explaining that I was an old friend and had not been able to contact her. The doorman told me in a quiet voice, "She was found dead in her apartment over a year ago. I guess she had a heart attack. She was a very nice person, and all the building employees miss her."

I doubted a heart attack was the cause of her death and assumed she had happily and willingly gone for a final, permanent trip with St. Anthony. I hope she is now helping him with his good works on a full-time basis and still taking joy in singing heavenly songs.

Blessings on you, lovely spirit.

Sparky's Death

In April of 1968, I bought a country house in Ridgefield, Connecticut, and Sparky and I started going there every weekend. We both needed something to help us get over the sad events of the past few years, and we both enjoyed the new property. Sometimes the neighbors' cows would get through the fence and wander into the yard, which excited both of us. Sparky liked Lovely Lady, one of the resident ghosts, and disliked Thumper, the other ghost.

He developed arthritis and disc problems, as is common in dachshunds. He developed complete paralysis in his hind legs, a very sad sight, and spent three months at Dr. Herman's Dog Bath Club on Fifty-Seventh Street, which featured a therapeutic heated swimming pool for dogs, which Sparky used twice a day. He eventually recovered enough to trot and even run and jump a little. His appetite was always good, and he especially loved eating pieces of raw rutabaga, not a usual canine favorite.

One evening in July of 1972, we were at home in New York. Sparky came in from the terrace, walked over to me, and had a bowel movement right in front of me, something he had never done before. At the same time, he stared at me with a puzzled look. He seemed to be in pain, whimpering slightly and not moving as freely as usual. That evening, I would not let him get into bed with me as he usually did. I was afraid he was having a relapse of his disc problem and that he might jump out of the bed in the night, as he usually did, and paralyze himself again. He looked at me for a while, whimpering, and then crawled under the bed.

In the morning, I found my dear little dog lying dead on the floor, his body already cold and stiff. I started to cry as the awful grief feeling began to rise up from my stomach to my chest and into my head.

"Presumably," the veterinarian said, "Sparky had had a heart attack, which was the cause of the unusual behavior of the night before." I was so sorry that I had not let him come into the bed with me, so he could at least have died lying next to someone who loved him. I had to go to work at the hospital that morning and was able to hold myself together there, trying to conceal my feelings.

Later that day I wrapped him in a blanket and took him up to the Ridgefield house and buried him in a spot just outside my bedroom window. A lilac bush hung over the grave, and there was a long, open vista toward the west. For over a year, I went outside every weekend to sit by his grave and cry.

Four years later, when I sold the Ridgefield house and bought another place in Danbury, I carefully dug up Sparky's bones and transferred them to the new house, burying them just outside the walled garden, where they remain permanently.

Sparky's death started another period of mourning for me. It seemed to me that I loved Sparky more than I had ever loved any person, with the possible exception of my grandmother, and I knew that Sparky loved me more than any living person did.

Sparky at the new house, Ridgefield, 1968.

MMMMMMMMMMMMMMMMMMMMMMMMMMMMMMMM

SPARKY

November 15, 1958–July 28, 1972

A GOOD DOG

MMMMMMMMMMMMMMMMMMMMMMMMMMMMMMMM

Intermission:
Good-Bye to Innocence

A major chapter of my life had closed. I had lost my grandmother, my parents, my first lover, and my closest friend, Sparky. I had just met a new and dashing lover, supposedly fatally ill and living 1,400 miles away. I was established in my psychiatric practice and had also become a successful businessman. The business had grown every year, often doubling the revenues of the previous year.

It was 1972, and I was thirty-nine years old, still struggling with severe feelings of inferiority and inadequacy, healthy except for a moderately severe and yet unrecognized alcoholism, enjoying an inherited income and a new house, free of burdensome responsibilities, and I still had a sense of adventure unconstrained by caution, prudence, or wisdom. Even so, I was sad and felt rootless. But the future looked promising, and I still hoped to find real love.

This story will continue in Volume II, *Lost Hearts*.

CPSIA information can be obtained at www.ICGtesting.com
Printed in the USA
LVOW062114100512

281154LV00002B/64/P

9 781440 198236